A Cultural History
of TIBET

A Cultural History

of TIBET

DAVID SNELLGROVE
HUGH RICHARDSON

1995   SHAMBHALA   BOSTON & LONDON

To Giuseppe Tucci
who has revealed so many hidden treasures
of Tibetan life, art, and learning

SHAMBHALA PUBLICATIONS, INC.
Horticultural Hall
300 Massachusetts Avenue
Boston, Massachusetts 02115

9 8 7 6 5 4 3 2 1

Printed in the United States of America
Distributed in the United States by Random House., Inc.
and in Canada by Random House of Canada Ltd

Library of Congress Cataloging-in-Publication Data
Snellgrove, David L.
  A cultural history of Tibet.
  Reprint. Originally published: Rev. ed. Boulder :
Prajñā Press, 1980, c1968.
  Bibliography: p.
  Includes index.
    1. Tibet (China)—Civilization.   I. Richardson,
Hugh Edward, 1905–   . II. Title.
DS786.S6 1986   951.5   85-27861
ISBN 1-57062-102-0 (pbk.)

Contents

List of Illustrations

The monastery of *Rva-sgreng*, founded in 1056 by *'Brom-ston* (photo: H. E. Richardson)

Sa-skya monastery, founded in 1073 by *dKon-mchog-rgyal-po* (photo: A. J. Hopkinson)

The tower of *Sras*, built by *Mi-la Ras-pa* at the command of his teacher (photo: H. E. Richardson)

'Bri-khung monastery, founded in 1179 by *'Jig-rten mGon:po* (photo: H. E. Richardson)

sTag-lung monastery, founded in 1185 by *sTag-lung Thang-pa* (photo: H. E. Richardson)

Stūpas at the monastery of *Tshal Gung-thang* (photo: H. E. Richardson)

A chain suspension bridge in the upper *sKyid-chu* Valley attributed to *Thang-ston rGyal-po*, 1385–1464 (photo: H. E. Richardson)

Seat of the district governor at *rGya-ma* near Lhasa (photo: H. E. Richardson)

Gu-ru lha-khang in *Lho-brag*, founded by *Gu-ru Chos-dbang* (1212–73) (photo: H. E. Richardson)

The Great *Stūpa* (*sku-'bum*) of Gyantse, fifteenth century (photo: H. E. Richardson)

dGa'-ldan (Ganden) monastery, founded by *Tsong-kha-pa* in 1409 as his own retreat (photo: H. E. Richardson)

Houses in Lhasa (photo: India Office Library – Bell)

'Bras-spungs (Drepung) monastery, founded near Lhasa in 1416 (photo: Chapman-Paul Popper)

bKra-shis lhun-po (Tashilhunpo) monastery, from the seventeenth century onwards the seat of the *Pan-chen* Lamas (photo: H. E. Richardson)

The *Potala*, residence of the Dalai Lamas, on a hill dominating Lhasa (photo: India Office Library – Bell)

Complex of monastic buildings at Tashilhunpo (photo: India Office Library – Bell)

Temple façade and roof decorations at Tashilhunpo (photo: India Office Library – Bell)

Interior temple architecture at Tashilhunpo (photo: India Office Library – Bell)

A holiday tent used by high-ranking Tibetans for summer parties and picnics (photo: India Office Library – Bell)

Enshrined image of *Tsong-kha-pa* at Tashilhunpo (photo: India Office Library – Bell)

The simple house of a village-lama in Dolpo (photo: D. L. Snellgrove)

Pages 81–88

Eleventh-century fresco of the Supreme Buddha at the old monastery of Tabo in Spiti, once part of Western Tibet (photo: D. L. Snellgrove)

Stucco image at Tabo typical of the Buddha *Vairocana*, the 'Illuminator' (photo: D. L. Snellgrove)

Decorated ceiling at Tabo, possibly eleventh century (photo: D. L. Snellgrove)

Eleventh-century fresco of *Phyag-na-rdo-rje* in the neglected monastery of Tsaparang (photo: G. Tucci)

Carved wooden doorway at Tsaparang (photo: G. Tucci)

Fourteenth-century lion beam-ends at *rGya-gnas* near Gyantse (photo: G. Tucci)

Carved wooden capital at rGya-gnas (photo: G. Tucci)

Fresco at Iwang near Gyantse representing *Śākyamuni* Buddha (photo: G. Tucci)

Fresco at Gyantse representing one of the kings of the four quarters (photo: G. Tucci)

Fresco at Gyantse representing an Indian devotee (photo: G. Tucci)

Fresco at Gyantse representing male and female divinities (photo: G. Tucci)

Image of *Atiśa* at the monastery of *sNye-thang* (photo: H. E. Richardson)

Image of *Srong-brtsan-sgam-po* in the *Potala*, possibly from the fourteenth century (photo: H. E. Richardson)

Image of *Srong-brtsan-sgam-po*'s Nepalese queen (photo: H. E. Richardson)

Pages 121–128

Ceremony of despatching of 'scapegoats' in the courtyard in front of the *Jo-khang* in Lhasa at New Year (photo: H. E. Richardson)

Simple monks who served tea to the community at *bKra-shis-lhun-po* (Tashilhunpo) (photo: Colonel Steen)

Monk dignitaries at *bKra-shis-lhun-po* (photo: India Office Library – Bell)

Traditional postures during a monastic debate (photo: India Office Library – Bell)

Annual parade of horsemen in traditional armour (photo: H. E. Richardson)

rNying-ma-pa lama of Tarap (Dolpo) reciting the daily office (photo: C. Jest)

Bon-po lama reading in his chapel in Tarap (Dolpo) (photo: C. Jest)

Villagers on pilgrimage in Dolpo (photo: C. Jest)

Village festival on the occasion of erecting new prayer-flags on the shrine *Ri-bo bum-pa* above Tarap (Dolpo) (photo: C. Jest)

Ceremony in a nomad's tent performed by laymen led by a married lama (photo: C. Jest)

A nun on pilgrimage with her staff and prayer-wheel (photo: India Office Library – Bell)

A meditating yogin, probably *rNying-ma-pa* (photo: India Office Library – Bell)

A beggar making the rounds of the sacred site by a continual series of prostrations and thus inviting alms (photo: India Office Library – Bell)

Pages 161–168

Herd of yaks transporting grain in small sacks made of local homespun (photo: C. Jest)

Ploughing in Dolpo with a single ox (photo: C. Jest)

Winnowing grain (photo: C. Jest)

Carrying in the barley harvest for threshing (photo: C. Jest)

Threshing with wooden flails (photo: C. Jest)

Weaving homespun on a domestic loom (photo: C. Jest)

Interior of house belonging to a painter of temple-banners (photo: C. Jest)

Wooden effigy of a local protecting divinity (photo: Sir G. Taylor)

Village doctor attending patient (photo: India Office Library – Bell)

Village youth playing a 'guitar' (*sgra-snyan*) (photo: C. Jest)

Village woman of *gTsang* tying up the watch-dog in front of her house (photo: India Office Library – Bell)

Wooden ferry with a wooden horse as its traditional figure-head (photo: India Office Library – Bell)

Coracle made from willow-boughs and yak-hides (photo: India Office Library – Bell)

Pages 185–192

A 'magic-dart' (*phur-pa*) used for the ritual slaying of the human effigy (*linga*), who represents the foe under attack (photo: Horniman Museum)

A domestic brass ladle as used in a well-to-do Tibetan family (photo: Horniman Museum)

A Tibetan 'guitar' (*sgra-snyan*) (photo: Horniman Museum)

A conch-shell, most commonly blown to summon monks to a ceremony (photo: Horniman Museum)

A conch-shell with a plaque of worked silver showing *Mahāmāya*, the mother of *Śākyamuni* Buddha (photo: Horniman Museum)

Three Tibetan 'horns' – two of copper embossed with silver and one made of a human leg-bone (photo: Horniman Museum)

Tibetan temple drum

A teapot of copper decorated with brass used only on ceremonial occasions (photo: Horniman Museum)

Mask and dress of brocade silk used in monastic dances (*'cham*) (photo: Musée de l'Homme, Paris)

A conch for blowing adorned with a worked silver plaque (photo: Horniman Museum)

Two 'horns' (*rkang-gling*), as used by yogins, of human leg-bones (photo: Horniman Museum)

A 'horn' of copper decorated with silver (photo: Horniman Museum)

Pages 209–216

A Tibetan 'guitar' (*sgra-snyan*) as used by wandering minstrels (photo: Horniman Museum)

A Tibetan 'shawm' (*rgya-gling*) of wood and copper bound with silver (photo: Horniman Museum)

A wooden printing-block (photo: Horniman Museum)

Decorative dragon-head of a 'guitar' (photo: Horniman Museum)

A painted scroll illustrating the Great Religious King *Srong-brtsan-sgam-po* and events in his life (photo: Horniman Museum)

Detail of lotus-flower pattern from side-table (photo: Horniman Museum)

A Tibetan side-table, carved and painted, for domestic use (photo: Horniman Museum)

Group of men from an aristocratic estate dressed in old military costume for New Year ceremonies (photo: H. E. Richardson)

Ceremonial dress as supposed to have been worn by the early kings (photo: Paul Popper – Chapman)

A copper teapot decorated with designs in silver and gold (photo: Horniman Museum)

An ornamental belt made of leather and silver as worn by nomad women (photo: Musée de l'Homme, Paris)

A steel and tinder pouch (photo: Musée de l'Homme, Paris)

An inkpot of copper decorated with silver with a wooden lid (photo: Musée de l'Homme, Paris)

A quiver-shaped bamboo container for sticks of incense (photo: Musée de l'Homme)

A metal pen-case (photo: Musée de l'Homme)

A long Tibetan dagger (photo: John Freeman)

Set of eating instruments in a case (photo: Musée de l'Homme, Paris)

Pages 249–256

Carved Tibetan book-covers (Ashmolean Museum, Pitt-Rivers Loan, formerly collection of Mrs. H. G. Beasley. photo: Ashmolean Museum)

Temple-banner: *Padmasambhava* in his paradise, *zangs-mdog dpal-ri* —'Glorious Copper-coloured Mountain' (Ashmolean Museum, Beasley loan. photo: Ashmolean Museum).

Temple-banner: *Śākyamuni* before he abandoned his princely life (Ashmolean Museum, loaned by Mrs. P. B. Knight. photo: Ashmolean Museum).

Temple-banner: *bSod-nams dbang-phyug*, the Dolpo lama, with events from his life (photo: D. L. Snellgrove)

Temple-banner: *gShin-rje* skr: *Yama* — 'Lord of Death' with his female partner and attendant demons (Ashmolean Museum, collection of E. M. Scratton Esq. photo: Ashmolean Museum).

Temple-banner: a pilgrimage to an unidentified *stūpa* and surrounding holy places (Ashmolean Museum, loaned by Mrs. P. B. Knight. photo: Ashmolean Museum).

Dur-khrod bdag-po — 'Lords of the Cemetery' — performing a macabre dance over a human corpse (photo: Musée de l'Homme, Paris)

Image of the tantric divinity *'Chi-bdag 'joms-pa* skr. *Yamāntaka* — 'Destroyer of Death' clasping his female partner (Ashmolean Museum, gift of Dr and Mrs W. A. Hislop. photo: Ashmolean Museum).

sGrol-ma skr. *Tārā* — 'Saviouress' — most popular of feminine divinities (Ashmolean Museum, Scratton collection. photo: Ashmolean Museum).

gSeng-ge gDong-ma — 'Lion-headed Goddess' — who plays a leading part in rituals centring on *Padmasambhava* (Ashmolean Museum, Scratton collection. photo: Ashmolean Museum).

Dam-can — 'Oath-bound' — protector of the doctrine *rDo-rje Legs-pa* (Ashmolean Museum, Scratton collection. photo: Ashmolean Museum).

Section of Tibetan carpet: dragon and bird designs (photo: D. L. Snellgrove)

Silver bowl, presumably of Central Asian origin, brought out of Tibet about 1950 (photo: D. L. Snellgrove)

Preface to the 1995 Edition

Twenty-seven years have passed since the first publication of this work, and fourteen years since a revised paperback edition first appeared with an extra chapter, "Aftermath," and an additional bibliography to bring it up to date.

By now the traces of the old Tibetan civilization that survive in Tibet itself are largely confined to some religious buildings, some traditional domestic architecture, mainly in outlying towns and villages, the little-changed nomadic life of Tibetan herdsmen, and the religious devotion of people generally who have maintained their Buddhist faith during the long years when its outward practice was prohibited. The *Jo-khang*, the "cathedral" of Lhasa, was reopened to the public in 1980; the images that had been stolen, defaced, and destroyed have been replaced by replicas, but fortunately the main structure is scarcely damaged. The massive wooden pillars of the sanctuary survive together with some carved lintels as relics of the seventh century, and a curious silver jar—doubtless of the same period—showing Sassanian influence. Although an entry fee is now imposed and the hours of opening are fixed, it draws large crowds of pilgrims at the New Year and other important dates in the Tibetan Buddhist calendar, while at all times large numbers of people are seen outside, prostrating themselves by the entrance and making the traditional circumambulations as signs of their devotion and respect.

The former great monasteries of Drepung and Sera and even the once totally devastated monastery of Ganden have now been allowed to recruit monks, but the number remains severely limited, and this concession has seemingly been made by the Chinese as part of their efforts to encourage foreign tourism with the valuable foreign currency that it brings. Elsewhere and doubtless for much the same reason they have restored and in some cases—notably Sam-yä (*bSam-yas*)—even totally rebuilt temples and monasteries, for the destruction of which they were responsible. Old paintings have been painted afresh and others renewed in rather garish colors. These efforts, whether intended to placate the Tibetan people or to serve the interests of tourism, have not succeeded very well so far as the Tibetans themselves are concerned. There have been frequent anti-Chinese demonstrations, usually led by monks and nuns, who have suffered as a result savage prison sentences, beatings, and torture. Such actions as carrying a picture of the Dalai Lama, waving a Tibetan flag, or chanting nationalistic slogans incur the severest penalties.

While on the one hand, the Chinese have restored some of the holy places that they destroyed, with the other they are vigorously obliterating the domestic architecture of the old city of Lhasa. The great houses of the former nobility, the houses and shops of more simple people built in traditional style—in short, all the old domestic architecture—is being bulldozed out of existence in order to be replaced by ugly concrete buildings, while wide straight streets replace the former narrow lanes and back alleys. The *Jo-khang*, formerly almost inconspicuous in its surroundings of harmonious buildings will now be set in a bleak modern piazza. Meanwhile, Tibetan life and culture is increasingly impaired by the continual increase in the number of Chinese settlers, officials of all kinds, and technocrats who come to manage the new industries and public services. The Tibetans find employment as low-grade officials and workers or in the usual activities of petty commerce, shopkeeping, and farming. Traditional arts and crafts have by no means disappeared, as fortunately image-makers, metalworkers, and artists and painters have been required for the restoration of temples and monasteries, as mentioned above. Music and drama have been popularized under increasing Chinese influence.

As for agriculture, although some private holdings are now allowed, a fixed quota of produce has to be sold yearly to the Chinese authorities at a fixed price. Planning and planting policy is largely in Chinese hands, and although there seems to have been a great increase in production, one may well wonder how much of this benefits the Tibetan farmer directly. Recently some Chinese farmers have been settled on land leased from the Tibetans, or brought into productivity by Tibetan prison labor. After an unsuccessful attempt to control livestock herding—a way of life unfamiliar to the Chinese—the lot of nomadic herd owners has become much easier and they sell their produce freely after delivering a fixed quota to the Chinese authorities. As for forestry, travelers report that the timber wealth of the lower valleys is being ruthlessly exploited without proper reforestation.

Fortunately, there have always been some Chinese scholars interested in the history and ways of life of their neighbors. Nowadays, a few such Chinese, with the cooperation of educated Tibetans, are conducting archaeological research into early sites, such as burial grounds and early Buddhist rock-carvings. Such activities, however, are inevitably linked ideologically with the Chinese "Motherland." Valuable literary work is also being done, and a new Tibetan–Chinese dictionary, a most substantial work in three volumes, has been published. When the work of adding the equivalent English terms to all the entries has been completed (a work now underway at the School of Oriental and African Studies in London), this dictionary will replace all earlier ones for scholars worldwide who are concerned with Tibetan studies.

Also on the credit side, one notes the ever-increasing number of scholars worldwide who now specialize in Tibetan studies. A Tibetan seminar held in Oxford in 1979 was attended by seventy such experts, while at a more recent seminar held in Oslo no less than 170 papers were read by the participants. One gains an immediate idea of the range of subject matter covered by glancing through the "Bibliography to the 1995 Edition," now added to the two previous ones.

Impressive exhibitions of Tibetan art and culture are frequently held in one place or another in Europe and North America, when examples of Tibetan arts and crafts are available for all to see: religious images and paintings, ritual vessels, domestic artifacts, tapestries and handwoven carpets, manuscripts and printed books. Herewith is a sampling of such exhibitions:

> 1977–78, Paris and Munich: catalogue by Gilles Béguin, *Dieux et démons de l'Himâlaya*, Paris 1977; German version: *Tibet, Kunst des Buddhismus*, Paris 1977.

> 1981–82, London: catalogue by Wladimir Zwalf, *Heritage of Tibet*, London 1981.

> 1989–90, Cologne and Munich: Gerd-Wolfgang Essen and Tsering Tashi Thinggo, *Die Götter des Himalaya—Bestandkatalog* and also *Götter des Himalaya—Tafelband*, Munich 1989.

> 1990–91, Paris: catalogue by Gilles Béguin, *Art esotérique de l'Himâlaya: la donation Lionel Fournier*, Paris 1990.

> 1991–92, San Francisco, New York, and London: catalogue by Marylin M. Rhie and Robert A. F. Thurman, *Wisdom and Compassion: The Sacred Art of Tibet*, New York 1991.

> 1994, Milan: catalogue by Erberto F. Lo Bue, *Tesori del Tibet, oggetti d'arte dai monasteri di Lhasa*, Milan 1994.

The mere sight of such things should suffice to convince any doubter that the Tibetan people possess not only a language of their own, but also a culture and a way of life quite distinct from the Chinese. What the Tibetans now chiefly lack is the right of self-determination. In this respect one notes a growing sympathy and understanding, again mainly in Europe and America, for the present plight of Tibetans in their own land. To a considerable extent this is due to the charismatic presence of the revered fourteenth Dalai Lama, Tenzin Gyatso, who travels tirelessly in so many different countries. He is now welcomed almost everywhere by heads of state, government ministers, parliaments, and national assemblies. His presentation of the Tibetan right to self-determination and freedom of religion has always been in very moderate terms and he has been willing to accept Tibet's continuance as a part of China if only real local autonomy is conceded, replacing the Chinese direct-rule of the unhappy present. The demand for full independence has been more vocally expressed by other Tibetans, especially the younger generation, and by Tibetan supporters in many countries, but while several governments are prepared to vote for resolutions condemning violations of human rights in Tibet, none has so far been willing to champion the cause of full independence.

The Dalai Lama has now been in exile for twenty-five years, acting through his government-in-exile to alleviate the problems and difficulties of so many of his subjects (more than 100,000) who have fled abroad, mainly to India and Nepal, in the hope of finding new means of livelihood free from Chinese domination. In India, many such refugees live in agricultural settlements arranged as villages, each with its monastery, hospital, and school, all supported with remarkable generosity by the Indian government, as well as by friends of Tibet in many countries.

Tibetans have also constructed monasteries and temples in sacred Buddhist places in India, such as Bodhgaya, Sarnath, Sanchi, and Lumbini (in Nepal). The whole area around the famous stupa of Bodhnath in the Kathmandu Valley is now covered with Tibetan Buddhist monasteries, representing all the various religious orders.

At the Dalai Lama's headquarters in Dharamsala, centers of every branch of Tibetan culture are maintained. There is an extensive library, a printing press, schools for the training of artists and craftsmen, for music, drama, medicine, and now even a school for technological developments. The Dalai Lama himself is readily accessible to ordinary people, giving simple, impressive sermons and lectures. He conducts religious ceremonies in monasteries and temples far and wide, thus holding together his people in exile, whether monks or layfolk, with his inspiring presence. One must surely hope that this amazing wealth of cultural heritage, so carefully nurtured in exile, will find its way back eventually to the land of its origin.

We express our thanks to Dr. Erberto Lo Bue, who has assisted us considerably, mainly with the preparation of the additional bibliography.

H. E. Richardson and D. L. Snellgrove
30 November 1994

Preface to the 1968 Edition

To write the cultural history of any country might seem a formidable task, for the term 'culture' covers so many human activities that it is scarcely possible for any writer, or even two writers, to cover all the various historical manifestations of a people's cultural interests over long periods of time. It would be easier if one could draw more widely upon the writings and researches of others in the various fields where one does not feel competent oneself, but serious Tibetan scholars have always been scarce and the ground they have been able to cover has been correspondingly small. Even to draw upon Tibetan literary sources, and this we have done as far as was practicable, involves one continually in interesting but distracting side-issues, for so much is still virgin ground. Aware of present limitations, we have sought to write without false pretensions, and we hope that this work may serve for a few years to come as an adequate survey of the history of Tibetan civilization within the terms set by present knowledge. We remain aware that some of our colleagues in other countries could have written of some aspects of this whole study with far greater competence than ourselves, and we ask them to be patient when we pass over in a few words matters which mean so much to them. Reference to their specialized works, and our own for that matter, are given in end-notes, which we have otherwise kept to a minimum.

We have taken upon ourselves to write this book at this time because the civilization of the Tibetan people is disappearing before our very eyes, and apart from a few gentle protests here and there the rest of the world lets it go without comment and without regret. Many civilizations have declined and disintegrated in the past, but it is rare that one has the opportunity of being an informed witness of such events. If we succeed in awakening the interest of our readers in this tragic drama, which affects us so closely in the human problems involved, the task of writing this book will have been well repaid.

Its symmetrical arrangement into three parts and nine chapters does not represent a preconceived scheme. In fact we began rather differently, and it came almost of its own accord into this arrangement, as we put our material together. As the earlier course of Tibetan civilization is so little known, comparison of the various parts of our work with similar periods in Western history may help to put the subject into a more familiar context for those who come to it for the first time.

The Tibet of the early kings (Part One) shows significant analogies with Anglo-Saxon England and Western Europe under the Franks, Lombards, Visigoths and other Germanic peoples during more or less the same period (fifth to ninth centuries AD). We note the existence of the same kind of settled agricultural system, supported by cattle and sheep rearing, and much the same kind of established monarchic rule. Despite the earlier occupation of parts of Europe by the Romans (for which there is no parallel on the Tibetan side), cultural and technological levels were probably comparable. In the sphere of religion striking comparisons might be made: both in Western Europe and Tibet indigenous religious practices, based on oral traditions, remained strong, while a great universal religion, Christianity on the one hand and Buddhism on the other, was beginning to establish itself with the occasional support of interested local rulers, but largely through the efforts of small and determined monastic communities.

Tibet of the Middle Ages (approximately tenth to fifteenth centuries) bears many analogies with our European Middle Ages. On both sides the great universal religions triumphed, bringing in their train a whole new range of philosophical ideas, literary themes, arts and crafts, largely Greco-Roman for us and largely Indian for the Tibetans. By absorbing and reworking all this new material, both Western Europe and Tibet developed vigorous and colourful civilizations, in which the established religions of Christianity and Buddhism often played a very worldly part, despite the extraordinary sanctity of some of their devotees.

It is only when we come to Part Three that analogies break down. The European Middle Ages ended with the Renaissance, leading to the exploration of new fields of learning, which soon began to threaten all the traditional assumptions upon which the earlier stages of our civilization were based. But as the old forms disintegrated, we were ever striving to rebuild them anew, so that although an entirely new kind of civilization came into existence, it still managed to keep some firm roots in the past. The Tibetans, on the other hand, in common with all other oriental cultures, experienced no such renaissance; lacking fresh inspiration from without, they continued to live within the terms of what were now becoming stereotyped forms. One by one the great oriental civilizations have been forced to come to terms with the resilient but forceful modern Western world. Tibet was almost the last country in Asia to have its doors forced open (in the event by the

British), and it is to its great tragedy that the perpetrators of the actual rape are humourless Chinese Communists, who show little interest in compromising with their own traditional cultural values, let alone with those of the Tibetans.

Of the materials used for our study we must mention especially the texts and documents brought to light from the caves of Tun-huang in Chinese Turkestan at the beginning of this century. We have written of them in more detail (pp. 76–77) and here it is sufficient to note that before this material became available, knowledge of Tibetan history was largely derived from the later writings of Tibetan Buddhist historians, who wrote from their own particular religious point of view. They were little interested in the Tibet of the pre-Buddhist period except in so far as they might relate it to Buddhist themes. Using the Tibetan texts from Tun-huang, now divided between London and Paris, we have tried to give in the first chapter a succinct account of the early Tibetan period (sixth century AD onwards) of which the Tibetans themselves know little.

We hope our readers who do not know Tibetan will not be too perturbed by our spellings of Tibetan names. The spellings used throughout are the correct Tibetan spellings, transliterated into the Roman alphabet.* Written Tibetan has a number of unpronounced prefixes, and thus the radical consonant of any syllable may be the second or even the third letter. Since Tibetan dictionaries list words under their radical and not their initial letters, we have used capitals for the radical letter in the first syllable of all names, e.g. *bsTan-rgyas-gling* which is pronounced something like 'Ten-gye-ling'. It will be noticed also that final consonants are not always pronounced as they are written, although rules of pronunciation are far more regular than in English. It may be asked why we have not made matters easier for our readers by using simplified phonetic spellings but the answer is that while it may appear to make them easier, in effect it makes them far more difficult. Previous writers, ourselves included, have used all kinds of phonetic spellings for Tibetan, some ingenious and some haphazard, and they all suffer from the same great disadvantage of being so various in their forms. It is often impossible to recognize the identity of a name from the 'phonetic' spelling which some writer has chosen to give it. One can easily imagine the chaos that would result if we started writing French names as we thought we heard them or in accordance with our favourite method of phonetic transcription. Tibetan is not like Chinese, written by means of complex characters. It has a simple alphabet of thirty consonants and four vowel signs, and apart from the rather unmanageable appearance of much of its vocabulary when represented in the letters of our alphabet, there is no valid reason why it should not be written just as it is spelt. To help our readers we have inserted in brackets approximate phonetic spellings from time to time in the text and in the index. In order to distinguish correct literary spellings from these 'phonetic' ones, we have used *italics* for the former and ordinary roman type for the latter. Guiding rules for the pronunciation of the literary spellings are given on pages 291–2.

We acknowledge with thanks the help given by Dr Katherine Whitaker and Dr D. C. Lau in the checking of translations from Chinese source material. Thanks are due to Mr Philip Denwood for preparing the maps and the appendices and assisting us in a whole variety of ways, to Miss Averil Thompson for kindly offering to read proofs and make the index, to Miss Winifred Large for helping with the illustrations, and to Miss Eleanor Curzon and Miss Nora Shane for getting the typescript into presentable order.

A cogent reason for writing this book has been to contribute to the finances of the Institute of Tibetan Studies, recently established at Tring, of which we are founder-trustees. We hope too that it will draw attention to the range of Tibetan studies which are in great need of far wider interested support, both financial and scholarly, if anything valuable is to be preserved from the present wreck of Tibetan civilization.

Tring,   H. E. Richardson and D. L. Snellgrove
18 February 1967

---

* The system of transliteration used is set forth in D. L. Snellgrove, *Buddhist Himālaya* (Cassirer, Oxford, 1957), pp. 299-300.

A Cultural History
of TIBET

PART ONE

The Early Kings

Chapter 1

Manifestation of Tibetan Power

The Physical Scene Tibet is renowned as the most remote as well as the most inaccessible country in the world. It is surrounded to the south, the west and the north by massive mountain ranges, ranging from six to eight thousand metres above sea-level along the Himalaya and the Karakoram, and from five to seven thousand metres along the Kun-lun Range. The general level of western and central Tibet is from four to five thousand metres above sea-level, and the whole country is traversed by subsidiary mountain ranges which reach to six thousand metres and more. This great mountainous area, as large as the whole of Scandinavia, is tilted towards the east, where it is drained by the Tsangpo (Brahmaputra) which flows almost the whole southern length of the country, and by the Salween, the Mekong and the Yangtse, which all rise in the remote eastern parts of Tibet. Although there is no single well-defined mountain barrier to the east, the centres of Tibetan civilization were as much cut off from the rest of the world on this side as on the other sides, because of the vast distances to be travelled across uninhabited wastes and a whole series of subsidiary mountain ranges. Until the middle of the present century the journey from Lhasa to Peking normally took eight months.

The northern part of Tibet, representing about three-sevenths of the whole country, is a virtually uninhabited wilderness of mountain spurs and ranges, interspersed with bleak barren plains, stretches of soda-encrusted soil, and innumerable small lakes and pools of brackish water. Although subject to short spells of heat, it is usually a country of intense cold and bitter winds which prevent the occasional snow from lying in any but sheltered valleys. Here live the wild yak (*drong*), the ass (*rkyang*), the antelope (*gtsod*) and the wolves that prey upon them. These regions are visited rarely by hunters and gatherers of salt, soda and borax, but they were traversed in the late nineteenth and early twentieth centuries by several adventurous foreign explorers. A further two-sevenths of the country, still high and cold but tempered by a more southerly situation, lying approximately between latitudes 30° and 32° North, is a land of sparse grazing and rolling plateaux, lofty ranges of snow-capped mountains, and great lakes. Here small and scattered groups of nomadic herdsmen, a people of extraordinary hardiness and endurance, wander with their tents, tending great herds of yak, sheep and goats. On the higher pasture lands live such animals as gazelles (*dgo-ba*), blue sheep (*gna'*), bears (*dred* and *dom*) and foxes (*wa-mo*).

The remaining two-sevenths of the country comprise the extensive valley system of the Tsangpo and the valleys of the Salween, the Mekong and the Yangtse. These southern areas of Tibet lie on the same latitude as Cairo, and since they represent the only favourable agricultural lands in the whole country, it is here that the sparse population of Tibet (estimated approximately as two and a half million) is naturally concentrated. Here there are many scattered villages, a few towns for traders, officials and landed nobility, and everywhere are the temples, monasteries and nunneries of the various religious orders. The staple crops are barley, wheat, peas and buckwheat, and various root-crops, but peaches, apricots, pears and walnuts are all well known. Further eastwards grapes are grown and in the extreme south-east rice and maize.

The two basic ways of life in Tibet are the agricultural and the nomadic, and the products of the nomad-herdsmen – meat, butter, cheese and wool – complement the food supplies of the valley-people. In intermediate areas there are those who practise both agriculture and animal husbandry, and almost all Tibetan farmers keep animals of some kind, thus sharing the attributes of the herdsmen. Similarly the nomads who live nearest to the farmlands have contacts with the ways, arts and artefacts of settled communities. The severe conditions of travel in the remoter parts of the country, as experienced and reported by foreign travellers, suggest rather false conceptions of the way of life of most Tibetans. The majority live in the southern valleys and on the gentler pastures, and with so small a population and such simple basic requirements, they seem to have achieved for themselves one of the higher living standards in Asia. But since travel in all directions is long and difficult, they have been easily isolated from surrounding cultures.

Northern Tibet is wildly, even terrifyingly, magnificent in its great solitudes, but descending eastwards from central Tibet, the Tsangpo passes through wide valleys with willow, poplar and walnut, and then later through steep gorges whose higher slopes are forested with conifers and shelter rare shrubs and flowers. If we think only of the northern wastes, it is all too easy to conceive of Tibet as a high treeless land, but in fact the lower river valleys, such as *Dvags-po* and *sPo-bo* on the lower Tsangpo, have all the wood they can possibly require. Little is known about the potential mineral wealth of Tibet, although gold, silver, copper, iron, lead and various kinds of semi-precious stones all seem to be present. The limited quantities of gold, silver and semi-precious stones which were produced were used primarily for religious and personal embellishment.

The convenient threefold division of Tibet into valley-lands, pasture-lands and northern wastes omits only the extreme western areas which, lying westwards from Mt Kailas, drain through to the upper waters of the Indus and the Sutlej, as well as a few low-lying fertile valleys bordering on Nepal, of which two important ones, *sKyid-grong* and *Nya-lam*, drain to the south through Nepal, so that their waters eventually reach the Ganges. In this history of Tibetan culture we are fortunately not concerned with political frontiers, which frequently cut through cultural units, and we may therefore include in our survey the regions of Ladakh, Lahul and Spiti in the far west, which now come under Indian administration, the lands of Dolpo and Mustang, which since the end of the eighteenth century form part of western Nepal, and still further east the states of Sikkim and Bhutan. In recent centuries Tibetan culture has pressed hard against the mountain barriers to the south, for these are comparatively close to the main centres of Tibetan civilization. Thus in many places besides those just mentioned Tibetan cultural influence has made itself strongly felt amongst peoples who are of related Tibetan stock, even though they live in separate communities south of the main Himalayan range, such as the people of extreme north-west Assam and the Sherpas and Tamangs of eastern Nepal. Tibetan cultural influence continues to make itself strongly felt in the very capital of modern Nepal.

Tibetan Origins The origin of the Tibetan people is generally sought among the nomadic, non-Chinese Ch'iang tribes, who herded sheep and cattle in eastern Central Asia up to the furthest north-west borders of China many centuries before the Christian era. The legacy of this origin is seen in the extensive nature of Tibetan farming with its ever-present element of animal husbandry, in the readiness of the Tibetans to travel great distances, in their seemingly inborn ability to handle and look after horses, yak and other animals, and in their delight in open air and open spaces coupled with their sturdy individualism. But the most obvious part of the legacy is the large number of true nomads, depending entirely on their flocks of sheep and goats and their herds of yak. They rove throughout the year, in wide but well recognized limits, living in tents, and, apart from some small remote monastery, some of them may scarcely see four walls in the whole of their lives. In the nomads the racial stock is far less mixed than among the settled Tibetans of the southern valleys, and they may preserve a way of life hardly changed for at least two thousand years.

Tibetan-speaking peoples seem to have made their way ever further westwards across the southern part of the Tibetan uplands round about the beginning of the Christian era. This is confirmed to some extent by rather later literary sources, which enable us to trace by name the movements of certain important clans from north-eastern Tibet to the centre of the country. The early advance of Tibetan-speaking people westwards and southwards through the Himalayas and into what is now northern and central Nepal is also confirmed by the persistence in these areas of ancient dialects of Tibetan origin.

Thus there would seem to have been a continuous movement of rival clans from the general complex of tribes in the far north-east of Tibet, some of whom gradually made their way towards the more fertile valleys of central and southern Tibet, where they adopted a more settled and partly agricultural way of life. From the sources at our disposal it is impossible to be precise about the exact nature of these 'clans', but they may well have resembled those of Scotland (whence we borrow the term), and thus may have consisted of a chief with his family and hereditary retainers and bondsmen. As they became more sedentary the chief's family gradually became a kind of established aristocracy which may not have differed in essentials from the type of local hereditary rulers who continued to exist in Tibet right up to 1959. In the early period before the sixth century AD we may envisage a continual process of more vigorous 'nomadic' clans displacing those who had already become more or less settled, while during the period of the Tibetan kingdom (early seventh to mid-ninth centuries) when central Tibet took the offensive, 'infiltration' from the north-east seems to have continued by means of marriage alliances. In view of the generally unhistorical and metaphorical nature of our limited source-material for this early period, it would be rash to attempt to be too precise. Local traditions were formulated, recited, retold and reformulated to the greater glory of those who finally triumphed, and handed down by a succession of bards, until some of their recitations were committed to writing in the eighth and ninth centuries, and then happily preserved for us in the sealed caves of Tun-huang (see pages 76–77).

The earliest literary records suggest a world of rival chiefs living in fortified strongholds in the valleys of the central and eastern tributaries of the Tsangpo. Each chief had his noble vassals, and chief and nobles were served by bondsmen and subjects. Agriculture was practised, and sheep and cattle were reared. To the north of these nuclei of civilization were nomadic peoples, living much as they live today. We begin to enter recorded datable history only when some local chiefs combined to support as their overlord the chief who ruled in the Yarlung Valley, building him up into a powerful king, of whom his neighbours were soon forced to take account.

The Founding of the Yarlung Dynasty The chief of Yarlung, whose confederacy was to form the nucleus of Tibetan power, was known by the title of *sPu-rgyal bTsan-po*. The term *bTsan-po*, meaning 'Mighty One', was used regularly afterwards as the title of the king of Tibet, and this central Tibetan kingdom became known as *sPu-rgyal's Bod*. *Bod* may be an old word referring to Tibet as the 'native or original place', and it has ever since been the name by which Tibetans know their own country. The first king of Tibet, like his successors, had a distinct sacral quality, being known also as 'Divine Mighty One' (*lha-btsan-po*) and 'Divine Son' (*lha-sras*). Like other early cultural ideas, its origin may well be Persia, and have been received by the Tibetans through the medium of the Central Asian peoples on their northern borders. The divine king of Tibet, however, was supposed to have descended from the zenith of the heavens by means of a 'sky-cord', which passed through the various atmospheric levels. This notion forms one of the regular themes of praise of Tibetan royalty, occurring both in the Tun-huang documents and on the early stone inscriptions:

> From mid-sky seven-stage high,
> Heavenly sphere, azure blue,
> Came our king, lord of men,
> Son divine, to Tibet.
> Land so high, made so pure,
> Without equal, without peer,
> Land indeed! Best of all!
> Religion too surpassing all!*

There are several versions of a legend which first appears in the fourteenth century, telling how the first king of Tibet descended upon the sacred mountain of *Yar-lha-sham-po* in Yarlung where he was received by a circle of twelve men, whose identity as chieftains, shepherds, sages etc. varies in different versions. Because he came from the sky, they resolved to make him king, and carried him in a palanquin on their necks. So he was called the 'Neck-Enthroned Mighty One' (*gNya'-khri bTsan-po*).† Popular as this story seems to have been, it was simply based upon a piece of folk etymology which sought to make sense of an unfamiliar name sounding something like *Nya*. As we learn from elsewhere in the documents from Tun-huang, the original name of this first king of central Tibet seems to have been *Nyag-khri*. Before reaching the Yarlung Valley south of the Tsangpo and the homeland of future Tibetan kings, he probably established himself first in *Kong-po*, north of the Tsangpo and further to the east, for plausible identifications of place-names are possible in this area.

One of the pleasing features of this early literature is the sense of wonderment and pride that these first inhabitants of a united Tibet seemed to feel for their country. The following translation of a passage about the manifestation of the first king of Tibet is typical:

> He came from the heights of the heavens,
> Descendant of the Six Lords, the Ancestral Gods
> Who dwell above the mid-heaven,
> Three elder brothers and three younger,
> Seven in all with the 'Seventh Enthroned One' (*Khri-bdun-tshigs*).
> The Mighty Enthroned One *Nyag-khri*,
> Son of the 'Seventh Enthroned One',
> Came as lord-protector on the face of the earth,
> Came as rain which covers the face of the earth.
> He came to the Holy Mountain *Gyang-do*,
> And the great massy mountain bowed low, bowed low.
> The trees came together, came together
> And the springs rippled with their blue waters
> And the rocky boulders and the like did him honour
> And the cranes made him salutation.
> He came as lord of the six parts of Tibet,
> And when he first came to this world,
> He came as lord of all under heaven.
> This centre of heaven,
> This core of the earth,
> This heart of the world,
> Fenced round by snow,
> The headland of all rivers,
> Where the mountains are high and the land is pure.
> O country so good,
> Where men are born as sages and heroes,
> To this land of horses ever more speedy,
> Choosing it for its qualities he came here.
> O King, whose religion is equalled by none,
> Who is saluted by worshipping cranes,
> And who takes the light as his cloak!
> Those who are his nobles
> Are clad in lordly garments.
> Their greatness and nobility
> Are all derived from him!

> Of all trees the pine is the tallest,
> Of all rivers the Yarlung the bluest,
> And *Yar-lha-sham-po* is god supreme!*

Being sons of the gods, the early kings were supposed to have returned to heaven by means of their 'sky-cord', leaving no mortal remains on earth. The change to the normal mortality of historic personages was explained by a story about *Nyag-khri*'s successor in the sixth generation. By some mistake he was given at birth the ill-omened name of *Dri-gum* ('Slain By Pollution!'). As a divine being he was possessed of magical powers and grew up proud and contentious. When he continually challenged his relatives and subjects to fight with him, one of them, *Lo-ngam*, the Master of Horse, finally agreed, on condition that the king would divest himself of his magical weapons. The rivals met in *Lo-ngam*'s territory of *Myang-ro-sham-po*. Meanwhile *Lo-ngam* had prepared a strategem by fixing gold spear points on the horns of a hundred oxen and loading sacks of ashes on their backs. When the oxen struggled together the bags burst and the air was filled with ashes; in the confusion *Lo-ngam* killed the king. In this way the evil omen of the king's name was fulfilled. *Dri-gum*'s sons were dispossessed but eventually avenged their father by killing the usurping *Lo-ngam*; the younger son then went to rule in Yarlung while the elder remained as lord of *Kong-po*. Later historians, developing and reshaping a tradition which must have been orally transmitted, represented the name *Dri-gum* by the similarly sounding *Gri-gum* ('Killed by a Sword').

Very little historical significance can be attached to these stories, but this particular one may represent some memorable crisis when the established rulers were worsted by an invader from outside. At all events, it is said that from that time onward the kings left their mortal remains on earth where they were entombed in the royal burial ground at '*Phyong-rgyas*, not far from Yarlung, overlooked by the ancient royal castle of 'The Tiger Peak of *Phying-ba*' (*Phying-ba'i sTag-rtse*).

In fact the early rulers of this small Tibetan kingdom of Yarlung (*sPu-rgyal*'s *Bod*) can have been little more than princelings whose local power and influence fluctuated with their personal ability. When one of them first appears in a setting which can fairly be described as historical, he is quite overshadowed by two powerful neighbours. These two princes became involved in internecine war after which the vassals of the victor defected and chose to offer their allegiance to the ruler of Yarlung, whose name was *sTag-bu sNya-gzigs*. The nobles were leaders of the *Myang* and *dBa*'s clans which continued to play an important part in Tibetan history for the next two and a half centuries. Their choice of the king of Yarlung as their *bTsan-po* ('Mighty One') may perhaps be ascribed to the sacral character attaching to his line rather than to his ambition. *sTag-bu sNya-gzigs* was in fact reluctant to have power thrust upon him, but he died – probably by violence – before matters were decided. The nobles renewed their allegiance to his son and proceeded with vigour and determination to build up the new king, *gNam-ri slon-mtshan*, into the powerful ruler of a greatly extended domain.

Tibet's Neighbours When the Tibetans began to make their impact on the outside world in the early seventh century, they found that their country was practically ringed by well-established Buddhist civilizations. Buddhism, already firmly rooted in the middle Ganges valley by the time of the great Emperor Aśoka (third century BC), had spread during his reign to the far north-west of the Indian sub-continent, the area corresponding approximately to modern Kashmir, Gilgit and Baltistan. From there it had followed ancient trade-routes, and, crossing the Pamirs, made its way gradually to northern China along the trade-routes which passed both north and south of the Takla-makan. The southern route passed through the small kingdoms of Shan-shan and Khotan with their flourishing Buddhist civilizations,* while the northern route passed through the cities of Kara-shahr, Kucha and Kashgar, all, like Khotan, garrisoned by the Chinese, for this whole area had been under their control since the first century AD. It was during the Sui dynasty (581-618), as Ma Tuan-lin records, that the name of a Tibetan king became known in China for the first time. This was King *gNam-ri slon-mtshan*.

South of Tibet was the little kingdom of Nepal, consisting then of little more than the area marked as the 'Nepal Valley' on our maps. This had been open to strong Indian cultural influence at least from the fifth century AD onwards, and several Buddhist monasteries were established during the following centuries in Pātan, old Kathmandu and old Bhatgaon. Since this Nepal kingdom owed its existence to the trade passing north and south through it, it is fairly certain that there were already trading connections between Nepal and Tibet long before the Tibetans became a recognized political power. In any event, once we enter an historical period, Nepal begins to become a kind of half-way house between Tibet and central India.

To the west of our young civilization, developing in the valley of the Tsangpo, was a country of rather vague definition, known as Shang-shung (*Zhang-zhung*). Its capital was at *Khyung-lung* to the west of Mount Kailas, and it seems to have consisted of the whole area which we now call Western Tibet, and possibly extending further to the east. This ancient land of Shang-shung was probably already in contact with the neighbouring Indian regions of Kulu and Jalandhara across the same Himalayan passes which are still used today. It seems to have been already inhabited by a Tibetan-speaking people. Still further west lay

Kashmir, renowned as a great Buddhist land and much visited by Chinese Buddhist pilgrims, especially from the fifth to eighth centuries.

Until the newly developing Tibetan power began to make contact with all these various neighbours, its chief cultural link was apparently with those Ch'iang tribes on China's north-western borders who lived within reach of the Takla-makan trade-routes. These routes linked China, not only with India, but also with Persia and ultimately with Byzantium. All kinds of cultural ideas and motifs made their way along these ancient routes, and, as will be observed, quite a number of these seem to have reached the Tibetans in pre-historical times.

A Great Tibetan King On the assassination of *gNam-ri* (c. 627) his famous son *Srong-brtsan-sgam-po* (Song-tsen-gam-po) succeeded as a minor. He had the support and protection of a powerful minister of the *Myang* family until he was himself able to take over the work of warlike expansion. In a surprisingly short time, using their new subjects as allies, the Tibetans were ranging from the plains of India and the mountains of Nepal to the frontiers of China; they may even have already established contact through their new Shang-shung subject-allies with Khotan and the great international trade route that passed through it on the south side of the Takla-makan. To T'ang China *Srong-brtsan-sgam-po* became a presence on their borders, to be viewed with apprehension and seriously reckoned with. His friendship was won by the grant of a Chinese princess as bride (AD 640) and his reign, which lasted till his natural death in AD 650, was one of such exuberant military prowess and such personal prestige that it established the kingship on a firm basis and prepared it for two centuries of stable succession and almost imperial greatness. His reign is the first subject in the Tun-huang documents to be treated in clear historical terms. The 'Annals' give details of the events of his reign, and the 'Chronicle', in addition to poetic praises of his achievements, add a great deal of local colour by describing such practical details as an oath of fealty sworn to him by the leaders of the *dBa's* clan in return for the king's oath of protection and maintenance of their rights.

The father, the *dByi-tshab* and his sons made the following oath:

> 'Never will we be faithless to King Song-tsen-gam-po, to his sons and his descendants!
> Never ever at any time will we be faithless to the King and his offspring, whatever they do!
> Never will we seek other overlords among other men!
> Never will we be at ease with others who are faithless!
> Never will we interfere with food and mix poison with it!

Never will we address the first word to the King!

If one of our offspring, male or female, acts faithlessly, never will we not
  confess that such a one is faithless!

Never shall our sons befriend those who are faithless!

If we perceive that anyone else is faithless to the King, never will we not
  confess it!

Never shall there be calumny or envy towards our comrades who are
  without fault!

If we are appointed as officials, never will we act unfairly towards those
  who are subject to us!

Never will we be disobedient to whatever command the King may give.'

Such was their oath.*

   This oath gives some indication of the strength and stability of royal authority
at that time. *dBa's* and *Myang* had been the king-makers, but within a generation
it was possible for the king to cast off one of those powerful vassals and to receive
at the same time the most solemn pledge of loyalty from the other. Throughout
its span of some two centuries the kingly power clearly relied on the support of
the great nobles who acted as ministers of state, but by a skilful balance and
manipulation of rivalries among the nobles the kings succeeded in preserving their
independence from anything like a permanent noble oligarchy. In this game of life
and death – for most of the kings died young and by violence – the maternal
relations (*zhang*) were an important factor, since the protection of a young successor to the throne fell to the kinsmen of his mother. Several of the royal mothers
appear to have come from clans or tribes well beyond the Tibetan homeland and
this imported yet another element into the internal rivalries in the competition
for first place between the clans of Tibet proper, headed by the king-making *dBa's*
clan, and those of the maternal relations from beyond the borders, among whom
the *'Bro*, of Yang-tung origin, played the leading part. But skill in playing off one
party against another does not seem the whole explanation of the long viability of
the kingship, and we may look again to that sacral quality by which the king
became a religious symbol and the guarantor of the unity which was essential to
national strength. Full advantage was taken of this in songs and legends glorifying
the divine nature and origins of the line of kings. But the risks of the position are
also hinted at in a suggestion that it was the lot of the sacred king in the earliest
days to withdraw, perhaps to a ritual death, 'when his son was able to ride a horse'.
That custom became humanized later by a ceremonial association of the heir with
the kingship when he reached the age of thirteen, accompanied perhaps by some
pressure on the king himself to withdraw from active life. The royal title 'Divine

Mighty One Magically Manifest' (*'phrul-gyi lha-btsan-po*) served to emphasize the sacred and mystical nature of the ruler. This was further emphasized by the elaborate ceremonies of burial, where their own special possessions and at one time even their personal companions were buried with them in their tombs. As late as 790 there is mention of a group of sworn companions of the king whose duty it was to accompany him in death.

Contact with foreign countries began to have a marked impact upon this rather rough and warlike people, who certainly showed themselves receptive to cultural influences from borderlands. The records of the T'ang Dynasty of China provide us with the earliest descriptions by outsiders of Tibetan life and manners:*

> We are told that the country has a very cold climate, that oats, barley, wheat and buckwheat grow there, and that there are yaks, excellent horses, and dogs, sheep and pigs. The capital is known as Lhasa, where there are city-walls and houses with flat roofs. The king and his nobles live in felt tents which are joined together as one large one. They sleep in unclean places and they never wash or comb their hair. For the most part the people lead a pastoral life with their flocks and herds without fixed habitation. They dress in felt and leather. They like to paint themselves with red ochre. The women plait their hair. They worship the heavens and believe in sorcerers and soothsayers. They do not know the seasons, and their year begins when the barley is ripe. Their games are chess and dice, and for music they have conch-shells and drums. They have no writing for official purposes, and they fix arrangements by means of knotted cords and notched tally-sticks. They make vessels by bending round a piece of wood and fitting in a leather bottom, or they make basins of felt. They knead roasted grain (*viz. tsam-pa*) into little cups, and they fill these with broth or curds and eat it all together. They drink their beer in their cupped hands.
>
> There are hundreds of thousands of men ready to bear arms, and in order to levy troops they used a golden arrow (as insignia of authority). In order to give warning of enemy attacks they use fire and smoke signals. There is a watch-post every hundred *li*. Their armour and helmets are excellent. When they put them on their whole body is covered, with holes just for the eyes. Their bow and their sword never leave them. They prize physical strength and despise old age. A mother salutes her son, and a son has precedence over his father. When they go out and in, it is always the young men who go first and the older men afterwards. Military discipline is strict. In battle it is not until the troops in front have been completely wiped out that the troops behind come up into line. They prize death in

battle and hate to end their lives by sickness. Those families of whom several generations have died in battle are considered of highest rank. But when someone is defeated in battle or runs away, they fix a fox-tail to his head to show that he is cowardly like the fox. A great crowd will assemble and he is certain to be put to death. According to their customs they feel great shame in this matter, and they consider that it is far better to be dead.

As punishments, even for a small fault, they take out the eyes, or cut off the feet or the nose. They give floggings with leather whips just as they see fit and without any regulated number (of lashes). For prisons they dig down into the earth several dozens of feet, and they keep their prisoners there for two or three years.

The king and five or six of his followers are bound in friendship and they are called 'living in common'. When the king dies, they are all killed sacrificially. His garments, his treasure, the horses he has ridden, are interred, and a large chamber is made which is covered with a mound. Trees are planted there, and it is in this place that ancestral sacrifices are performed.

This may be to some extent an expression of a general Chinese view of 'barbarians', and indeed almost exactly similar terms are used of some of the neighbouring nomadic peoples. It is also rather a composite picture. The statement that the Tibetans had no writing, for example, can relate only to a time before about AD 640, whereas the information about Tibetan crafts and military prowess would have been acquired later. Nevertheless much of it can be confirmed from other sources. Some families still preserve ancient plates made of leather of just the kind described, and some Tibetans still eat their broth by taking it up in little cups which they mould skilfully out of moistened *tsam-pa* (roasted barley meal) as they eat. Lhasa can only just have been founded by King *Srong-brtsan-sgam-po*, and the brief descriptions of the way of life of the people are probably accurate enough. Of Tibet's military preparedness more will be said, and as for the use of red ochre as a face-paint, a text from Khotan regularly refers to the Tibetans, who invaded their country in AD 665, destroying temples and shrines, as the 'Red Faces'.

In addition to the general description of Tibet, the T'ang Annals give an account of the relationship between China and Tibet from the seventh to the ninth centuries, and so provide much evidence of Tibetan behaviour during a time when the two countries came to know one another quite well. Both *Srong-brtsan-sgam-po* and one of his successors married Chinese princesses, and occasional marriages may also have taken place between Tibetan nobles and Chinese brides. The granting of Chinese princesses to neighbouring 'barbarian' rulers was an instrument of Chinese diplomacy, and the Tibetans, adopting the same policy, made similar alliances with other neighbouring peoples, with the Turks and the *'A-zha* and the *Tu-yu-hun*, with Nepal, Shang-shung and *'Bru-zha* (Hunza).

Tibetan Military Power From the seventh century onwards Tibet begins to enter an entirely new period of growth and development. The political history of the period of the Yarlung kings (seventh to ninth centuries) is one of constant warlike activity. China was the principal rival and the Tibetans pressed further and further into the borderlands of what are now Kansu, Szechwan, Yunnan and Shansi. On one occasion they even captured Ch'ang-an (Sian) which was then the capital of China. By occupying strategic points on the routes through Central Asia they cut China's communications with the West, and the strain on Chinese resources and spirit are echoed in the war-weary poems of the great T'ang poets Po Chü-i, Li Po and Tu Fu. There were of course periods of peace, when Tibetan and Chinese envoys passed between the courts and between the generals on the frontiers. The Chinese began to hold their 'barbarian' enemies in far greater respect.

On one occasion the Tibetan envoy asked for copies of Chinese classics, and an anxious Chinese minister supplicated the throne, saying:

> How can we give the contents of our classics to these barbarian enemies of the West? I have heard that these Tibetans have a fierce and warlike nature, yet are steadfast in purpose, intelligent and industrious, intent on learning undistractedly. If they were well read in the *Book of History*, they would know about war-strategy. If they were well versed in the *Odes*, they would know how fighting men should be trained to defend their prince. If they were well read in the *Book of Rites*, they would understand seasonal programmes for the use of arms. If they studied the *Tso Chuan* ['commentary to the Spring and Autumn Annals'], they would know that in warfare it is usual to employ deceitful stratagems. If they studied the *Wen hsüan* Anthology, they would know how to compose and exchange letters and state-despatches. In what way would this differ from giving weapons to brigands or one's possessions to thieves?*

The Tibetans were now certainly a formidable enemy, and their country was organized on a war-footing with a system of general military service. The earliest organization was into three 'horns', right, centre and left, covering the eastern parts of Tsang (right), the Lhasa valley and surrounding country (centre) and Yarlung, Kong-po and thereabouts (left). By about 733 growing military and administrative responsibilities, the result of conquest and expansion, led to the addition of a fourth 'horn' (*Ru-lag*) to the west, and also to further formations to deal with Shang-shung and the north and north-eastern border areas. An account in one of the 'rediscovered texts' of the fourteenth century,* which purports to contain early material, describes further subdivisions within the various 'horns' and quotes figures which would produce 700,000 men available for each of the four 'horns', a very large figure indeed. Chinese sources represent the Tibetan armies in the field as numbering up to 200,000, and even if this is exaggerated, it must be remembered that China was only one of the fronts on which the Tibetans were engaged. Each division had its distinguishing flag, and it is interesting to note that the upper division of the 'left horn', namely the one that comprised the royal seat of Yarlung, had as its emblem two lions facing one another. These are still the main feature of the national flag of Tibet.

There seems to have been no basic distinction made between military and civil organization, and the same word (*sde*) refers both to district and to regiment. The districts were subject to the authority of the local forts, and although the commander was necessarily assisted by ministers responsible for various internal affairs, such as the collection of taxes, the hiring of animals, legal agreements and so on, the main effort of the whole administration was clearly directed towards maintaining the country on an efficient war-footing. The only ancient Tibetan forts that have been excavated were in the occupied Takla-makan area, where relations with the subject populations must have been rather different from conditions within the four provinces (as listed on page 31) of Tibet proper. In the occupied areas the ministers attached to the commanders were primarily concerned with the levying of supplies for the maintenance of their war-effort, for the Tibetan army was maintained entirely on local exactions. Within the provinces of Tibet proper they were primarily concerned with the levying of troops, and it is hard to understand how the economy of the country was not weakened by a constant demand for fighting personnel, unless, as seems likely, the call-up was efficiently arranged and care taken to ensure that agriculture and animal husbandry, upon which the whole life of the country ultimately depended, were not allowed to suffer unduly.

It seems barely possible that from so secluded a beginning in the little Yarlung Valley, the Tibetans should have been able to sustain so vast a series of military enterprises over a period of some 250 years; yet such was the case. Further north and west of the Chinese border the Tibetans were in touch with the then (early eighth century) diminished power of the great early Turkish empire, and they often joined forces with the Turks in attacks on the Chinese power, or, as it suited them, made alliances with one Turkish section against another. For long periods they made their presence felt in Turkestan (the Takla-makan area) from Hami to

Landscape and architecture

The castle of *Yum-bu bla-sgang* in Yarlung, reputedly the home of early kings and the oldest surviving dwelling in Tibet (see page 46)

(*left*) The 'cathedral' (*Jo-khang*) of Lhasa, founded by King *Srong-brtsan-sgam-po* in the seventh century and containing *Jo-bo Rin-po-che* (the Precious Lord), the holiest image in Tibet (see page 73)

(*centre*) The old chapel of *dBus-ru-ka-tshal*, a small seventh-century religious building which retains its early style and appearance (see page 74)

(*below*) The *Khra-'brug* chapel, reputedly founded by *Srong-brtsan-sgam-po* in the seventh century, is the largest and most imposing of surviving royal foundations in the Yarlung Valley (see page 74)

Site of the tombs of the early kings of Tibet at *'Phyong-rgyas* in the Yarlung Valley. On the mountain-side beyond is the ancient fort of *'Phying-ba sTag-rtse*, 'Tiger Peak' of *'Phying-ba*

The royal tombs at *'Phyong-rgyas*. There are ten tumuli identifiable as the tombs of eight kings and two princes who died during the period from AD 650 to 815 (see pages 50–54)

(*left*) *Kva-chu*, an eighth-century chapel near *bSam-yas*. Massive inward-sloping walls are typical of Tibetan buildings from the earliest times onwards

(*centre*) The first Tibetan monastery at *bSam-yas*, founded in the eighth century. The central temple has three main storeys and is surrounded by symmetrically arranged buildings with a great *stūpa* at each of the four points of the compass (see page 78)

(*lower illustration*) *Has-po-rgyab*, an eighth-century chapel near *bSam-yas*. It is noteworthy as an early temple which has seemingly preserved its original plan (see page 89)

(*below*) This stone lion which now stands on the tumulus of King *Ral-pa-can* at '*Phyong-rgyas*, seems to be a unique survival from the ninth century (see pages 53–4)

(*above*) The *Zhol* stone pillar below the *Potala* (see page 91)

(*below, left*) This stone pillar at *bSam-yas* stands on a typical lotus throne and is topped by a well-proportioned canopy and a finial with the 'sun-moon-union' symbol (see page 91)

(*below, right*) One of the two stone pillars at the *Zhva'i lha-khang*. They have severe-looking canopies and stand on solid stone bases decorated with the signs of the crossed powerbolt and swastika

(*below*) The *sKar-cung* stone pillar at *Ra-mo-sgang* near Lhasa. It has an elaborate fluted stone canopy and a shell-like finial. The base is decorated by a Chinese-inspired mountain design

(*above*) Extract of the *sKar-cung* inscription (see previous page). This temple was founded, and the stone inscription set up, by King *Khri-lde-srong-brtsan* in the early ninth century. Translated, the inscription reads as follows:

'As for the matters arising from the oath taken by succeeding generations not to abandon or destroy the practice of the Buddhist religion, I the king and my son, ruler and ministers together, having all sworn an oath, do act in accordance with the words of the edict and with that which is written on the stone pillar. Thus this founding of shrines of the Three Precious Ones (the Buddha, his Doctrine and his Community) by the generations of my ancestors and this practice of the Buddhist religion is to be held in affection and in no way for no reason whatsoever is it to be destroyed or abandoned, whether because people say it is bad, that it is not good, or by reason of prognostications or dreams. Whoever, great or small, argues in that way, you are not to act accordingly. The kings, grandsons and sons, from the time of their earliest age onwards, and even after they have assumed authority, should appoint teachers of religion from among the ordained monks, and should absorb as much religion as they can learn.'

(*above*) The stone pillar in Lhasa which bears a bilingual inscription recording the treaty made in 821/822 between China and Tibet

(*below*) A group of eighth- to ninth-century chapels at *gNas-gsar* between Gyantse and Shigatse

(*above*) Tomb of *rNgog Blo-ldan shes-rab* (eleventh century). An early example
of a tiled pagoda-style roof combined with normal Tibetan building (see pages 141 and 160)

(*below*) The monastery of *Rva-sgreng*, founded in 1056 by *'Brom-ston*, who lived
there until his death in 1064 (see page 131)

(*right*) *'Bri-khung* monastery, founded in 1179 by *'Jig-rten mGon-po*, rose to great religious and political importance during the thirteenth century (see page 137)

(*below*) The nine-storeyed tower of *Sras*, built by *Mi-la Ras-pa* at the command of his teacher and master *Mar-pa* as a kind of 'initiation by suffering' (see page 135)

(*above*) *sTag-lung* monastery, founded in 1185 by *sTag-lung Thang-pa*, became the centre of one of the smaller *bKa'-rgyud-pa* schools (see page 137)

(*above*) *Sa-skya* monastery, founded in 1073 by *dKon-mchog-rgyal-po* and destined to become the powerful centre of one of the most important religious orders in Tibet (see page 132)·

(*below*) *Stūpas* at the monastery of *Tshal Gung-thang*. This special type of Buddhist shrine (see pages 80 and 89) tends to develop in clusters around any sacred Buddhist place

(*right*) Seat of district governor at *rGya-ma* near Lhasa, a fine example of thirteenth- to fourteenth-century domestic architecture

(*lower right*) *Gu-ru lha-khang* in *Lho-brag*, founded by *Gu-ru Chos-dbang* (1212–73), a famous 'text-discoverer' (*gter-ston*)

(*opposite*) The Great *Stūpa* (*sku-'bum*) of Gyantse (fifteenth century). There are four storeys containing symmetrically arranged sets of chapels with vast collections of images of divinities and holy persons.

(*below*) A chain suspension-bridge in the upper *sKyid-chu* Valley attributed to *Thang-ston rGyal-po* (1385–1464)

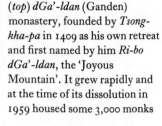

(*top*) *dGa'-ldan* (Ganden) monastery, founded by *Tsong-kha-pa* in 1409 as his own retreat and first named by him *Ri-bo dGa'-ldan*, the 'Joyous Mountain'. It grew rapidly and at the time of its dissolution in 1959 housed some 3,000 monks

(*upper left*) Houses in Lhasa. These flat-roofed, two-storeyed dwellings represent typical Tibetan town housing

(*lower left*) In the background is '*Bras-spungs* (Drepung) monastery founded near Lhasa in 1416. It rapidly became the foremost of the great *dGe-lugs-pa* establishments. In the foreground is *gNas-chung*, famous as the seat of the oracle regularly visited by the government

(*below*) *bKra-shis lhun-po* (Tashilhunpo) monastery, founded by *dGe-'dun-grub* (the 'first Dalai Lama') in 1445, and becoming from the seventeenth century onwards the seat of the *Pan-chen* Lamas. *gZhis-ka-rtse* (Shigatse) Fort is visible beyond

(*above*) The *Potala*, residence of the Dalai Lamas, constructed by the Fifth
Dalai Lama from 1645 onwards on a hill dominating Lhasa. There had been a
fortress-palace of more modest proportions there from the seventh century
onwards (see pages 199–200)

Fully developed
Tibetan temple architecture
of the sixteenth and seventeenth centuries. The same
styles and motifs have remained unchanged to the
present day:

(*top*) Complex of monastic
buildings at Tashilhunpo.
The tiered roof houses one of
the *Pan-chen* Lama's tombs

(*centre*) Temple façade and
roof decorations (victory-
banners and shaivite tridents)
at Tashilhunpo

(*bottom*) Interior temple
architecture at Tashilhunpo

(*above*) A holiday tent used by high-ranking Tibetans for summer parties and picnics

(*right*) A lavish Tibetan altar-piece as found in so many prosperous monasteries. Enshrined image of *Tsong-kha-pa* at Tashilhunpo

The simple house of a village-lama in Dolpo. Firewood is stacked around the edge of the roof which is decked with prayer-flags

Kashgar, and here they were in close contact with the cosmopolitan city-states along the great trading routes that passed from the West to China. These city-states had themselves inherited a whole variety of cultural influences, those of Buddhist India, of the old Persian Empire and of the Hellenized satrapies of Bactria and Sogdiana. Trade brought all and sundry together, and the territories that the Tibetans now occupied were the melting-pot of all the great religions of the world. There were Zoroastrians and Manichees, Buddhists and Moslems and Nestorian Christians. As they took stock of their new territories, the Tibetans must have been amazed at the existence of such material and cultural wealth; that they were by no means unappreciative of the latter is proved by the efforts that they promptly made to develop a literary language of their own, devised primarily for purposes of translation (see page 74).

Even further west they impinged on the Arab conquerors of the old Persian dominions in western Central Asia, and made contact with the local viceroys. They developed with them a relationship of guarded co-operation, broken for a time by the Calif Haroun ar Rashid, when it seemed that the Tibetan power was growing too great. From the Arabs they may have gained their first hearsay knowledge of Byzantium and Rome; they adopted the form *Khrom*, based on the Arab form of the name, to refer to some mighty empire, of whose actual location they were never really sure. Later the great epic hero of the Tibetans, the King of Ling, became known by the title of *Ge-sar* of *Khrom* ('Caesar of Rome'). This probably represents the very extreme limit of remote cultural penetration into Tibet.

Towards the south the Tibetans made their presence felt in Hunza and Swat and Kashmir. They reached the plains of India itself, dominated Nepal for a time, and penetrated the whole cis-Himalayan region. It was ultimately from this side that they were to become involved in one of the greatest deliberate importations of a foreign culture in which any country has ever engaged.

Difficult as it must have been to wage campaigns on such a variety of different fronts, one must remember that soldiering was still a seasonal occupation, taking place usually during the winter months after the harvest was gathered. Also, by their conquests the Tibetans were able to draw on the armed services and food supplies of their neighbours, who to the great advantage of the Tibetans were during this period all in varying states of disruption and internal dissension.

Early Tibetan Crafts We do not propose to detail the domestic history of Tibet. It is enough to note that from the death of *Srong-brtsan-sgam-po* in 650 until the murder of *Glang-dar-ma* about 842 there was a succession of eight kings (see page 289), and although most of them succeeded as minors, each can be recognized in the Tibetan and Chinese records as a distinct personality. The power and influence of the nobles, especially of the king's maternal relations, stands out vividly, but there was never a complete domination of the palace by the nobility. The astute manipulation of rival interests amongst the nobles, rendered easier by the new influence exerted by fresh royal relations from neighbouring countries and border peoples, enabled the kings to exert their authority and to maintain during this early period the effective unity of the whole kingdom. Wide-ranging foreign contacts began to enlarge the mental horizon of the Tibetans and brought in diverse influences in architecture, art and literature, as well as in ways of living; but the event which was to have the most profound and the most long-term effect on the cultural and political life of Tibet was the introduction of the seeds of Buddhism in the time of *Srong-brtsan-sgam-po* and its powerful reinforcement by *Khri-srong-lde-brtsan* (Trhi-song-de-tsen) in the following century. The first introduction of Buddhism, traditionally ascribed to *Srong-brtsan-sgam-po*'s Chinese and Nepalese wives, may be compared with the bringing of Christianity to the Scottish court by Queen Margaret, and in the early days it was probably little more than a polished aristocratic hobby. We shall write in more detail of the new religion later, for now we are still concerned with Tibetan ways of life in their pre-Buddhist setting.

Contemporary records and survivals are mostly aristocratic, and the life of the ordinary man can only be deduced from occasional indications and reconstructed by comparison with his life in more recent times, for this has probably changed little in its main essentials. The common man was farmer and herdsman. He built the castles and raised the royal funeral mounds. He made earthenware pots and metal vessels and figures of animals. He made tents of felt and armour of leather and metal, which he wore in campaigns on distant battle fronts. His wife helped look after the fields and the animals, and wove the woollen homespun, just as she does today. In later times Nepalese craftsmen brought many skills to Tibet, especially that of metal work, but it is clear that the Tibetans already possessed their own traditions of metal work, especially of arms and weapons, and in eastern Tibet in particular the local metal crafts have continued right up to the present time. It is possible that noble families from these eastern regions brought these crafts to central Tibet when they won these new lands for themselves in the fifth and sixth centuries. Once again we touch upon a pre-historic period of which we can write with no certainty, but there are sure indications that however much Tibetan metal crafts may owe to Nepalese influence, the craft itself must have existed in a still earlier period. Yet authentic survivals of metal work from the royal period are rare. In the Lhasa Cathedral (*Jo-khang*) there is a silver jug with a long neck surmounted by a horse's head. This is said to be a recent outer covering, made in replica and containing an original piece dating from the time of *Khri-srong-lde-brtsan*. Once a year a pottery drinking vessel, said to have been

used by *Srong-brtsan-sgam-po* and now enclosed in silver, was carried cere-
monially round the houses of the older nobility. A bronze cauldron traditionally ascribed to the time of *Srong-brtsan-sgam-po* is preserved in the noble
house of Phunkhung, who acquired it as part of an estate near Lhasa, which is
said to have been a summer retreat of the king. Similar relics from the royal period
are believed to be stored in treasure-chests in the Cathedral and the *Potala*. It is
said that ancient ornaments, swords and weapons are kept there, and an expert
search in the royal chapels of the Cathedral might reveal genuinely old objects
among the offerings there. The T''ang Annals refer to all kinds of presents made
of gold, a suit of gold armour, a golden goose seven feet high and holding ten
gallons of wine, a miniature city decorated with gold lions, elephants and other
animals, a gold wine vase, gold bowl and agate wine-cup, a gold duck, plate and
bowl. Gold animals are also mentioned as decorating the camp of the Tibetan king
(*Ral-pa-can*) on the occasion of the visit of a Chinese envoy in 821 (see page 64).

We have no certain picture of the Tibetans as they appeared at this time, nor of
their way of dress, but for their own idea of how their early kings looked there are
a number of images in the *Jo-khang* and *Potala* at Lhasa and in the old castle of
Yum-bu-bla-sgang. However, old as these may be, they can scarcely be contemporary. Another traditional survival from the age of the kings is a style of dress
worn on a few ceremonial occasions and known as the 'ancient adornments'
(*ring-rgyan*); there is another ceremonial dress which is worn more frequently
and known as the 'garments of royalty' (*rgyal-lugs-chas*).

Of more substantial survivals, the traditional sites of many ancient castles are
known, but only one of them is anything more than a heap of ruins or an obvious
later reconstruction. This one is *Yum-bu-bla-sgang*, by repute the home of the
kings and the oldest dwelling house in Tibet (page 33). This may well be an
authentic survival from the seventh or eighth centuries, and the name *Om-bu
Tshal* occurs in the Tun-huang Annals in connection with royal residences in that
area. The tower recalls the defence-towers with which the southern part of Tibet
is scattered. The interior has been converted into a chapel and the golden
pinnacle is certainly a later addition, but the stone-work is indubitably old, while
the tower itself makes an interesting comparison on the one hand with the remains
of an ancient circular tower at *Pho-brang** and on the other with one of greater
sophistication, which is not far distant and forms part of a religious foundation
ascribed to the eleventh century (*viz Sras*, p. 40). The connection of the ancient
royal line with the Yarlung Valley is beyond doubt, and not far from the castle of
Yum-bu-bla-sgang is the impressive burial ground of the kings at *'Phyong-rgyas*.

Tombs According to Tibetan tradition all the kings from *Dri-gum* onwards are
buried at *'Phyong-rgyas*, but as the site now presents itself, there are just ten

tumuli, identifiable as the tombs of all the kings from *Srong-brtsan-sgam-po* to *Khri-lde-srong-brtsan*, including two princes (page 35). Animal sacrifices were still offered at these tombs even during the early Buddhist period, and only excavations would show whether the close associates of any of these kings of the historical period were buried with them, as certainly seems to have been the case in pre-historical times. As was noted, the Chinese assert that this was so, but they may have been simply recounting what they had been told of the past. However, as late as the year 800 there is mention in the history of Nan-chao of an adopted son of the Tibetan king who surrendered to the Chinese to escape the duty of being interred along with his deceased lord. The Tibetan accounts were mainly written during a later period, when with the exception of the 'heretic' *Glang-dar-ma*, this line of kings was presented as fervent patrons of Buddhism, and all reference to pre-Buddhist rites at their tombs is suppressed. An early document from Tun-huang does contain a large fragment with detailed prescriptions for funeral rites. Obscure as many of the terms and references may be, the officiating priests are clearly *Bon* ('invokers') and *gShen* ('sacrificers'), and it is likely that these representatives of the old religion continued to preside over such ceremonies throughout the whole royal period. Another early text, which merits quotation in full, suggests that in this later period the companions of the royal dead were not killed, but lived within the precincts of the tombs, acting as though they belonged to the dead. This isolated fragment occurs in a later compilation of the fourteenth century, which purports to contain rediscovered texts hidden in the ninth.

> After *Srong-brtsan-sgam-po* had bestowed great favours on Tibet, he withdrew his physical manifestation according to three different showings. In the sight of the Buddhas he just withdrew his physical form. In the sight of the palace-officials he disappeared into a sacred statue. But his royal descendants built a tomb at Yarlung sMug-ra, and having covered the king and his two wives with gold leaf they placed them in silver caskets. The king was placed on his throne on the central square of the tomb and they piled up in front of him a load of gold, of silver and of turquoises as well as all the wealth from his treasury. They set up silk hangings, canopies, parasols and banners of victory, and having arranged everything properly so nothing was missed, they affixed a sevenfold series of seals so nothing should be broken open. The charge rested with the palace-officials [of the deceased king] who were appointed as his ministers, and all these palace-officials had to protect the king's tomb. They played the part of dead men and were consecrated as the subjects of the [royal] corpse. A distinction was made between the living and the dead, and they kept apart from the company of men. They did not come into contact

with living members of the royal line, and except at times of worship, living men, horses and cattle had no right to wander in the outer enclosure of the tomb. Whatever men or property made their appearance there, were seized by the 'dead men' who protected the grave. If they were touched by the keepers of the grave, they could not return to the company of the living. They received the mark of the dead and became the servants of the keepers of the grave. They had no work to do for others. They protected the holding and the treasure in the corpse-chamber of the tomb. Barbarian kings sent miscreants and the messengers of these kings would slink in to the corpse in the tomb. That is why the palace-officials protected it after the seals had been affixed.

As for times of worship, they worshipped the tomb of *Srong-brtsan-sgam-po* on the 'royal' day on which he departed for the heavenly spheres, and afterwards whenever it was his anniversary the princes, lords, subjects and followers brought wonderful and precious things as offerings. They entered the temple he had founded and blew a conch. Then they sent to the lord [of the tomb] saying: 'Tomorrow we shall worship the tomb of *Srong-brtsan-sgam-po*. All the people of the dead must go away.' Having said this, they perform the worship on a large scale. When they have finished their worship with the first offerings [of crops], with treasure and garments and so on, with horses and cattle and other animals, with items of worship [such as these], they pile up what remains in the place they are leaving, saying:

'O dead ones, come and eat these things. They are consecrated to
    you.'

Then they go home without looking back, and the keepers of the grave who had gone away, now return. They relish these offerings and left-overs and other foods. They enjoy these garments and animals and other things. They plant crops for their maintenance on the spacious lands. They have offerings and left-overs, food and drink in great quantities. They are not poor in wealth. They have no fears and troubles. They have no military service or any work at all, They are happy where they are, that company of palace-officials.*

This literary fragment gives a sudden view of the past, like a small section of a pageant glimpsed through a castle loophole. Already towards the end of the ninth century the royal tombs had been broken open and desecrated by looters, and they soon fell into total neglect. Of architectural motifs there is one quite unique survival in the form of a lion carved in stone, which now stands on the tumulus traditionally identified as that of King *Ral-pa-can* (page 36). It is manifestly of Persian style, and we may safely presume that it is typical of the kind of sculpture of which Tibetan craftsmen were capable up to the early Buddhist period. Excavations would doubtless provide us with some very interesting relics from the past, for it seems that the earlier traditional crafts must have suffered through lack of patrons during the period of political chaos that followed upon the assassination of the last of the line of the Yarlung kings in about AD 842, and then were later replaced by a whole new range of arts and crafts introduced from India and Nepal. The pillars that were set up by the royal tombs betray some Indian influence as early as the eighth and ninth centuries in the carvings of sun and moon or lotus-flower or in the jewel finial with which they are adorned, but some of them display other motifs, a free design of a lion, a dragon in the Chinese manner, or a foliage pattern reminiscent of designs from sites in Central Asia. These stone pillars are important not only because of these scanty remains of decorative art surviving from the royal period, but also because they preserve the earliest known records of Tibetan as a literary language (see page 74).

There are other burial grounds besides those of the Yarlung kings at '*Phyong-rgyas*, and complex funeral rites were certainly performed for the nobility and quite possibly for lesser folk as well. King *Srong-brtsan-sgam-po* promises (in the Tun-huang documents, p. 144) to build a tomb in a sanctified place for a faithful minister and to sacrifice on his behalf one hundred horses. The offerings made at the tombs of the deceased represented goods and chattels which were thought of as being useful to them in the life beyond, and this idea has persisted right through the Buddhist period down to the present day, certainly so far as the 'Old Order' of Buddhism is concerned. Thus in a present-day Buddhist ceremony relatives offer symbolically food, drink, clothes, etc., with the words:

> Listen, noble son deceased, your parents, brothers and sisters, your cousins and uncles and aunts, your devoted friends, are dedicating to you all these splendid things, food and drink and clothes and jewels, horses and elephants and foot-attendants, gold and silver, copper, iron, grain of all the different kinds, jewelled carriages, and platforms for mounting, couches, parks and castles, fields, implements, bright lamps for overcoming darkness, friends as protection against fear, in short all desirable things belonging to the categories of form, sound, smell, taste and touch. They are dedicated for ever as the property of your shrine.*

Several of the terms in this list, such as elephants and jewelled carriages, betray their Indian origin, and we have here simply an extension of the more ancient list of offerings made at the tomb in pre-Buddhist times. Even the reference to 'friends' points back to the very early period when the close companions of a chief were killed and entombed with him. Thus although these offerings are quite meaningless in the new Buddhist context, the Tibetans have never lost contact with pre-Buddhist ideas of the state after death.

Indigenous Religious Beliefs Apart from the belief in very early kings as divine beings who ultimately returned to the celestial spheres, leaving no mortal remains behind (thus they had no tombs), there is never any suggestion of transference to heavens or hells until Buddhism later on suggests such ideas. The deceased simply belong to the realm of the dead, probably rather like a kind of Hades. Pre-Buddhist religion in Tibet seems to be entirely concerned with the affairs of this life. Its purpose is to discover, usually by means of sortilege or astrological calculation, the causes of human ailments and misfortunes, and then to prescribe a suitable cure. The main causes of trouble to human beings are local gods, demons and sprites of all kinds, and the normal way of counteracting their attacks is to make ransom-offerings.

> For all living beings, afflicted with attacks by the eight kinds of sprite, by hating and consuming gods and demons, you must perform the Exchange Rite of transposing two equal things. Prepare the ritual devices and ritual items, the right-sized figurine as ransom for the [patient's] body, the sky-symbol, the tree-symbol, the arrow, distaff and the ritual stakes, the male figure, the female figure, the plant Ephedra and mustard-seed, a model of the house and its wealth, the things one desires. If they are exchanged as equal things, the ransom will be good. If they are transposed as equivalents, they will be chosen as payment.*

It is the function of prognosis, whether performed by sortilege, by trance or by dreams, to identify the god or demon who is causing the trouble, and it is the function of the rite to make amends. The divinity towards whom the rite is directed is sometimes conjured into a ritual device, known technically as the 'sky'.† This is a contraption made of sticks across which coloured threads are stretched. The simplest and most common type is diamond-shaped, consisting simply of crossed sticks with threads connecting the arms, but far more complex ones, wheel-shaped or box-shaped or a combination of several different shapes, may be employed. The god or demon is caught in this device like a bird in a cage. He is given his ransom-offerings, and then dismissed by being hurled away. These contraptions are still used by the Tibetans, usually nowadays as part of Buddhist ceremonies, but their use goes presumably back to pre-Buddhist times.

There is no suggestion that temples of any kind existed in this pre-Buddhist religion. Such descriptions of early ceremonies as exist assume a knowledge on the part of the reader which we no longer possess, but obscure as many of the references certainly are, we may gain some idea of the scope of these rites.

> As for the place, one must face towards the lower part of a valley and a cross-roads.
> (There must be) a lofty mountain, an amphitheatre (formed by surrounding cliffs), some good ground and some cross-roads.
> Turn your back to the lofty mountain and make preparations in the amphitheatre.
> As good ground a raised place is commendable, and at the cross-roads you must leave (your ransom-offerings).
> The items should be good ones and various:
> birds' feathers, coloured wool, sacrificial barley,
> a wish-granting cow and feathery fowl,
> a white monkey and a white badger,
> a bat and other things should be gathered together.
> Furthermore an offering of green barley,
> the three milk-products, the three sweet offerings, flesh and blood and other desirable offerings,
> these are the excellent necessaries to be gathered together.
> Set up as an aid the original exorcizing ring.
> The three great high vales of being above,
> The three great low vales of non-being below,
> And in between the place where gods and men may meet,
> (Here) on the white sacred mat
> Place the 'sprinklings' of green barley.
> Set up as symbol the sacred arrow with the white feather.
> Prepare the necessaries for offering to the pure divinities of the exorcizing rite.
> The great speaker of the original exorcizing *bon*
> Binds the turban on his head.
> In his mouth he receives the draught to be drunk.
> In his hand he offers the thing to be offered.
> With his voice he intones with ululations the exposition.
> Unsuitable ritual items must be avoided
> And the exposition must be done carefully in full.*

An essential part of these rites was the 'exposition' of a sacred archetype in the form of myth. These 'expositions' consisted in the recitation by the invoking priest (*Bon*) of ancient myths recounting the origins of existence, of gods, demons, genies and all the rest. The 'exposition intoned with ululations' served to invoke the help of the powerful beings whose nature and function might be described. This was an entirely oral tradition, but some examples of such invocations have been preserved in later literature. Similar rituals with exactly similar recitations of ancient myths survive to this day among peoples of old Tibetan stock who penetrated the Himalayas in pre-Buddhist times and have since escaped the full impact of the later Tibetan Buddhist culture. Thus from a Nepalese people like the Gurungs we can probably even nowadays gain some impression of the workings of such rituals in early Tibet. For an example of an 'exposition' of myth we can quote from Tibetan sources:

> Formerly by the magical power of the gods, the *gSas* and the *dBal*,
> An egg formed of the five precious gems
> Burst open by its own innate force
> From the celestial womb of the empty sky.
> The shell became protecting armour.
> The tegument defending weapons,
> The white became a strength-potion for heroes,
> The inner tegument became a citadel for them to dwell in,
> That obscure citadel the 'Sky-Fort of the Waters of Wrath',
> It stole the sun's light, so bright was it.
> From the very inner part of the egg
> There came a man of magical powers.
> He had the head of a lion and the ears of a lynx,
> A fierce face and an elephant 's nose,
> A crocodile's mouth and a tiger's fangs,
> Feet like swords and feathers like sabres,
> And between his horns which were those of the King of Birds
> He had a head-ornament a wish-granting gem.
> No name was given him, so he had no name,
> But the 'Primeval Priest of Perfect Power' (*Ye-gshen-dbang-rdzogs*)
>   conjured him with magical force,
> Giving him the name Great Hero *Wer-ma Nyi-nya*.
> He is the foremost of all the powerful ones,
> Protecting the doctrines of *Bon* and of *gShen*,
> Overcoming the hordes of foes and opponents.
> Acting as friend of goodness and virtue.*

The myth of the primeval egg occurs again and again in these ancient ritual recitations. Thus the egg is the origin of the physical universe, of primeval man, and of gods and of demons:

> The egg burst open and its outer shell
> Became the realm of sprites and parasites,
> Its inner tegument became the eighty-one evil portents and the three hundred and sixty injuries.
> The white of the egg spilled on the ground and became the four hundred and four kinds of disease.
> The centre of the egg became the three hundred and sixty classes of evil spirits, *etc.**

The early Tibetans conceived of men as being continually beset by a whole variety of spiteful demons, who were presumed to be directly responsible for human ailments and misfortunes. The main classes of these lesser divinities are known to us by name from early texts, but it has long since become impossible to distinguish between them, as must clearly have been possible once. On the side of health and happiness were certain great beings known as *gSas* and as *dBal*. Of their original nature we know nothing, but since they were equated in Buddhist times, the *gSas* with the more gentle Buddhist divinities and the *dBal* with fierce manifestations, we may presume that these equations correspond to their previous nature. Below the *gSas* and the *dBal* come various categories of divine heroes, who were probably originally the guardian divinities of the various Tibetan tribes.

> There was a Foe-God (*dGra-lha*) for each lineage of men,
> And for each Foe-God there was a divine army,
> And for each army an overseer,
> And for each overseer a leader.†

Each tribe must have possessed its own particular variations of these many myth-motifs.

Certain mountains were regarded as sacred, and it is likely that each tribe or group had its own sacred mountain. The mountain-gods belong usually to a category of 'hero-gods' known as *bTsan* ('Mighty'), a term which recurs significantly in the title *bTsan-po* ('Mighty One') referring to the early kings of Tibet. The close connection between these kings and certain sacred mountains has already been noted in some quotations (see pages 23–5). The sacred mountain of the chiefs of Yarlung, who became the kings of a united Tibet, was *Yar-lha-sham-po,* and the king is explicitly identified with this mountain. As Tibet became a united country and ever more conscious of its inherent unity and its military might, the ruling chief, from being a kind of 'hero-god' associated with a particular mountain, became a special son of the gods (of which all the various categories of 'hero-gods' were offspring), who descended onto the mountain from the celestial spheres with the special function of ruling Tibet. Early Tibetan beliefs in local divinities and their special theory of sacral kingship fit together well enough.*

Between harmful demons on the one side and hero-gods on the other there are other categories of local divinities who merit special mention as they have survived right up to present times. Closely connected with the mountain-gods are the local 'gods of the soil' (*sa-bdag*) or 'gods of the place' (*gzhi-bdag*) who inhabit conspicuous rock-features in the mountains, and the 'serpent-divinities' (*klu*) who inhabit streams and springs. In all kind of buildings and agricultural labour men are liable to come into conflict with these local divinities, who easily take offence if they are not propitiated in compensation for the use that men make of their domains. Any misuse of them, such as polluting a spring, provokes spiteful reactions from them which result in disease and death.

The priests who performed the ceremonies at the tombs and who invoked and made offerings to various classes of divinities were known as *Bon* (probably meaning 'Invoker') and *gShen* (probably meaning 'Sacrificer'). The whole practice of such religion was referred to as 'sacred conventions' (*lha-chos*), as contrasted with 'human conventions' (*mi-chos*), or as 'the pattern of heaven and earth' (*gnam-sa'i lugs*). Later Tibetan writers as well as some western scholars have referred to this early religion as *Bon*, but the word never seems to appear with any other meaning but 'priest' in really early Tibetan literature. Later on the term *Bon* came to be applied to the new religious developments, which incorporated some old beliefs and a very great deal of Buddhism, but this is a subject for the next chapter. Judging by later accounts, the priests of Shang-shung seem to have been reputed for their special skills and knowledge, and there are many references to their making special missions to central Tibet.

Non-religious Literature There would seem to be no connection between religious rites of the kind described above and moral values, but these were by no means lacking in early Tibetan society. Morality, however, belongs rather to the sphere of human affairs. There are some collections of sage sayings and moral maxims which have been preserved from the pre-Buddhist period.

> If there is one pine-tree standing, the forest has not ended.
> The slight blue waters of a spring are the substance of the ocean.
> A sharp knife for cutting meat, and with every cut the taste is better.
> A faithful mate, and at every tale the smiles are larger.†

Or again:

> Do not conceal your words from one who speaks honestly.
> Do not reply to deceiving words.
> Do not follow after false rumours.
> Although you reach a high position, protect lowly people.
> Although you are clever, guide those who do not know.
> Although you are experienced, watch your own measure.*

Pithy sayings of this kind have had a very long history in Tibet, and several renowned Buddhist teachers later produced collections of their own.

A large number of early songs are preserved in the Tun-huang documents. By the nature of the material these tend to be aristocratic in content and flavour, but sometimes they are simple and personal, such as the lament of the Tibetan princess who was married to the King of Shang-shung:

> The land that has fallen to my lot is the 'Silver Castle' (*dNgul-mkhar*) of
>   Khyung-lung.
> All around others say:
> 'Seen from without, it's a rocky escarpment!
> Seen from within, it's all gold and treasure!'
> But as for me and my opinion,
> I wonder, is it good to live in?
> How sad I am and lonely!
>
> The servants who have fallen to my lot
> Are these serfs of *Gu-ge*.
> I wonder, are they good as servants?
> In *Gu-ge* they are familiar, but dislike us!
>
> The food that has fallen to my lot
> Is fish and wheat.
> I wonder, is it good as food?
> Fish and wheat are hard to eat.
>
> The animals that have fallen to my lot
> Are wild deer and wild asses.
> Are they suitable to take to pasture?
> These deer and asses are too wild to care for.†

A common feature of this early poetry is the constant use of metaphorical allusions which have sometimes lost all meaning for us. Sometimes these songs are in the form of a challenge and reply between two rivals, in which the taunts are concealed by the use of metaphor. Such taunting songs of challenge still found a part in the Tibetan New Year ceremonies up to 1959, when the leader of one rank of soldiers would chant provocations at another rank. Many of the early songs were full of life and colour and reveal the countryman's interest in animals and the beauties of the land. As an example of Tibetan pre-Buddhist literature we quote at length an exchange of taunts in lilting prose attributed to a Tibetan minister and a Chinese minister who were holding a parley some time towards the end of the seventh century.

> The Tibetan minister *Khri-'bring btsan-brod* of *mGar* and the Chinese minister *Wong-ker-zhang-she* exchanged words of disputation. General *Wong-ker-zhang-she* led the mighty Chinese army forward, and when his troops had reached their objective, he sent a message addressing *Khri-'bring btsan-brod* of *mGar* who was in the region of the Kokonor:
> 'I have sent a load of millet and a load of mustard-seed, for I have [as many troops as these], while your numbers may be counted as tigers or yaks may be counted. Just measure your heads and make caps. Measure your feet and make boots. The Tibetan troops flow on to their maximum capacity, but my forces are so many. Once one has made room through the narrow neck, one can count on entering the great stomach. When our lightning strikes, not one will escape.'

Khri-'bring of *mGar* replied:

> 'There is no disputing the matter of numbers. But many small birds are the food of a single hawk, and many small fish are the food of a single otter. The deer has a multitude of horns, but are they upstanding? The yak has [just two] short horns, and we see how upstanding they are. A pine-tree has been growing for a hundred years, but a single axe is its enemy. Although a river runs ceaselessly, it can be crossed in a moment by a boat six foot long. Although barley or rice grow over a whole plain, it is all the grist of a single mill. Although the sky is filled with stars, in the light of a single sun they are nothing. If a single fire spreads from the lower valleys, all the trees of both valley and mountain are burned. If a flood emerges from the source of a single spring, all the trees of both mountain and plain are carried away. If a stone is rolled into a whole plain of pebbles, one will see whether the stone or the pebbles are broken. If one leaves a load of hay and a single iron rake bound together in a great field, one will see whether the hay or the iron rots first. If one throws a pinch of salt into a full cauldron, one will see whether there

is a taste of water or a taste of salt. As for thunder and lightning, although thunderbolts are few in number, there is a mighty great noise to the four limits of the sky. Your troops are like gnats over the surface of a lake. They would be useless for working our fields. Like mountain mists, they do not press upon men. My army will cut its way through just as a single scythe cuts its way through numerous blades of grass. If a single arrow is shot into a yak, one can count on the yak being killed.'

Wong-ker-zhang-she replied:

'If a heavy mountain crushes a small egg, one can count on its being broken. If the waves of a great lake extinguish a blazing fire, one can count on its being extinguished.'

Khri-'bring of *mGar* replied:

'On the great mountain there is a rock. On the rock there is a tree. In the tree there is a nest. In the nest there is an egg. If the mountain does not fall, the rock will not split. If the rock does not split, the tree will not break. If the tree does not break, the nest will not be destroyed, and if the nest is not destroyed, the egg will not be broken. The mountain does not break the egg just like that. If the fire blazes on the mountain and the water descends the valley, it cannot reach it to extinguish it. *sPu-rgyal* of Tibet is like the sun. The Lord of China is like the moon. Although he is certainly a great king, his splendour is of a different kind.'*

It is difficult to recapture in English translation the style and spirit of Tibetan verse, partly because the word-order in the two languages is almost totally reversed. The unaccented particles which serve as conjunctions and grammatical endings always follow the noun or verb on which they depend. The following verses consist of two feet of three syllables each, and the stress falls thus:

FIRST FOOT	SECOND FOOT
— ‿ ‿	— — ‿
or	or
— — ‿	— ‿ —

They are attributed by some royal bard to the King *'Dus-srong* who is supposed to have sung them at the time of the defection of his minister *mGar*. All we can preserve in the translation is something of the terseness of style as well as the poetic imagery of this early Tibetan verse.

> Oh at the very beginning
> In the most ancient times

All was so well ordered
Beneath the zenith blue
Upon this earthy surface.
The sky did not collapse.
The earth did not cave in.
The sun shone in the sky.
The earth was nicely warm.
The feathers were well fixed (to our arrows).
If you looked at them, how fine they were!
If you let them fly, the deer lay dead!
As deer were slain, so men had food.

Oho but nowadays
The earth-bound beetle
Aspires to act like a bird.
It tries to fly in the sky,
But it has no wings for flight.
Even if it had wings to fly,
The zenith blue is much too high.
It could not pass the clouds.
Neither reaching the heavens
Nor gaining the earth,
Neither high enough nor low enough,
It serves as food for the hawk.
In the little land of *Bya-pu*
A subject aspires to be king,
A frog indeed aspires to fly!*

Early Chinese Reactions to the Tibetans Before the quite recent discovery of this wealth of early material from Tun-huang, students of Tibetan history had to rely upon later Tibetan histories, heavily biased by Buddhist pietism and lacking for the most part any critical appreciation of earlier records. The Tibetans also remained largely ignorant of Chinese contemporary records concerning their country, although these are of immense value not only for their general historical reliability, but for the careful descriptions that they often give of particular events. They confirm the Tibetan tradition about Chinese princesses being given as brides to Tibetan kings, and they provide a continuous history of warfare, embassies and treaties between the two countries during the Tibetan royal period. The light they shed on early Tibetan ways is unique. A few Tibetan nobles are described as educated persons of pleasant behaviour, implying some knowledge of Chinese, but in general the tone is one of apprehension and disapproval of barbarian ways. Their military prowess is duly and sincerely admired; the size of their armies is frequently recorded, and probably inflated; their persistent and skilful methods in securing what they want are remarked on, and we have seen from a quotation (page 31) that some Chinese ministers warned against letting the Tibetans have copies of Chinese literary works in case they learned too much; we may fairly presume that at this early period there were a few Tibetan scholars of literary Chinese at the Tibetan court. This is worth commenting on, for from the end of the royal period (approximately AD 842) onwards Chinese studies were never fostered in Tibet, and the Tibetans have remained to this day as ignorant of Chinese literature and philosophy as of Chinese historical records. Chinese cultural influence in Tibet has been so slight compared with what it might have been, and is virtually limited to just a few artefacts. As early as 640 they sent ink and paper, as well as silks and jewels. Tea was probably also introduced into Tibet about this time, although it would have remained for the time being an aristocratic drink. A document of the eighth century seems to refer to some kind of tea-making utensil. We know from their own records that the Tibetans were already brewing ale from rice and grain and they certainly knew of wine made from the grape. It is likely that *Srong-brtsan-sgam-po*'s Chinese wife, to whom is attributed so fervent a zeal for Buddhism, had a far greater influence at the court in introducing gentler manners. It is related in the T'ang Annals* that she greatly disliked the way in which the Tibetans painted their faces red, and that *Srong-brtsan-sgam-po* formally forbade this custom at her instance. He himself gave up his clothes of felt and rough homespun and adopted Chinese manners, and he arranged for the sons of the great families to receive a Chinese education.

We quote from the T'ang Annals the description by a Chinese ambassador of his reception at the Tibetan court in 821.†

> The valley to the north of the River Tsang-po is the king's headquarters for the summer. It is surrounded by stakes fixed together, and at intervals of one hundred paces a hundred lances are set up with a great banner fixed in the centre of them. There are three gates one hundred paces apart, which are guarded by soldiers clad in armour. Priests with feathered head-dresses and girdles of tiger-skin beat drums. Anyone who would enter is searched before he is allowed in. In the centre there is a high platform surrounded by a jewelled balustrade. The king sits in his tent which is decorated with gold ornaments in the form of dragons, tigers and leopards. He is dressed in white cloth, and wears a turban, the colour of the morning clouds, bound round his head. He bears a sword

inlaid with gold. The Great Religious Minister stands on his right, and the ministers of state are in a row at the foot of the platform.

As soon as the T'ang Ambassador arrived, the honourable minister Si-ta-jo came to discuss with him (the protocol of) the alliance. A great feast took place to the right of the tent, and the manner of the serving of dishes and passing of wine rather resembled Chinese customs. Music was played to the air of 'The Prince of Chin breaks the phalanx', as well as other tunes of the Liang Prefecture. It is recorded that all the songs and entertainment were done by Chinese. The altar for the pact was ten paces wide and two feet high. The T'ang Ambassador and more than ten of the alien ministers faced more than one hundred chiefs who were seated below the altar. A throne was placed on the altar, and the Great Religious Minister, having ascended the throne, pronounced the oath. Someone at his side translated it and passed it on to those below. When he had finished, they drew their blood (in confirmation of the oath), but the Great Religious Minister did not. However, he repeated the oath in the name of Buddha, and drank to the T'ang Ambassador from a cup of saffron water. The Ambassador returned the compliment and they descended from the altar.

We have deliberately avoided mentioning Buddhism in this first chapter, because its importance has been so much over-emphasized by later Tibetan historians, whose only real interest is in the fortunes of their religion. It was little more than a court interest to begin with, but by the end of the royal period (*c*. 842) Buddhist prelates were beginning to occupy positions of power. We must now go back over the ground already covered and trace the development of Indian religious influence. In any case this subject is so complex that it requires separate consideration.

Chapter 2

Introduction of Buddhism

Previous Developments in India Nowadays we think of Tibet as preserving a strange form of Buddhist civilization, isolated culturally from her neighbours, who for the most part are indifferent or even hostile to Buddhism in any form. The one small exception are the Newar Buddhists of Nepal, who, like the Tibetans, represent a strange survival of Indian Buddhist civilization, which since about AD 1200 has disappeared almost entirely from the land of its origin. Yet in the seventh century AD, when the Tibetans were emerging as an ebullient self-confident power in Central Asia, the situation was completely reversed. Tibet was then indifferent and even hostile to Buddhism, as the inmates of the monasteries of Khotan learned to their cost, while all her neighbours, with the exception of the Arabs who were just then making their presence felt on the western confines of Central Asia, were supporters of Buddhism in its various forms.

Buddhism had progressed a very long way since the fifth century BC when its teachings were first promulgated throughout the cities of the upper Ganges Valley by the faithful followers of the Enlightened One, the Lord *Śākyamuni*. It began as a special way of life for gentle ascetics, men, and later women, who deliberately forsook their homes and normal responsibilities for the homeless life of religious mendicants. Thanks probably to the directing force of *Śākyamuni* himself, their self-discipline and kindly demeanour soon won them the support of wealthy patrons, especially among the merchant classes. They received lands and buildings as gifts, which first they used as fixed retreats for the three months of the Indian monsoon, and which only later became the permanent headquarters of self-constituted orders of monks. In the third century BC the Emperor *Aśoka* seems to have bestowed special favours on the Buddhist communities, and they spread far and wide throughout the length and breadth of India. Merchants and monks were common travelling companions in ancient India, just as they were in Tibet until very recent times.

The Buddhists began as one order of Indian ascetics among many others, but it happened to be the one that succeeded (for reasons that we have no space to analyse here) beyond all others. Whatever sound spiritual values a successful religion may continue to maintain, it is bound at the same time to come to terms with the world on which it depends for its support. Thus while the core of Buddhist practice, as exhibited by a minority of devotees throughout all the later period, remains a strict asceticism as much in the intellectual as the physical sphere, the great majority of those who call themselves Buddhists have played their normal part in human activities. Apart from certain basic philosophical principles which early demanded attempts at precise definition, the first bands of monks were not much concerned with literary and academic pursuits. But they soon found it necessary to justify their rules and customs by recalling whole sets of oral traditions attributable to their founder, and as the order spread and split into separate schools (as was inevitable, if only because of the distances that separated them), they found it increasingly necessary to justify by appeal to tradition the changes that were imperceptibly taking place in their beliefs and their practices. From using local Indian dialects they quite naturally took to using Sanskrit, the classical and literary language of India, as the main medium for the texts that they now committed to writing. Over the centuries a vast literature began to develop, concerned not just with the teachings and rules of their order but with vast philosophical problems; these problems became ever more developed and complex as the Buddhists came into conflict with other philosophical schools, and so sought to restate their fundamental philosophical position in terms that suited fresh arguments. Similarly the early ascetics might have been little concerned with Indian divinities and the ritual needs of the local layfolk, but as Buddhism became the religion of the many, it became increasingly necessary for its accredited representatives to attend to the wants of its lay supporters. Thus Buddhist monks began to act as priests, acknowledging, as did the Brahmans, the power and influence of local gods. They became skilled in the medical knowledge of their times, adding whole series of medical works to their ever-growing literary collections.

Yet the greatest change that Buddhism was to undergo seems to have been largely an internal development, for it concerned the actual goal and forms of practice of those who were seriously devoted to Buddhism as a religion in its own right. Round about the beginning of the Christian era there came into existence schools of practising Buddhists, who claimed that the way that had been followed before them was all very well so far as it went, but that it was really only a 'lesser way', leading at best to a kind of selfish salvation for oneself alone. This was not the true way of the Enlightened One, the Lord *Śākyamuni*, who had sought not just salvation for himself alone, but the salvation of all other sentient beings as well. The essential corollary of his perfect wisdom was precisely his universal compassion, and it was in the unity of wisdom and compassion that his enlightenment consisted. He may well have taught a 'lesser way' to those of weak understanding, it was argued, but the only true way for a perfect follower of his law was to strive to be a *buddha*, an enlightened one, like him. Those who subscribed to these new and ambitious theories referred to themselves as followers of the 'Great Way' (*Mahāyāna*). The theories involved a radical shift in Buddhist philosophy and morality, and it is a hard task to resume satisfactorily in a few short paragraphs processes that evolved over several centuries. But since it was this later form of Buddhism that the Tibetans received from their neighbours from the seventh century AD onwards, some description of it forms a necessary part of Tibet's cultural history.

It had been taught from the start of Buddhism that normal life was a round of suffering, leading inexorably from one rebirth to another. Phenomenal existence was composed of apparent conglomerations of physical and mental elements, which disintegrated on death in order to reform with others to make yet another physical entity, as impermanent and therefore ultimately as unreal as any other. The worthy Buddhist monk (*arhat*) was one who reduced the elements of his personal existence to such total quietude that at his death they disintegrated never to reform any more. The philosophers of the early Buddhist schools were much concerned with the actual nature of the basic physical and mental elements, which were only finally dispersed in *nirvāṇa* (which means a blowing out or dispersal); however much they may have disputed on this subject, they were all agreed that physical bodies had no real existence at all, in so far as they were composite and impermanent. A common simile for the human body is a cart that can be dismantled into various component parts. It is argued that just as there is ultimately no such thing as a cart, so there is no such thing as a human person. We may see flaws in such an argument, but no orthodox Buddhist, whatever his school, seems to have disputed this matter.

The followers of the 'Great Way' went beyond the earlier Buddhist teachings by insisting that the elements themselves, in short whatever names could be named, were as empty of ultimate significance as the physical entities of which they formed a part. They taught a doctrine of 'universal emptiness', empty not in a nihilistic sense (their opponents were quick to accuse them of this and they refuted the charge), but empty in the sense that nothing could be predicated of anything. In Western terms it might be better called a doctrine of universal relativity. They continued to use and indeed to develop the earlier philosophical theories and structures, but they used them simply as a means to an end, much as we might use grammatical exercises in order to master a language, and then put our grammar-book away for ever, once the language has been mastered. What is extraordinary is the insistence with which they found it necessary to preach their doctrine of universal emptiness, this 'Perfection of Wisdom'. Whole new series of texts, claiming to be the teachings of *Śākyamuni* himself, came into existence, and they reiterate interminably the absolute emptiness of every conventional concept from that of a *buddha* to a mere element of phenomenal existence. There is a 'Perfection of Wisdom' text in 8,000 verses, a longer version in 25,000 and a still longer one in 100,000. There are short versions, of which the most popular is the 'Diamond-Cutter', well known in English translations. These supposedly canonical texts, of which the actual origin remains unknown, provide the philosophical basis of all *Mahāyāna* Buddhism. The Tibetans later made them into a separate section in their voluminous Buddhist canon, and it would be a very poor Tibetan temple indeed which did not possess the set of eighteen volumes of these 'Perfection of Wisdom' texts.

Teachings which deliberately reduced every possible statement to nonsense would have been entirely destructive of all conventional religious practice, were it not for the convenient theory of two kinds of truth, relative and absolute. Whereas all concepts might be ultimately meaningless in the tranquil mind of an enlightened sage, lesser beings who were still struggling along the path towards enlightenment needed firm supports on the way, and these were provided by conventional philosophical notions and moral teachings. It was admitted from the start that such supports had an entirely relative value, and those that were suitable for one kind of person might well be quite unsuitable for another. The primary need now for a 'would-be buddha' was to find a teacher whose methods suited the propensities of his pupil. The perfect teacher took the place of the Buddha himself in the eyes of a devoted disciple, and absolute faith in one's chosen teacher became the foremost requirement in the later forms of religious practice.

The *Mahāyāna* teachings developed in normal monastic settings, and at one time monks who followed the 'lesser way' and those who professed to follow the 'Great Way' sometimes lived side by side in the same monasteries, but before long the new teachings were bound to have the most disruptive effects. According to the old morality, one could only be a real follower of the Buddha if one renounced the world and became an ascetic; by practising conscientiously one might within a series of a very few human lives succeed in tranquillizing the elements which made up the stream of one's own existence, and so bring the process of suffering to a stop. But according to the new morality all this was changed: the goal now was not just to save oneself but to realize final enlightenment for the benefit of all others as well as one's self. This would involve one in heroic striving through myriads of existences, where one's primary function would be the selfless service of others. Clearly therefore not only monks, but virtuous laymen who had taken the vow of a 'would-be buddha' were equally on the way towards final enlightenment. Buddhism as an active religious force was no longer the preserve of life-denying ascetics. It was this realization that made for the main practical differences between early Buddhism and the *Mahāyāna*, but this process, unfortunately perhaps for the subsequent history of Buddhism, did not stop even here.

As a pan-Indian religion Buddhism was now ready to adopt any religious practices whatsoever, so long as they might be used as a means towards the perfection of enlightenment, and since the decision about what was usable or not depended upon no recognized authority, but upon those practising the religion, there was no form of Indian religious practice that did not now have some Buddhist equivalent. From the earliest times Buddhist monks had used recognized methods of physical and mental self-control, usually referred to under the general term of *yoga*. Regulated control of the breath and concentrating one's gaze were very ancient techniques. Later the general acceptance of Indian divinities, although under special Buddhist names, meant that they too could be brought into play for meditative purposes. They were conceived of as beings of power, sometimes even consubstantiated in buddhahood, and the powers of spiritual grace at their disposal could transfer their devotees to the higher spheres of extra-sensory experience. The primary means of establishing personal contact with such a divinity was by means of his 'spell' (*mantra*), which was repeated thousands and tens of thousands of times during long periods of meditation upon the envisaged physical form of the god. The great gods and goddesses were envisaged conventionally as resembling kings and queens. They were enthroned in the centre of a palace, surrounded by an entourage of lesser divinities and controlling the four quarters of the world. Any such particular set of divinities, as envisaged at any particular time, possessed total control over the whole of existence, and the skilled meditator, by calling them forth in his mind, identified himself through the concentrated use of the requisite 'spell' with the central divinity in the heart of the universe. Thus through the medium of his chosen divinity, he himself was temporarily consubstantiated in buddahood itself. Methods such as these, which Westerners might dismiss as mere self-hypnotism, could be used quite legitimately within the terms of the new philosophy, which taught that all forms were ultimately unreal and empty, the gods themselves as much as those who meditated upon them. The criterion by which any method was judged was its success in gaining its object, and those who used such methods were convinced that by their means they could experience the real nature of things which lay beyond all forms and names. New forms of Buddhist literature, known as 'tantras', were developed, and in these the various sets of divinities were described and praised, the rituals were referred to and the states of supreme bliss that might be experienced were extolled.

These new practices of Buddhist *yoga* were not necessarily monastic, and so they were developed as much by free-roaming schools of yogins as by monks. The yogins, not being bound by monastic rules, were free to marry, and they introduced yet other forms of *yoga* involving the controlled use of the sexual processes. These sexual forms of *yoga* concentrated upon divinities in male and female pairs, and in so far as their methods were found effective for the realization of a kind of transcendent bliss that was identified with enlightenment, the pairs of gods and goddesses were logically conceived as possessing buddha-rank.

The changes and developments within Indian Buddhism between the first century AD and its general disappearance from the land of its origin at the end of the twelfth century were enormous; it was during this long period that it gradually became the religion of the greater part of Asia. It had already reached China across the Central Asian tracks in the first century AD and thereafter a whole succession of monk travellers and scholars, both from the Indian and the Chinese side, maintained Buddhist cultural contacts through the city-states of the Takla-makan (generally under Chinese control until the seventh century, when the Tibetans appeared on the scene) as well as in the two great countries that were the main centres of pan-Asian civilization. From China Buddhism passed to Korea and Japan. Meanwhile it passed direct from India and Ceylon to Burma, Siam and Indo-China and to the islands of South-East Asia. Tenuous links were maintained throughout this whole vast area by Chinese monk travellers who made the long journey to and from India by way of Central Asia and by sea via South-East Asia. It spread to these various countries in the whole variety of its forms, Ceylon, Burma and Siam receiving it mainly in its earlier forms which were known later by their opponents as the 'lesser way'. Meanwhile central and north-western India became the main centres of the developed teachings of the 'Great Way', and since it was from north-western India that Buddhism spread across Central Asia to China, most of its later Indian versions became known throughout the city-states of the Takla-makan and in China and Japan. Although it does not affect later developments in Tibet, it is interesting to note in passing that these later teachings also spread by sea-routes across to Indo-China and the islands of South-East Asia. Being so close a neighbour, Nepal received the full full force of Indian Buddhist developments. Buddhism became established here both in its earlier and *Mahāyāna* forms by the fifth century AD, and from then until the end of the twelfth century its many monastic centres, concentrated mainly in Pātan and old Kathmandu, remained in constant contact with the great monastic centres of central India. Later Tibet inherited the Indian and Nepalese traditions intact.

Despite the extraordinary developments that were taking place in Buddhist theory and practice, and despite the important part played in these by non-celibate yogins, the great strength of Buddhism as an organized religion still lay in its monasteries. But these had changed a great deal from the very early times when they were quiet retreats for small groups of meditating monks. Such small religious centres certainly continued to exist (just as they still existed in Tibet right up to 1959), but the main Buddhist centres of central India during the eighth to twelfth centuries were the great monastic universities of Nālandā, Bodhgayā, Odantapuri and Vikramashīla, housing thousands of monks and learned men, those who had taken monastic vows and those who had not, and attracting scholars from every Asian country which had developed an interest in Buddhism. From the fourth to the eighth centuries Chinese monk scholars were frequent visitors, and from the eighth century to the final eclipse of Buddhism in India at the end of the twelfth the Tibetans were constantly visiting Nepal and India for texts, instructions and initiations. Even in later centuries Tibetan pilgrims continued to visit the holy places.

This brief survey of general Buddhist developments will assist in explaining the whole new course of cultural development upon which the Tibetans began to embark rather hesitatingly in the seventh century, and to which they had committed themselves quite wholeheartedly by the twelfth century. There is sad irony in the whole historical situation. When the Tibetans were in two minds about adopting a foreign religion, all the countries surrounding them were enthusiastic about its practice, and were still practising it mainly in its conventional monastic forms. Yet by the time the Tibetans had firmly made up their minds to introduce everything Buddhist they could find, Buddhism had disappeared under Moslem pressure from north-western India and Central Asia, while the Buddhist teachers from Nepal and central India who had now become their chief authorities instructed them (seldom freely but willingly enough in return for substantial payments of gold) in all the available texts and practices that went under the label of Buddhist in the latter days of Indian Buddhism. Thus the great Canon which the Tibetans eventually put together for themselves in the thirteenth century was the most composite in its extraordinary range of teachings that any group of Buddhists had produced. Thereafter Buddhism disappeared from India and so dwindled in Nepal, where it was subjected constantly to the social pressures of a brahman-dominated society, that the Tibetans soon found themselves the sole representatives of forms of Buddhist practice in which no one else in Asia was seriously interested; the only exceptions were the Mongols, whom they succeeded in converting, and occasionally the Chinese court as part of its policy of reassuring those whom it chose to regard as its Tibetan and Mongol subjects. The Tibetans became in effect the inheritors of the whole Indian Buddhist tradition, and thus from the seventh century onwards it becomes increasingly difficult to write of the historical development of Tibetan culture without constant reference to Indian forms of literature, Indian religious practices, Indian religious orders and monastic organization, Indian medicine, Indian styles of painting and architecture, even though so far as medicine, painting and architecture were concerned, the Indian forms were not the only ones of which the Tibetans made use.

We must now attempt some historical survey of this whole long development, remembering always that what interests us particularly is just how much the native Tibetan genius turned all these foreign influences in specifically Tibetan directions and how much of the original Tibetan indigenous culture remained as a coherent part of the new Tibetan Buddhist civilization that gradually developed.

The First Buddhist Temples in Tibet There is good evidence that Buddhism was first established in Tibet, albeit on a very small scale, during the reign of *Srong-brtsan-sgam-po* (Song-tsen-gam-po) who died in AD 650. In later Buddhist tradition he was accounted as the first of the three great religious i.e. Buddhist, kings, the other two being *Khri-srong-lde-brtsan* (Trhi-song-de-tsen) who ruled throughout the second half of the eighth century, and *Ral-pa-can* who ruled from 815 to 836. To the latter day Tibetans the remains of ancient royal greatness, although accorded a vague sentimental respect, were regarded as of far less importance than anything connected with Buddhism. Although they glorify the greatest of their early kings as religious rulers, their burial mounds have been neglected for a thousand years or more, and the contents of the early inscribed royal pillars are almost unknown, while the one surviving palace has been converted into a chapel. But a special aura of sanctity and antiquity still surrounds the principal Buddhist foundations ascribed to the Religious Kings, however much they have been changed from their original form. The holiest of them is the *Jo-khang*, often referred to as the 'Cathedral of Lhasa' (pages 34 and 121), which contains the most sacred of Tibetan images, that of *Jo-bo Rin-po-che*, the 'Precious Lord'. This image is supposed to have been brought to Lhasa by the Chinese wife of *Srong-brtsan-sgam-po*. Tibetan tradition records the removal of the image in the following century and the closing and desecration of the *Jo-khang* in the ninth. It is now so encrusted with gold leaf and jewels that no one, however qualified, would hazard a guess at its actual age. However the *Jo-khang* itself was certainly founded by *Srong-brtsan-sgam-po*, for it is specifically mentioned and ascribed to him under its old name of *'Phrul-snang* of *Ra-sa* (Lhasa) in several ancient inscriptions. Also ascribed to him are the *Ra-mo-che* and *Khra-'brug* chapels, as well as twelve 'boundary and limb-binding' chapels, supposedly built to bind and subdue the anti-Buddhist demons of Tibet. The authenticity of these traditions has been questioned by some Western scholars, but if the *Jo-khang* is accepted as a seventh century foundation, there is no good reason to reject the others out of hand.

However, these first Buddhist temples, possibly built to please his wives by a king who continued to follow the beliefs and practices of his non-Buddhist ancestors, were at first very small affairs. It is certain that the main foundation, the *Jo-khang*, has been frequently restored and enlarged throughout later centuries. It retains, however, a central basic lay-out similar to other early chapels and it also contains some very early wood-work, especially the lion beam ends and the carved capitals of some of its pillars; but even these resemble work which can be ascribed with greater confidence to the thirteenth century.

The most convincing of the old religious foundations is the tiny temple of *dBu-ru-ka-tshal*, one of the 'limb-binding' chapels (page 34). Having escaped an excess of veneration (unlike a later foundation alongside it, attributed to *Khri-srong-lde-brtsan*), it bears no sign of restoration or pious embellishment. It is solid and austere, and behind the altar there is an enclosed ambulatory of the kind which occurs in other recognizably old temples, like those that have survived unchanged from a slightly later period in Western Tibet (see page 140). The old *Ra-mo-che* temple, built according to tradition as the first resting place of the image brought by *Srong-brtsan-sgam-po*'s Chinese wife, has certainly been enlarged during later centuries, but being a smaller and more compact building, it is likely to contain more early work than the *Jo-khang* nearby. The *Khra-'brug* temple is built in the Yarlung Valley, the homeland of the early kings of Tibet (page 34). It is the largest and most important of the surviving royal foundations in that area, and there is no reason for not accepting its traditional ascription to *Srong-brtsan-sgam-po*. There is an old bell in the verandah bearing the name of *Khri-song-lde-brtsan*, but it is not necessary to ascribe the original foundation of the temple to him, for it is just as likely that he simply enlarged and embellished a foundation of his famous ancestor.

But however small these beginnings, *Srong-brtsan-sgam-po*'s royal patronage of Buddhism is not subject to doubt. It is quite possible that the Tibetans were aware of the existence of Buddhism in even earlier times, for there is a tradition that in the reign of *Srong-brtsan-sgam-po*'s fourth predecessor certain religious books fell from the heavens on to the roof of his palace, but no one could understand them. Maybe some intrepid Buddhist monk from Nepal found his way to Tibet in the company of trading companions, only to find that the few books he brought with him were quite incomprehensible in this strange country.

The Literary Language It is certain that *Srong-brtsan-sgam-po*'s main achievement, so far as the history of Tibetan Buddhism is concerned, was the fixing of a new script for the Tibetan language. It may be questioned whether some parts of Tibet were altogether without writing of some sort before this time, but whatever the reasons for the introduction of the new script, whether primarily for administrative purposes or for the translation of Indian Buddhist works (as later Buddhist pietism would have us believe), it was this readaptation to the needs of the Tibetan language of a northern form of the Indian Gupta alphabet which set the Tibetans on their long and successful literary course in the Buddhist field.

The Tibetan alphabet, as then devised and as still used, consists of thirty basic letters, including the vowel *a*, and four extra vowel-signs on the Indian model for *i*, *u*, *e* and *o*. As it is now fundamentally a monosyllabic language (in the sense that with few exceptions words of more than one syllable can be immediately split up into their component parts, each of which has a recognizable meaning), Tibetan word-syllables have been subject to considerable phonetic decay. Thus, the word for 'eight', *brgyad*,which is spelt with a whole complexity of initial consonants and was presumably once pronounced something like 'bragyad' (scarcely monosyllabic), is now pronounced in the dialect of central Tibet as simply 'gyay'. Several sets of combined consonants, such as *gr*, *dr* and *br*, are pronounced nowadays in most parts of Tibet as a single sound; the three quoted now sound not very different from an English *d*. Nevertheless the original spellings, as fixed in the time of *Srong-brtsan-sgam-po* and his successors, have usually been preserved as the correct ones. There is thus often a considerable difference, far greater than in English and French (although for example our present-day pronunciation of the English word 'knight' may serve as an analogy) between the way Tibetan words are spelt and pronounced. There are both advantages and disadvantages in this. Once one is sufficiently skilled in the use of the script, one can attempt to read Tibetan texts of any period from the eighth century (the earliest surviving example of Tibetan script is a stone inscription, the *Zhol rdo-ring*, of about 767) to the twentieth century, usually with far greater ease than an English reader can read Anglo-Saxon or even Middle English. Nevertheless serious difficulties in vocabulary (to which we have already referred in the previous chapter) arise in the indigenous literature of the earliest period, and we do not yet possess all the scholarly aids that are available to students of European languages.

There are sure indications that Tibetan as a literary language was most flexible in the first centuries after the introduction of the conventional methods of spelling, and some of the ancient texts from Tun-huang, from which short selections have already been quoted, possess a freshness and freedom of style which is rare in later literature. The reason for this is a simple one. Tibetan *literati* were primarily interested in Buddhist texts, and so they developed their vocabulary and their style to suit the translations from Indian Sanskrit works on which they were working for several centuries. Thus even when they began to produce independent works of their own, almost invariably on Buddhist subjects, they continued to use constructions and styles modelled as far as possible on Indian works. Fortunately, however, there are exceptions, and earlier traditions of Tibetan story-telling and verse-making have not died out altogether. But it should not be thought that we are deprecating the extraordinary achievements of whole generations of Buddhist scholars in Tibet. Using entirely their own linguistic materials (direct borrowings of Sanskrit terms are very rare indeed), they produced a highly complex religious and philosophical vocabulary, capable of rendering in faithful translation the whole vast range of Sanskrit Buddhist literature, and usually so accurate that modern European and Indian scholars are able to produce an adequate reconstruction of any lost Indian Sanskrit work from its Tibetan translation. This is made all the easier in that, by the early ninth century, the Tibetans had drawn up lists of fixed equivalents for the translation of Sanskrit Buddhist terms into Tibetan; in order to ensure absolute conformity they retranslated into Tibetan all the texts previously translated that did not conform to the new rules. From then onwards the conventional equivalents, carefully taught by one generation to the next, have been used unerringly up to the present day. Such a system ensures the precise and unalterable statement and restatement of unchanging religious and philosophical notions, but it does not encourage the development of imaginative and poetic literature such as we now take for granted in the modern Western world, and which other Asian languages, such as Chinese and Japanese, have produced in good measure. In writing of Tibetan literature it is tempting to select just those parts of it – the Tun-huang material, the *Ge-sar* Epic, the songs of some schools of non-monastic yogins, and popular ditties – which are free or at least relatively free from the strait-jacket of Sanskrit idiom; but this inevitably gives a false impression of the whole range of Tibetan literature, which remains for the greater part dry and scholastic. However, in the early period with which we are immediately concerned this whole long process was still in its beginnings, and the new script was still being used to record local historical and even non-Buddhist traditions. It is significant that this type of early literature does not always adhere to the approved styles of spelling.

The first literary records to throw direct light on Tibetan culture of this early period became available only at the beginning of this present century, thanks to the remarkable discoveries of two great scholar-explorers, Sir Aurel Stein and Professor Paul Pelliot, at various sites in Chinese Turkestan. As well as Buddhist temples and shrines, containing some fine well-preserved murals, ancient Tibetan forts were excavated, revealing fragments of armour and clothing, scraps of official papers and stacks of inscribed tally-sticks which the occupying Tibetan troops of the eighth and ninth centuries used for local records and message plaques. But the most important finds came from the ancient Buddhist cave temples of Tun-huang at the far eastern end of the Takla-makan. Here there had survived for ten centuries and more collections of ancient manuscripts, hermetically sealed from the ravages of the outside world. The collections which were subsequently brought to Europe were divided between libraries in London (the India Office Library) and Paris (Bibliothèque Nationale). Only a small part of the material is Tibetan, most of which consists of Buddhist texts, but there are some non-Buddhist records, one of which summarizes events of the royal court and the principal affairs of state (referred to by us as the '*Annals*'), while others contain rather more literary and poetic versions of those occurrences and also legends relating to the mythical origins of the country (the '*Chronicle*'). There are also ritual texts of various kinds, laws of hunting, rules for working out prognostics, as well as a whole collection of ancient sage sayings. Most of this material is recorded, rather irreverently it would seem, on the backs of some of the Chinese Buddhist scrolls. By contrast the Tibetan Buddhist texts, the earliest available to us, are written in the usual oblong form of later Tibetan books on paper that is manifestly inferior to the paper of the Chinese scrolls. Out of this medley of early Buddhist and pre-Buddhist records, surviving from a time when Buddhism had not yet acquired the dominance which later cast its religious colour over all Tibetan history, we have attempted in the previous section to extract a coherent account of pre-Buddhist Tibet and to draw significant contrasts with the Buddhist Tibet which is so much better known.

Buddhism during the reign of *Srong-brtsan-sgam-po* was probably restricted to the court, and its priests were Indian or Chinese. A few Tibetans may have studied the new faith and helped in the first translations of religious books, but even this is not certain. *Srong-brtsan-sgam-po*'s next successors showed no great enthusiasm for Buddhism, although two of them, '*Dus-srong* (676-704) and *Khri-lde-gtsug-brtsan* (704-54), are credited in an eighth-century inscription with the foundation of chapels; the latter also had a Chinese wife, who presumably followed the faith, for thanks to her intercession a large number of refugee monks from Khotan were hospitably received and seven monasteries were built for them, where they stayed in peace for three years. When the queen died, they were driven away. Later Tibetan tradition makes a great deal of the suppression of Buddhism in the later part or immediately after the reign of *Khri-lde-gtsug-brtsan* and of its triumphant restoration under his son *Khri-srong-lde-brtsan* (740 to *c.* 798). That something of the sort took place is supported by ancient edicts preserved in the *History* of *dPa-bo gTsug-lag*, but the actions which are attributed in such later histories to irreligious ministers may have been instigated by practitioners of the indigenous Tibetan religion or may simply represent a spontaneous Tibetan reaction against the importation of foreign customs. At all events, the ban cannot have appeared so important to contemporary Tibetans as it did to the pious historians of later periods. The *Tibetan Annals* (from Tun-huang) make no mention whatsoever of Buddhism, and the *Chronicle* has the scantiest allusion to it, while the Chinese records note no cataclysmic upheaval in Tibet at this time. In short, religious questions were not of primary concern during the early royal period. Nevertheless, compared with its first beginnings during the reign of *Srong-brtsan-sgam-po*, Buddhism made rapid progress, both spiritual and material, thanks to the interest that *Khri-srong-lde-brtsan* showed in it.

The First Tibetan Monastery His great contribution was the foundation of the stately temple and monastery of *bSam-yas* (Sam-yä), in which Tibetans were trained as monks for the first time. It was constructed as a great complex of buildings arranged around a central temple, said to be modelled on the great Indian Buddhist monastery of Odantapuri in Bihar. Such a symmetrical arrangement of a central temple with four sides oriented to the four quarters had the symbolic significance of the 'sacred circle' (*maṇḍala*) enclosing the temple-palace of supreme divinity at the core of the universe. We have already referred to this notion (page 70) and more will be said about it further on. This *bSam-yas* temple is unlike other Tibetan temples in having three main storeys each traditionally in a different style, Indian, Chinese and Tibetan, surmounted by a small lantern-roofed chapel (page 36). It was inspired by the Indian teacher *Śāntarakshita*, known in Tibet as the 'Bodhisattva Abbot' (he was the master of *Kamalaśila*, who conducted the Indian case in the great *bSam-yas* debate), and, according to later accounts, the *Guru Rin-po-che* (Precious Master) *Padmasambhava*, a renowned yogin-sage, skilled in magic and mysticism, who probably came from Swat. These two teachers represent two rather different forms of Buddhist practice, the one conventionally academic and monastic, and the other mystical and ritual. Both forms permeated the other to some extent, and it is significant that *Padmasambhava* was supposed to have been invited to Tibet on the suggestion of *Śāntarakshita*, who found the country as a whole not so well disposed to the kind of teaching which he himself represented.

The great *bSam-yas* temple has been severely damaged by fire more than once, but Tibetan devotion to traditional forms probably ensured that the original pattern and the original objects of worship were maintained in any restoration. Several of the outlying chapels which surround the great temple appear to be original, and unmistakable survivals are an inscribed pillar recording the foundation (but without any mention of the king), and a fine bell still hanging in the verandah and bearing a pleasing prayer for the king inscribed by one of his queens.

The Great Debate Thanks to this new impetus, Buddhism, hitherto suspect as a dangerous foreign influence, began to become a truly Tibetan religion, and there followed a surge of activity in the translation of Indian and Chinese

Buddhist texts into Tibetan. A keen interest in doctrine began to develop, and this culminated in the great debate held at *bSam-yas* about 792 as to whether Indian or Chinese teachings should be followed. The Indian side, as represented in this debate, argued the conventional *Mahāyāna* teachings connected with the theory of the gradual course of a 'would-be buddha' (*bodhisattva*) towards buddhahood. The basis of these teachings was the assumption that it was necessary to accumulate vast quantities of knowledge and merit throughout innumerable ages, if one wished to progress towards the final goal of buddhahood; this was now proclaimed according to the *Mahāyāna* as the only true goal for the real followers of *Śākyamuni*, in that it benefited all other sentient beings as well as oneself. Such a doctrine argued in favour of the conventional intellectual and moral training which had guaranteed the stability of Buddhist monasticism since the days of its founder. The Chinese case concentrated upon the absolute nature of buddhahood, which could be realized by any practitioner who established himself in the state of complete repose. According to this, conventional morality and intellectual endeavour are irrelevant, and in some cases even directly harmful, if they obstruct the pure contemplation of the emptiness of all concepts whatsoever. Such teachings are a logical development of the philosophy of the 'Perfection of Wisdom' texts, as already described.

The verdict in this present case went to the Indian school, and contemporary dossiers show that it was a victory for a moralistic view skilfully defended by the Indian scholar *Kamalaśīla*, who had been specially invited for the occasion, supported by a recently converted Tibetan with his own blunt Johnsonian commonsense. Together they triumphed over the refined intellectual subtleties of the chief Chinese champion, the Hoshang, named *Mahāyāna*. Perhaps political considerations also weighed in this result, for at this time Tibet was openly at war with China. But even if the verdict went technically against the Chinese, they were certainly not the only champions of those Buddhist doctrines which we might describe as 'contemplation for contemplation's sake'. The idea of buddhahood as contemplation of absolute truth, spontaneously realized by means of certain contemplative techniques which could be learned from a teacher who was himself competent in such practices, without the need of moral and intellectual endeavour, exists certainly from the eighth century onwards right up to present times as one of the main streams of Tibetan religious life. The Chinese were the champions of such views on the occasion of the debate at *bSam-yas*, but it must not be thought that they represented Chinese Buddhism as a whole versus Indian Buddhism. There were already Indian teachers in Tibet who were teaching forms of Buddhism quite as 'absolutist' and with far less concern for conventional moral disciplines than the Hoshang displayed in his arguments. Buddhism was not only of far less importance in these centuries (seventh to the ninth) than later Tibetan historians would have us believe, it was also far more complex in the various forms in which it gradually permeated the country than the later official accounts imply. All this will become clearer later on.

The Stūpa The most typical monument of any Tibetan scene is the Buddhist 'cenotaph' (Sanskrit *stūpa*, Tibetan *mchod-rten*) and its introduction must date from the seventh century. We have already mentioned that such monuments were erected at the four corners of some early Tibetan temples, but the construction of such a *stūpa* (we will use the Indian word from now on) was an act of religious merit in its own right. The *stūpa* originally represented the funeral mounds under which the shared relics of *Śākyamuni*'s incinerated corpse once reposed, and it soon became the chief symbolic representation of Buddhism, just as the cross became the symbol of Christianity. At first the *stūpa* was felt to symbolize the person of the departed lord, and in very early Buddhist times it became an object of faith and devotion. With the loss of historical perspective, to which we have already referred, the *stūpa* easily became the symbol of buddhahood itself, and in a later period this symbolism was made even more pointed by the buddhas of the four directions which were set into its four sides. Thus it was no longer referred specifically to *Śākyamuni*, but rather to the very essence of buddhahood, as sometimes personified in the supreme central figure of the Buddha *Vairocana* ('Illuminator'). Its various parts became endowed with symbolic significance, and despite variations in local style and design, it generally retained certain essential features. The dome, rather changed in shape in the later models, remained the fundamental part, for it was in the dome that the sacred objects reposed. The *stūpa* has never lost its essential character of a reliquary, and in place of the relics of holy men the later ones often contained sacred images or books, or even just a few inscribed prayers. At the same time it has continued to be used as a cenotaph or even a tomb in the full sense of the term, for some contain the ashes, usually first moulded with clay into tiny miniature *stūpas* (known as *tsha-tsha*), of deceased lamas, or simply of the friends and relations of anyone who chooses to have such a monument erected. They may even contain whole bodies, presumably embalmed. The dome normally rests upon a five-tier platform, said to represent the five elements of existence (earth, water, fire, air, space), and this in turn may rest upon a decorated base, usually referred to as the 'throne'. The dome is surmounted by a kind of spire consisting of thirteen rings. Architecturally this device was derived from the ceremonial umbrellas which used to top the earliest Indian structures. First made of wood, they were later made all of one piece out of stone, and the number was finally increased to thirteen, when they were reduced conventionally to the appearance of simple ring-like steps and were said to symbolize the thirteen stages of a would-be buddha's advance

Images, frescoes and decorative motifs

An eleventh-century fresco at the old monastery of Tabo in Spiti, once part of Western Tibet (see page 113). The divinity is *rDo-rje-'chang* (skr. *Vajradhara*), 'Holder of the Powerbolt', the Supreme Buddha revered by Indian Buddhist tantric yogins and by the older orders of Tibetan Buddhism

(*opposite, above*) Stucco image at Tabo of uncertain date but possibly the eleventh century. The European seated posture and hands joined in the gesture signifying preaching typified the Buddha *Vairocana*, the 'Illuminator' in the early Indian *Mahāyāna* period. Later as *Vairocana* became the centre of a special tantric cult, the posture and gesture seems to have been taken over by *Maitreya*, the Future Buddha

(*opposite*) Decorated ceiling at Tabo, possibly eleventh century and presumably reproducing Kashmiri styles of that period. The goddesses are clearly Indian-inspired. The birds represent peacocks or even possibly the phoenix. The design of massed curls represent clouds. Such birds and clouds continue to be used as common motifs on Tibetan carpets, where they are usually assumed to be of Chinese origin. This ancient ceiling suggests an Indian origin (see page 113)

An eleventh-century fresco in the neglected monastery of Tsaparang. The divinity is *Phyag-na-rdo-rje* (skr. *Vajrapāṇi*) 'Powerbolt-in-Hand' in his yogin-like tantric manifestations known as *gTum-chen* (skr. *Caṇḍamaharoshaṇa*)

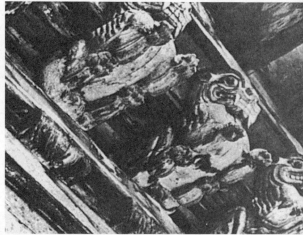

Carved wooden doorway at Tsaparang

(*above*) Lion beam-ends. Fourteenth-century woodwork at *rGya-gnas* near Gyantse. Such protruding lions are frequently used as decorations over doorways

(*below*) A carved wooden capital at *rGya-gnas*. The monster (*mahoraga*) head motif as top decoration of portals and capitals is found throughout all the areas influenced by Indian civilization

(*opposite*) Fresco at Iwang near Gyantse representing *Śākyamuni* Buddha, thirteenth to fourteenth century

(*above*) Fresco at Gyantse representing one of the kings of the four quarters (about fifteenth century)

(*right*) Fresco at Gyantse representing an Indian devotee

(*opposite*) Fresco at Gyantse representing male and female coupled divinities (*yab-yum*) from the entourage in the mystic circle (*maṇḍala*) of *sPyan-ras-gzigs* (skr. *Avalokiteśvara*)

(*above*) Image of *Atiśa* at the monastery of *sNye-thang* where he died (see page 130)

(*upper right*) Image of *Srong-brtsan-sgam-po* in the *Potala*, possibly fourteenth century (see page 154)

(*right*) Image of *Srong-brtsan-sgam-po*'s Nepalese queen (as above)

towards buddhahood. Being the most common of Buddhist monuments, they have undergone developments of design and symbolic meaning in every country in Asia where Buddhism has spread, and a great deal might be written about them, which would take us far beyond the needs of the present book.

The earliest Tibetan *stūpas* seem to have been simple solid affairs consisting of a compact drum-like 'dome', set on a five-tier platform which rested on a plain square plinth (page 41). The 'dome' was surmounted by the conventional thirteen ring 'spire', which in turn was topped by a solar disc resting in a lunar crescent. Resting on the solar disc was a small circular device known technically as the 'drop' (Sanskrit *bindu*, Tibetan *thig-le*), into which the sun, representing wisdom, and the moon, representing compassion, dissolved in the moment of enlightenment. These symbols were connected with the most developed of Buddhist tantric doctrines. Those who erected *stūpas* as acts of merit erected them in such a form simply because this was the conventionally acceptable way of constructing them. Because of their very great importance as a Tibetan cultural motif we cannot fail to mention *stūpas* at this point in our story, but as they were an entirely foreign cultural importation, there can have been little specifically Tibetan about them in the early Tibetan Buddhist period.

Other Temples and their Architecture There are several other chapels and temples ascribed to *Khri-srong-lde-brtsan* and his successors. Some, such as *sMra-bo lCog-pa*, *Thang-rgyab*, *mChing-phu* and *mKhar-chu* have obviously been much enlarged or rebuilt, but others seem to have retained their original plan, for example the *Tsan-dan-g.yu* Temple and the *Tshe-bcu Bum-pa* in Yarlung, the *Has-po-rgyab* Temple near *bSam-yas* (page 36), the *Lho-brag Khom-ting* Temple, the *'On-ke-ru* Temple, the *Zhwa'i* Temple (*Zhwa'i lha-khang*), and the three chapels at *rTsis-gnas-gsar*. These last appear to be almost neglected and remain as examples of the very humble scale of some holy places built at that time. The sites of *sKar-cung* (*Rama sGang*) and *'U-zhang-rdo* near Lhasa are also noteworthy in having large areas marked out with a *stūpa* at each corner – as at the great *bSam-yas* temple – but no original building survives. Here and in several other places excavation would probably yield interesting results.

All these early foundations, with the exception of a few hillside retreats, are situated on level ground in sheltered places. The spectacular cliff-hanging or castle-like buildings and the great monastic cities, often thought to typify Tibet, were a much later development. But the characteristic Tibetan style is apparent even in the earliest buildings – walls sloping inwards from massive foundations with windows tapering upwards so that the impression is that of a solidly based mass yet with an upward soaring movement. The effect is perhaps similar to that produced by reconstructions of the *zikurrats* of the ancient Middle East, and one is led to wonder if there may have been early influences in building styles from this direction. Roofs and decorative motifs were certainly produced on Indian and Nepalese models, but since Chinese religious architecture was being heavily influenced by Indian styles during this period, it would be hard to identify any of the early foreign influences in building as genuinely Chinese. The pagoda-style roof, so typical of Far Eastern architecture, was ultimately of Indian origin.

As well as the religious foundations in Central Tibet established during and after the time of *Khri-srong-lde-brtsan*, there were also many, of which we have little information, in Eastern Tibet. A document from Tun-huang gives an impressive list of monasteries in that area. Other documents suggest that the number of monks in these monasteries was quite small; there is similar evidence from Central Tibet, where the traditional number of original ordinands was just seven, and where a stone pillar recording the foundation of a temple at *lCang-bu* (in *sTod-lung*) by the noble family of *Tshes-pong* mentions provision for only four monks.

It is less easy to decide whether any of the images and ritual objects in the temples mentioned date from the eighth and ninth centuries. Mention has already been made of the bell at *bSam-yas*, and there are other similar inscribed bells at *Khra-'brug* (in Yarlung) and at *Yer-pa*.* The principal Buddha image is usually that of *Vairocana* (Tibetan *rNam-par-snang-mdzad*), the 'Illuminator', who is closely connected with a series of tantric texts that were popular at this time in the Buddhist centres of north-west India, of the Takla-makan and in China. In conformity with the new universal theories of buddhahood as preached by the followers of the *Mahāyāna*, and with the new philosophical teachings of the ultimate emptiness of all concepts whatsoever, the Buddha *Śākyamuni*, who had really lived in central India in the sixth to fifth centuries BC, now lost the central position of importance which had indisputably been his in the early days of the doctrine. Buddhahood as the ultimate goal for all sentient beings was now repre-sented by symbolic buddha-forms with generalized names, and five such were conceived of as a set of one central buddha with four others commanding the four directions in the typical pattern of the sacred circle (*maṇḍala*) already referred to. The arrangement varies in different series of tantric texts, but the most usual arrangement placed the Buddha 'Illuminator' at the centre, and so it is he who often occupies the central position in temples of this period. It may be assumed that Indian, Nepalese and Chinese examples of the same period are a guide to the nature of Tibetan iconography and artistic style at this time. In particular several of the wall paintings and painted scrolls from the caves of Tun-huang show characteristics and motifs which can still be found in later Tibetan religious and decorative art.

Stone Pillars In addition to these rather speculative remains there is the authentic but scanty artistic evidence of the inscribed stone pillars (pages 37–8). These show not only the proportions which Tibetans apparently found pleasing and their mastery of good ornamental lettering, but also the decorative motifs that were popular at this time. The oldest pillar and by far the most elegant and impressive is the *Zhol* pillar set up by a powerful minister *Ngan-lam sTag-sgra Klu-gong*, to record his services to his king, including victories over the Chinese, and the rewards he received.* It is interesting that a subject should have erected so proud a memorial; and that this particular monument celebrating a minister who was traditionally regarded as an opponent of Buddhism should have been allowed to stand after *Khri-srong-lde-brtsan* had restored the Buddhist faith underlines the comparative insignificance of religious issues at the time, and the relative weakness of Buddhism. Apart from its excellent proportions this pillar has little ornamentation. Any decoration that there may have been on the base has been effaced by time. It possesses a neat stone canopy topped by a carved finial representing the flaming wish-granting jewel (*cintāmaṇi*) of Indian mythology.

The pillar at *bSam-yas* stands on a typical lotus throne, and is topped by a well-proportioned canopy with upturned edges and a finial in the form of the 'sun-moon-union' symbol, such as is regularly found on the summits of Tibetan *stūpas* (page 37).

A pillar at *'Phyong-rgyas*, attributed to *Khri-srong-lde-brtsan*, bore an inscription which is now effaced but has recently been recovered from a medieval copy. This will be mentioned again later. On the other side of the pillar are carvings of a lion in light relief, and the remains of a dragon figure. There is a heavy canopy and a rather damaged finial representing either a lotus bud or a flaming jewel.

Two pillars at the *Zhva'i lha-khang* stand on rectangular stone bases decorated with the sign of the crossed powerbolt (Sanskrit *vajra*, Tibetan *rdo-rje*) and the swastika (Tibetan *g.yung-drung*). Their stone canopies are severe, lacking their upper parts and decorative finials. But a pillar of the same period, at *sKar-cung* near Lhasa, has an elaborate fluted stone canopy with a Chinese flavour and a well-carved shell-like finial, while its stone base is decorated with a Chinese-inspired conventional mountain design (page 37).

A third pillar of *Khri-lde-srong-brtsan*'s reign stands by his burial mound at *'Phyong-rgyas*. It is a massive monolith, of which the proportions cannot be properly appreciated, since much of its lower part is buried in the ground. The canopy is flattish, as at *Zhva'i lha-khang*, but its under part is carved with a leaf and scroll design and the finial is a solid ball-shaped object representing a lotus bud. The upper part of the pillar is decorated with two lightly carved circles depicting sun and moon.

Next in date comes a pillar at *mTshur-phu* commemorating the founding there of the temple of *lCang-bu*. It stands on a three-tier plain stone base, but has a well-shaped canopy with a carved decoration of small scrolls which show Chinese influence. The finial, rather too large for the canopy, represents a flaming jewel in Indian style. A similar finial surmounts a better proportioned canopy on the pillar at Lhasa. This is from the same reign and bears a bilingual inscription of the treaty of 821 between China and Tibet (page 38).

The earliest of them, the *Zhol* pillar, and one from *Kong-po*, make no mention of Buddhism, but the latter refers to the legendary ancestry of Tibetan kings as divine rulers. From both these inscriptions information can be gleaned about the contemporary Tibetan social order, the relative importance of official positions, the manner in which a successful general was rewarded, and the tax concessions on the several kinds of property held by a feudal prince.

Buddhism on the Defensive From all the other inscriptions information in differing degrees can be derived about the status and practice of the new religion and its relationship to earlier Tibetan beliefs. Other information about monasteries, especially in the north-east, their landed properties and their scholastic activities, is found in the manuscripts from Tun-huang in the London and Paris collections. Of the inscriptions dealing with Buddhism, that at *sKar-cung* is the most important. It confirms the authenticity of two edicts of *Khri-lde-srong-brtsan* and one of his predecessor, which are quoted in the religious history of *dPa-bo g Tsug-lag 'phreng-ba* (1565), and thus substantiates contemporary evidence about the suppression of Buddhism while *Khri-srong-lde-brtsan* was a minor. It also reveals Buddhism at that time as a cautious and conciliatory religion rather than the church militant, as later histories like to depict it. It was rather a matter of securing royal permission and protection for its practice, than of practising it confidently as the dominant religion.

The attitude of the early Tibetan kings was perhaps a precursor of that mixture of tolerance, syncretism and readiness to try any form of spiritual prophylaxis which was to be exemplified in the Mongol Khans of a later period (thirteenth century) when they in turn showed an easy-going willingness to learn of Buddhism from the Tibetans. This may have been particularly true of *Srong-brtsan-sgam-po* and his immediate successors. But even *Khri-srong-lde-brtsan*, that great champion of Buddhism according to later Tibetan accounts, appears in his inscription at *'Phyong-rgyas* as the defender and quasi-deity of the older faith and simultaneously as an 'enlightened' votary of the new. The titles accorded him are a combination of the ideals of both, and the attribution to him of the Buddhist term for enlightenment (*byang-chub*) suggests rather the princely associations of the 'would-be buddha' ideal. (The Tibetans translated the Sanskrit term *bodhi-sattva* by means of a Tibetan paraphrase meaning literally 'hero of the thought of enlightenment'.) *Ral-pa-can*, the third of the great 'Religious Kings', is represented in later histories as almost besotted in his adulation of Buddhism; yet he too was buried, presumably in accordance with the ancient pre-Buddhist rites, at the ancient *Bon*-dominated burial ground of *'Phyong-rgyas*, where his father another 'champion of Buddhism', was also buried and in his case celebrated by a funerary inscription, which although incomplete, gives in its surviving passages a strictly non-Buddhist account of his achievements.

It is interesting to compare the accounts in Chinese and Tibetan sources of the ceremonies at the conclusion of treaties between Tibet and China in 727 and 782 (namely before the strong growth of Buddhism) and in 821. At the first there is brief reference to the sacrifice of a dog. At the second there is a long description of sacrifices and of the participants smearing their lips with the blood of the victims. At the third the treaty inscription of 821/822 shows that a variety of deities, both Buddhist and non-Buddhist, including sun and moon and stars, were called to witness; and the Chinese accounts confirm that the principal ceremony was non-Buddhist and accompanied by animal sacrifices. It is, however, made clear that on this occasion the Buddhist participants abstained from smearing their lips with blood and that they afterwards moved into a temporary chapel for Buddhist rites.

It is quite clear that in those early days Buddhism was content to compromise, to secure peaceful coexistence, trying always to come to terms with the older faith. It was able to exploit such common ground as existed between some of the more worldly Buddhist tantric rites (e.g. rites for prosperity, for destroying enemies, etc.) and certain indigenous pre-Buddhist practices, as performed by the *Bon* and the *gShen*. This was probably the main achievement of such as *Padmasambhava*, who even if he incurred unpopularity at *Khri-srong-lde-brtsan*'s court, came to be venerated in Tibet far more highly than the gentle intellectual priest *Śāntarakshita*.

It is possible to trace a continuous rivalry and difference of view between a conservative group of Tibetan ministers, headed by the *dBa's* family, which represented the older indigenous Tibetan families, and on the other side a group from border countries, connected with the maternal relations of the kings. The former were generally supporters of the Tibetan king as *sPu-rgyal bTsan-po*, the sacred ruler of divine origin, and they were generally hostile both to China and to Buddhism as a foreign religion. The latter may have been acquainted with both Buddhism and the ways of the Chinese court before they came to central Tibet, and in several instances can be identified as supporters of Buddhism and as favouring a policy of peace with China. Once the differences of opinion among the Buddhists themselves, culminating in the great *bSam-yas* debate, had been formally settled to the discomfiture of the Chinese party, the political potentiality of the new religion seems to have been quickly appreciated. The seven original ordinands were recruited from the nobility, including those families which were apparently the most conservative. Some of them, e.g. the *Tshes-pong* and the *Myang*, are even found patronizing the new religion to the extent of founding temples, and within a very short time monk-ministers of noble rank were exercising power in the affairs of state. *Myang Ting-nge-'dzin bZang-po*, the founder of the *Zhva'i lha-khang*, was one of these. The climax was reached in the reign of *Ral-pa-can* (815-838) who according to later tradition was so lavish in his support of Buddhism that he allotted seven households for the maintenance of each monk, and so infatuated that he let the monks sit (as a sign of their superiority) on his outspread long hair. There is doubtless some exaggeration here. Contemporary Chinese records make no mention of the king's reputation for piety, but say only that he was weak and left the administration in the hands of his ministers. Chief of those ministers, as is seen in the Lhasa Treaty Inscription of 821/822, was the monk *Bran-ka dPal-gyi-yon-tan*. With the acquisition of such power Buddhism became a weapon in the ceaseless struggle for influence in the state and must have roused the jealousy of rival lay nobles concerned with maintaining their political rights against these new religious competitors. At all events in 836 a combination of ministers, led by the conservative *dBa's*, engineered the disgrace and death of the monk and Chief Minister *dPal-gyi-yon-tan*, and then assassinated the King. Within a short time *Ral-pa-can*'s brother and successor, *Glang-dar-ma*, who is infamous to later historians as the persecutor of Buddhism, suffered the same fate. There was no acknowledged heir of the royal line and the fading of the divine *charisma* of kingship left the nobles indifferent to the claims of both the candidates who were eventually put forward. The increase in the prestige of Buddhism, especially as it began to take over the magical arts of the old Tibetan religion, must have insensibly undermined the supremacy of those same kings who were the patrons of its more conventional forms.

There followed a long period during which rival groups of ministers, the *dBa's* versus the *'Bro*, fought for supremacy on the eastern borders, while Buddhism in central Tibet was virtually eclipsed, at least as a formal religion, in the internecine struggles of those who had formerly been its patrons. Such was the end of *Srong-brtsan-sgam-po*'s line in central Tibet. Some of his descendants migrated to found small kingdoms in western Tibet, where they became patrons of Buddhism once more. Others remained as small princes and lordlings in estates widely scattered throughout the country, and although Buddhism retained something of its formal monastic framework both in the east and the west, nothing is heard of it publicly in central Tibet for about 120 years.

Chapter 3

A Later Literary View

Early Historical and Later Quasi-historical Records Our estimate of the progress of Buddhism to date is based primarily upon contemporary or nearly contemporary evidence, the stone inscriptions, the Tun-huang documents and Chinese accounts. As we have already observed, this material is in the main aristocratic, centring as it does upon the interests of the court, the nobles and generals. Although both Buddhist and pre-Buddhist religious texts are found among the Tibetan manuscripts from Tun-huang, references to religion of any kind in the 'Annals' and 'Chronicle' (see page 18) are quite incidental; even the later Tibetan histories in their accounts of this early period write almost exclusively of those Buddhist teachers and foundations which were sponsored by aristocratic circles, and it is significant how little they have to tell us of the yogin-magician *Padmasambhava* who was supposedly disapproved of at court. Likewise the newly introduced means of writing was primarily at the disposal of the aristocratic and monastic circles where it was first introduced. Only gradually can others have availed themselves of the opportunities that it presented for the recording of local popular traditions. This process was, however, certainly well under way by the ninth century, as we know from the fragments of folk-literature that survived in the Tun-huang caves. Yet the general chaos that followed upon the break-up of the Tibetan kingdom in 842 and the gradual loss of Tibetan control and interest in Central Asia, which was now wide open to Muslim domination, seems to have driven all literary activities underground.

Thus in making a fuller estimate of religious developments during and after the royal period, we need to draw upon certain later literary compilations, which relate specifically to the earlier period. A large popular literature developed around *Padmasambhava*, and although the two main works which tell of his doings, the 'Padma Scrolls' (*Padma thang-yig*) and the 'Fivefold Set of Scrolls' (*bKa'-thang sde-lnga*), are compilations of the fourteenth century, they are clearly composed, at least in part, of very much earlier popular traditions. The compilers in fact claimed that they were merely reproducing rediscovered texts, which had been hidden during the political upheavals of the ninth century, and several lamas of this later period are famous as 'text-discoverers' (*g Ter-ston*). It is clear that popular forms of Buddhism, which were certainly not sponsored by the court, were becoming organized as local religious 'schools' with lines of succession of their own. But not only Buddhism organized itself on this kind of unofficial basis; those who practised the old religion of Tibet, making use of the new means of writing and also the new religious and philosophical literature which was now entering the country, began to organize themselves on an entirely new basis.

As we have mentioned, pre-Buddhist Tibetan religion is referred to in the earliest literary sources as 'sacred conventions' (*lha-chos*) or the 'pattern of heaven and earth' (*gnam-sa'i lugs*), but with the reorienting and development of the old ways in what amounted to an entirely new religious setting of Indian inspiration, the term *Bon* (previously used with the meaning of a class of indigenous Tibetan priests, perhaps meaning 'invoker') comes to be used of the religion as a whole, while the followers of these recast teachings are known as *bon-po*. The *bon-pos* themselves gloss the term *bon* by an old word *gyer*, meaning 'chant', and this would relate it with the word *bon*, meaning 'priest who invokes'. But whatever its earlier associations, *bon* comes to mean for the *bon-pos* all that *chos* (used to translate the Sanskrit term *dharma*) means to Tibetan Buddhists.

The great gap in contemporary literary evidence between the ninth and the thirteenth-fourteenth centuries makes it impossible for us to give a precise historical account of the actual development of the Buddhist groups which acclaimed the great sage-magician *Padmasambhava* as their lord and founder, and of the newly organized *Bon* religion, which soon began to honour as its founder and first promulgator a certain *gShen-rab*, a name which could originally mean simply 'Best of Sacrificial Priests'.

Padmasambhava In retrospect, as new Buddhist schools came into existence (and of these we will write later), the followers of *Padmasambhava* were referred to generally as *rNying-ma*, those of the 'Old Way'. However fantastic the stories of their 'founder', who was recognized in his own right as a self-manifesting buddha, born from a lotus-flower (which is what his name means) and nurtured by the king and queen of ancient Swat (known as *U-rgyan* in Tibetan from the old Indian name *Oḍḍiyāna*), *Padmasambhava* may have been a genuine historical character, an Indian yogin who visited Tibet perhaps at royal invitation towards the end of the eighth century. The stories told of him belong on the one side to the *genre* of fantastic tales related about a whole series of accomplished Indian tantric yogins (Sanskrit *siddha*, Tibetan *grub-thob*), and on the other to the tradition of demon-quelling rituals, bragging self-praise, and displays of magical powers and self-transformations, which seem to be typical of Tibetan folk-literature of all periods. The description of *Padmasambhava*'s meeting with *Khri-srong-lde-brtsan*, a comparatively restrained passage, will give some idea of how the *Padmasambhava* literature treats what may have been historical events.

> Then having given pleasure in Lhasa, he came to *sTod-lung*. The King had set up his camp by the side of the *Lohita*, and he sent as his representative *lHa-bzang Klu-dpal*, who had an entourage of five hundred horsemen in armour. When they met at the lower end of the *sTod-lung gZhong-pa* Valley, they could find no water for making their lunch-time tea. *Padmasambhava*, the Great One of *U-rgyan*, stuck his staff into the side of the *sTod-lung* pit, and he said: '*lHa-bzang*, the water has come out. Hold up a bowl', and so the place is called the 'Holy Water of the Bowl'. Then he went to meet the King in the *Zung-mkhar* Grove by the *Lohita* Palace. The King of Tibet was surrounded by all his courtiers, and they shimmered whitish grey like a flock of doves. The two queens were surrounded by their women, and they glowed with many colours like a silken tent. They went to the meeting with drummers and singers, with masked dancers and a lion procession. *Padmasambhava*, the Great One of *U-rgyan* thought to himself:
> 'I am not born from a womb, but was magically born. The king was born from a womb, so I am greater by birth. I am a Religious King who ruled the land of *U-rgyan*, and my lineage is greater than that of the king of this evil land of Tibet. As for our two aspects, he's in a confused state of ignorance, while I am skilled in all the five branches of learning. My buddhahood was acquired in one lifetime, and I know neither birth nor death, while he has only invited me, because he had need of me. This king must certainly salute me first. But I wonder, shall I return his salutation or not. If I return it, the greatness of the Buddhist religion will be lost. If I don't return it, he will be displeased. However although he is a great king, I cannot salute him.'
>
> King *Khri-srong-lde'u-btsan** was thinking:
> 'I am the lord of all the people of Tibet. The Bodhisattva Abbot made me salutation first. In the same way this Teacher should salute me.'
>
> Thus disagreeing about the act of salutation, they waited there with

hesitation. So the Teacher sang this song about his own strength and might.

'The Buddhas of Past, Present and Future emerge from wombs,
Accumulating stocks (of merit and knowledge) throughout three long
   incalculable world-ages.
But I am the Buddha who is Lotus-Born (*Padmasambhava*),
Possessing the precepts of the insight that comes from above.
I am skilled in the fundamental teachings of the Canon and Tantras.
I discourse fully on all the Buddhist Ways (*yāna*) without confusion.
I am the Law which is Lotus-Born,
Possessing the precepts of progressive religious practice.
Outwardly I wear the saffron robes of a monk.
Inwardly I am the highest of tantric yogins.
I am the Assembly which is Lotus-Born,
Possessing the precepts which unite insight and practice.
Even more, my knowledge is higher than the sky.
I understand the causes and effects of actions more minutely than finely
   ground flour.
I am the Lama Lotus-Born,
Possessing meaningful precepts as required sacramentally.
I explain the actual meaning and the implied meaning in the book of
   physical and metaphysical being.
I am the Friend-in-Religion Lotus-Born,
Possessing the precepts which distinguish good and evil.'
(*Padmasambhava* continues to explain who he is through a long succession of
verses, and the king is quite reduced to subjection.)

Then the King *Khri-srong-lde'u-btsan* confessed his fault and made
salutation, saying: 'Please remove such sin as I have committed in not
saluting so worthy a person as yourself.'

The Teacher replied: 'Listen, O King, in order to atone for this sacred
convention you have broken, you must construct five wonderful *stūpas*
made of clay. This will remove the sin.'

So they were erected adorned with lotus-flowers in the middle, and
the Great One of U-rgyan concealed sacred treasure in each of them.*

How far this quasi-historical narrative diverges from the true course of events,
the reader may be left to judge. Nevertheless as a piece of imaginative writing
based upon historical themes this 'biography' of *Padmasambhava* remains a quite
remarkable piece of medieval Tibetan literature. It is written throughout in a

form of blank verse, and although it inevitably makes use of all the new Buddhist technical vocabulary, it is a truly Tibetan piece of writing, free from the mimicries of Sanskrit Buddhist style which already characterize 'professional' Tibetan Buddhist works.

Bon as a Developing Religion There is no known historical character concealed in the legendary biography of *gShen-rab*, founder of *Bon*, and his 'life' is manifestly a fabrication modelled on the traditional Buddhist accounts of the life of *Śākyamuni*. Nevertheless the actual materials used for the 'life' are peculiarly Tibetan and suggestive of early cultural contacts with the regions to the west of Tibet, which we have no reason to dismiss out of hand as totally invalid. *gShen-rab* is supposed to have been born miraculously in the land which the Tibetans knew as *sTag-gzigs*, vaguely identifiable as Persia. It is said that he made one personal visit to Tibet, actually in quest of his horses which had been carried off by a Tibetan demon, but his doctrines are supposed to have reached Tibet later on through the medium of the language of Shang-shung. Shang-shung itself is a land of vague definition. In early historical times (seventh to eighth centuries) its capital was at *Khyung-lung*, and we have already quoted (page 60) a few verses from the lament of the Tibetan princess who was married to the King of Shang-shung. This region of western Tibet, known later as Nga-ri (*mNga'-ris*) had been conquered by *Srong-brtsan-sgam-po* in the first part of the seventh century, but nothing certain is known of its rulers then. It was not properly part of Tibet during the early royal period, and during the reign of *Khri-srong-lde-brtsan* it seems to have been an allied territory, recognizing the general overlordship of the king of Tibet. Historical references to Shang-shung in the Annals and the Chronicle are scanty and names tend to be confused. One of its kings, known as *Lig-mi-rhya* in the Tun-huang documents, reappears in later *Bon* tradition as *Lig-mi-rgya*, the main champion of *Bon* during the reign of *Khri-srong-lde-brtsan*. As an example of the new type of Tibetan narrative literature, vaguely historical and largely imaginative, we quote the story of *Lig-mi-rgya*'s defeat as told in the 'Oral Traditions of Shang-shung' (*Zhang-zhung snyan-rgyud*), which although not committed to writing in its present form until very much later, contains (like the *Padma thang-yig*) some genuinely early traditions of *Bon*, as it would seem to have been practised and understood in Shang-shung.

> At that time when *Lig-mi-rgya* was king of Shang-shung, it had a military strength of many hundreds of thousands of regiments and the realm of Nga-ri included the small regiment in the Sum-pa country, while Tibet had forty-two regiments plus one small one, making forty-three in all. Thus the King of Tibet could not overpower the

King of Shang-shung, but since he was black-hearted he thought he would overcome him by intrigue.

The King of Shang-shung had three wives, of whom the youngest was named Nang-dron-lek-ma (*sNang-sgron-legs-ma*); she was eighteen years old. An envoy of the King of Tibet, a man named *sNang-lam-legs-sgrub*, of evil disposition and a deceitful talker, brought a horn filled with gold dust and gave it to Nang-dron-lek-ma, saying: 'That such as you, Nang-dron-lek-ma, should be the junior wife of the King of Shang-shung! You are of very high lineage, and the King of Tibet finds this situation insufferable. Is there a way of overcoming it? If there is, you shall be the chief wife of the King of Tibet, and you shall be given two thirds of Nga-ri by Tibet.'

Nang-dron-lek-ma replied: 'The armies of the King of Shang-shung cover the land. The King of Tibet has only enough troops to cover the back of a heifer, so he cannot overpower him openly. But if you wish to overcome him by intrigue, then next month the King of Shang-shung, accompanied by his attendants, will be going to an assembly at *Glang-gi-gyim-shod* in the *Sum-pa* country, so wait for him and slay him. I myself will give you the signal.'

One does not expect a woman to show consideration, and so she spoke like this, and it was decided that she should place a sign on the top of the pass indicating what day he would come.

Then the King of Tibet and his ministers came with many regiments of troops, and *sNang-lam-legs-sgrub* and the King went first to the top of the pass, where they saw a full pan of water with a little gold, a little piece of conch and a poisoned arrow-head in it. The King of Tibet said: 'The full pan of water means that they will come on the full moon day of the next month. The little gold and the small piece of conch means "Prepare your troops and wait by the Gold Cave and the Conch Cave of *Dvang-ra*". The poisoned arrow-head means "Be ill-disposed to him and slay him".' So then they waited.

Thus the two kings met, and the Tibetan soldiers killed the King of Shang-shung. So the hundreds of thousands of regiments of Shang-shung were defeated, and the tens of thousands of regiments of Tibet were victorious.*

After a short insertion which gives a rather scurrilous account of the origins of *Śāntarakshita* (the 'Bodhisattva Abbot'), the story returns to Shang-shung, with an account of the extraordinary revenge taken by the chief wife of the King of Shang-shung. The word translated as 'bomb' (*bTso*) is a special *Bon* word, meaning literally something like 'concoction'. In effect the word means 'bomb' and it seems to have been a *Bon* speciality.

Khyung-za mTsho-rgyal, the chief wife of the King of Shang-shung, felt evilly disposed towards the King of Tibet, so she invited *Gyer-spungs* (whose full name was *Gyer-spungs sNang-bzher-lod-po*), and prepared for him a throne consisting of nine quilts of heavy silk. She erected a tent for him of fine white cloth patterned with deer, and she offered him clear rice-beer, and presented him with the nine savoury dishes and the nine desirable things. The tears of her suffering trickled down as blood, and she besought him with the words: 'The king who protects *Bon* is dead. The silken knot of *Bon* morality is destroyed. The golden yoke of government is smashed. The land of Tibet is going to pieces, while the doctrines of eternal *Bon* are in decline. Since times such as these have come upon us, I beg you to manifest an evil disposition.' *Gyer-spungs* said: 'I have one (kind of bomb) called a *sPu*. If I practise upon an ounce of gold for three years, and then let it off, I can have the land of Tibet swept away as by a gale. Shall I do this? I have one called a *Khyung*. If I practise upon half an ounce of gold for three months, and then let it off, Yarlung *Sog-kha* together with *Khri-srong-lde-brtsan* and his court will be destroyed. Shall I do this? I have one called a *rNgub*. If I practise upon a dram of gold for seven days, and then let it off, I shall slay the king himself. Shall I do this?' *mTsho-rgyal* said: 'I beg you to make the *rNgub*.' So the great *Gyer-spungs* set up the white tent, patterned with deer, on the island in the *Da-rog* Lake. He sat on the throne consisting of nine quilts of heavy silk, and practised (on the dram of gold) for seven days. Then he divided the dram of gold into three parts, and he hurled one part at the dusk of evening. He hit the lake on the side of Mount *Yar-lha-sham-po*, and the lake dried up and the serpent divinities fled. That is why it is called the 'Dry Lake of Yarlung'. He hurled one part in the middle of the night and it struck seven deer who were sleeping on Mount *Sog-kha-sPun-mo*. Two of the deer died and five of them went stiff. That is why it is called the 'Mountain of the Stiff Deer'. He hurled the last part at dawn and it struck the Castle 'Tiger Peak' of '*Phying-ba*, and the king was seized by sickness. The king was clever and said: 'The doctrines of eternal *Bon* have been suppressed and the king who protected *Bon* has been slain. Now as for the way this bomb came at dawn, it must be because the great *Gyer-spungs* is angry. Bring a horn filled with gold dust and make ready one hundred horsemen. *Gyer-spungs* has the means of curing me. If you do not invite him here, I shall probably die very quickly. Then the hundred horsemen went to the country of *Drva-bye*, and they sought information from a shepherd of Shang-shung, saying: '*Gyer-spungs* has been evilly disposed and the King of Tibet is ill. Since we have come to greet *Gyer-spungs* and to invite him, tell us where he is staying.' The shepherd said: 'He is there at the foot of that white cliff on the island in the lake, where he has erected his white tent patterned with deer. There is no certainty about his bodily form, for he may turn himself into anything.' Then they put out in a boat and went over there. He was there on his throne of nine quilts of heavy silk in the form of a crystal horn. They offered him the horn of gold dust, walked round him respectfully and made salutation. The crystal horn rose up in the form of *Gyer-spungs*, who said: 'The king who protected *Bon* has been slain. The doctrines of eternal *Bon* have been suppressed. Although I am evilly disposed to you on this account, yet if the King of Tibet dies, the whole realm of Tibet will decline. Now will you promise what I ask of you?' The envoys said: 'The Lord *Khri-srong-lde-brtsan* says: "In the first place it was not my fault that *Bon* was suppressed. This came about through the ill will of the Indian Teacher *Bodhisattva* and the ministers of the court. I will attend now to whatever you command." This is what he says.' *Gyer-spungs* replied: 'In that case you must assent to these four points. Firstly you must not suppress these 360 *Bon* texts of Shang-shung which I practise. Secondly, when members of the *Gu-rub* family go to Yarlung *Sog-kha*, they must be free from religious and state taxes and you must seat them on your right hand side. Thirdly for the Lord *Lig-mi-rgya* we want a golden shrine large enough to enclose his body and marked with a swastika two yards across, and fourthly we want full restitution for his loss (literally: for all twelve parts of his body and for his head making a total of thirteen). Do you assent to these four points?' Then the three envoys gave their word. Thereupon *Gyer-spungs* went to visit the king and performed a rite for reversing (the course of the disease). He drew out from the nine apertures of the king's body threads of gold like tangled cotton threads, and when it was weighed, it came to just one third of a dram. After that he extracted black blood and matter and pus and all the rest in great quantities, and thus the sickness was relieved. The king was very grateful, and he did not suppress the *Bon* texts of Shang-shung. He gave the land of Yarlung *Sog-kha* to the *Gu-rub* family, and he sent to the Queen (of Shang-shung) the wherewithal for the shrine to the king's size and the (gifts of) restitution.*

Gyer-spungs, the sage who made the 'bomb', is well known in the later *Bon* tradition. He belongs to one of several lines of meditating hermits who seem to have established themselves in western Tibet from the seventh century on, and possibly even earlier. *Bon* 'historical' accounts, in order to outdo the Buddhists, place the beginnings of these spiritual successions so fantastically far back in the past that no reliance of any kind can be placed upon them; and so we are left to make our own deductions from circumstantial evidence. There is no serious reason for doubting the existence of the *Bon* sages who come within the historical period, and at the same time there is no doubt of the Indian Buddhist origin of their philosophical theories and meditative practices. 'The Oral Traditions of Shang-shung' belong to the class of teachings known as the 'Great Perfection' (*rDzogs-chen*). Such teachings are common to both the 'Old Order' (*rNying-ma*) among Tibetan Buddhists and to certain followers of *Bon*, and there would seem to be a close connection between the *Bon* sages who practised them and the Indian Buddhist yogins who were perhaps already spreading in Tibet unconventional teachings of a non-monastic kind during the royal period.

There is very little contemporary evidence for all this, but as we have observed, the contemporary evidence is mainly aristocratic and interested in Buddhism only so far as it was sponsored by aristocrats. At the same time the quite extraordinary developments which had taken place by the thirteenth and fourteenth centuries both in the more popular forms of Buddhism and in the new *Bon* religion, which emerges provided with a whole wealth of varied literature which it claims as its own, imply the existence of a great deal of individual endeavour, unsponsored by wealthy patrons, which must have taken place during the preceding centuries. Taking these considerations into account, we cannot simply ignore the *Bon* traditions of their seventh- and eighth-century sages of Shang-shung.

It is related of *Gyer-spungs* that he spent most of his life meditating on an island in the middle of a lake, presumably receiving supplies from nomads and villagers only when the lake was frozen sufficiently for them to cross. Tibetan hermits have continued to live in this way right up to the twentieth century, and since *Gyer-spungs* was probably one of the first to whom there is any quasi-historical reference, we quote a story told about him from the 'Oral Traditions of Shang-shung'.

> As for the place to which he was attached all his life, it was the region called *Da-rog*, where there were water-sprites and other human and non-human creatures. As for the manner of his practising austerities, he took provisions and necessities and went to stay for one year with his disciple on an island in the middle of the lake. At the end of every repast *Gyer-spungs* placed a small bowlful of moistened meal aside. Then the ice

of the lake was in an unsafe condition, and so with each little bowlful of moistened meal, the master and his disciple made some broth which they drank. The sediment of each lot of broth, he poured on the rock which served as his pillow, but still the ice was unsafe. So they scraped off the sediment of the broth and put it in water and drank it. Thus three years passed. Then the servant thought: 'The two of us, master and pupil, will die some time whenever it may be. How if I just fall off a cliff and turn myself into a corpse?' So he said to his master: 'Worthy *Gyer-spungs*, there is a fresh human corpse.' 'Have you come upon one?' his master asked. 'Yes,' the servant replied. 'Well, go round the island, and see what there is.' So he went and returned with the news: 'There is the corpse of a wild ass.' 'As we are of undefiled stock, we may not eat it,' his master said. A few days later he went round the island again, and reported that there was the corpse of a woman with a bad goitre. 'We are not allowed to eat carrion,' his master said. 'Put our things together.' What is *Gyer-spungs* doing now, the servant thought, there will be no way of leaving tomorrow, and he was frightened. *Gyer-spungs* said: 'Hold on to me and close your eyes.' They travelled a long way, and then he thought 'I have left the cooking tripod behind', so he opened his eyes and looked back. A woman wearing jewelry was coming along, winding up a length of white cloth. Then he looked forwards, and there was a woman in front just like the other one, and she was spreading out a length of white cloth, on which the two of them, master and pupil, were advancing. But as soon as he looked, they pulled away the cloth and disappeared, and just as they would have reached the water's edge, they fell into the water. Then a number of laymen from those northern plains gathered around them, and the master said to them: 'I am *Gyer-spungs*.' But his flesh was withered and his hair had grown long, so they did not recognize him and said: '*Gyer-spungs* died many years ago. You are not he.' Then he told them the whole story and they believed in him. First they gave him lye, then the milk of a white goat and of a white *'bri* (female of the yak), and after that they gave them all the food they wanted, and so restored them to normal bodily strength.*

The willingness of the disciple to sacrifice himself for his master, once he was assured that his master would be prepared to eat the flesh of his corpse, belongs to Indian tantric tradition. So too do the women, dressed in jewelry and white clothes, for they are the *ḍākinī* (attendant goddesses) who administer to meditating yogins. Tibetan Buddhist literature of the 'Old Order' is filled with references to them. The religious practice of the 'Great Perfection', as practised by these sages, was a logical development of the basic *Mahāyāna* philosophical theories of absolute emptiness, and in fact it is very close to the theories argued by the Hoshang on behalf of the Chinese party at the great *bSam-yas* debate (see above, page 79). As we observed then, the two conflicting parties represented two ways of Buddhist *Mahāyāna* practice, rather than schools of specifically Indian and Chinese Buddhism.

Unconventional Forms of Buddhist Practice The *Mahāyāna* preached a new philosophy, namely, the absolute emptiness of all concepts whatsoever, and the universality of buddhahood. It was universal in the sense that it was the goal of any man who was prepared to devote himself wholeheartedly to its pursuit and its realization, while he remained free to choose how to go about the matter. Being a widespread religion with all kinds of schools and monasteries, Buddhism was able to absorb new philosophical teachings, however extreme, into its normal religious life, and by developing the theory of the two kinds of truth, absolute and relative, it was able to justify the practice of conventional monastic morality and discipline as well as new and strange practices. A faithful Buddhist could still pursue the goal of enlightenment through conventional ways, which he nevertheless knew to be empty of ultimate significance. But there were those other Buddhists who practised outside conventional monastic circles, and so could risk taking the teachings of absolute emptiness to their local conclusions. It was they who enunciated the theory of buddhahood gained in one human life by the strict dissociation of oneself from all concepts whatsoever. They claim to cut through the need for any kind of relative truth, for buddhahood is realized spontaneously once one knows its universal nature.

It is worth-while emphasizing the difference between these two ways of Buddhist practice, for they run through the whole history of Tibetan religion, and once grasped, they help to simplify our understanding of one of the world's most complex religions. Just as in the early period, so throughout the later ones, which we shall describe, the conventional monastic forms of Buddhism were those that received the support of kings and established rulers, for they were seen to play a necessary part in organized social life, just as European monasteries did in earlier centuries, and just as our universities do today. On the other hand the unconventional forms of religious practice, often the more impressive because of their far greater spontaneity and individualism, have been merely tolerated and allowed to develop at a far more popular level. Hence there has usually been a very close connection, at least in literary sources, between the free-practising man of religion (yogin or hermit) and tales of magic and imagination. Ordinary people believed in demons and monsters, and who else should be able to quell them, if not the sage who meditates serene and unharmed in wild remote places?

The yogins and hermits themselves, while doubtless believing too (in a sense) in demons and monsters, regarded them as unreal like all other phenomenal manifestations, for they had grasped philosophical theories which lay beyond the understanding of ordinary worldly people, and which they express as an ineffable mystery.

> The Teacher in his great compassion
> Released this essence from the core of his heart,
> These precepts taught by spiritual grace,
> Unsought, unique, these pondered precepts,
> Pre-eminent amongst all spiritual precepts.
> Like the great bird *Khyung* they are precise in their swoop.
> Like the mighty lion they hold with power.
> Like the sky above they are all-pervading,
> Just as the waves of the sea are everywhere wet.
> There are those who see, yet do not understand.
> To understand and not to understand, how great the difference!
> Those who understand are the blessed ones.
> Those who understand are enlightened sages.
> Those who understand are the best of priests.
> If there is no understanding, there is no enlightenment.
> Apart from these kingly precepts, no others produce enlightenment.
> The others are like a *Khyung* fledgeling that seeks the limits of the sky.
> They are like an elephant that pursues a mirage.
> They are like a child that runs after the rainbow.
> So go for these most kingly precepts (some verses omitted)
> They are precisely that, so go for them and look!
> Yet by looking nothing is seen.
> By means of them one sees just that.
> E-MA-HO!
> The elements of existence are like a dream or a mirage.
> Their sole validity is their essential vacuity.
> This truth which never came about
> Was never said to have been really taught,
> It is taught in forms of metaphor.
> Transcending sounds and terms and words.
> It cannot be taught for what it really is.*

These verses are extracted from an early *Bon* text, but they could easily be paralleled from *rNying-ma* sources, and their Indian Buddhist origin is beyond doubt. One may well ask why practisers of this kind of *Bon* appear to be such ardent enemies of Buddhism, the more so as from this time on the *Bon-pos* absorbed all they possibly could of Buddhist theories and practices. Presumably the main conflict was between conventional Buddhist religion, especially as sponsored by the court, and the free religious practice of those who adopted whatever teachings happened to suit their purposes. There is no doubt that *Khri-srong-lde-brtsan* (Trhi-song-de-tsen) was detested in *Bon* tradition, and this curse of one Shang-shung hermit has somehow a genuine ring.

> King Trhi-song-de-tsen is a foolish fellow.
> His ministers are monstrous rogues.
> Our blazing light is now withdrawn.
> Now is the time of these Buddhist monks.
> The princes have great faith in gold
> And our haloed *Bon* declines.
> May the king be a village beggar
> And his ministers be shepherds!
> May the land of Tibet break into pieces
> And these Buddhist monks lose their law!
> May these nuns bear children
> And these Buddhist priests lead fighting gangs!
> May their monasteries be filled with battle
> And their temples set on fire!
> May the princes sift their own gold!
> O may my curse be effective
> And may these books of mine be found by someone worthy!*

The Process of Religious Amalgamation Whether by power of this curse of the *Bon-po* Sage *Li-shu-stag-ring*, or for the reasons we have given above (page 94), within forty years of *Khri-srong-lde-brtsan*'s death the land of Tibet broke into pieces and all the other misfortunes listed came about. The *Bon-pos* claim that the old books which their text-discoverers unearthed in later centuries had been concealed during the persecutions of *Bon* in the reign of *Khri-srong-lde-brtsan*, while the *rNying-ma-pas* are supposed to have concealed their literary treasures during the chaos that followed upon the break-up of the Tibetan kingdom.

Later Tibetan historians distinguish between two separate 'spreadings of the Buddhist doctrine' in Tibet, the first one being carried out by the great 'Religious Kings' (seventh to ninth centuries), and the second being initiated by the kings of Western Tibet (see page 113) in the tenth century. But as we have observed, they were thinking primarily in terms of royal patronage. The slow penetration of Tibet by Buddhism must have gone on continuously, for far more was involved in the process than the founding of monasteries and the translating and transmission of Buddhist literature. Not only were those who called themselves followers of *Bon* busy absorbing all they could of Buddhist doctrines and practices, but many of those who called themselves Buddhist were occupied in fitting the old Tibetan gods and indigenous rites into the framework of the new religion. Of this whole process we can expect to find no ready historical accounts, and it is left to us Western scholars to try to unravel the amalgamations that must have begun to take place from the time that the two religions first came together. Nowadays a Tibetan Buddhist assumes that all that forms part of his religious beliefs and practices fits into the 'Buddhist Law', for which he uses the quite general term *chos*. This is the same word as was used in pre-Buddhist times in such terms as 'sacred conventions' (*lha-chos*) and 'human conventions' (*mi-chos*), but it is clearly now used with a greatly extended meaning. However, having since lost contact with Buddhism as practised in other Asian countries, the Tibetans have no means of contrasting their *chos* with other surviving forms of Buddhism, and they have never thought seriously of rejecting their own local gods and indigenous rites as un-Buddhist or 'pagan'. Likewise the *Bon-pos* have had no scruples about taking all they could from Buddhism. The traditional hostility which exists between *chos-pa* (follower of *chos*) and *bon-po* continues to be based upon a general lack of realization on both sides concerning the extraordinary amalgamations of which both religions consist. In fact since the *Bon-pos* accepted the idea of buddhahood as the supreme goal and posited the existence of quite as many 'buddhas', both human and divine, as the *chos-pa*, the general term of 'Buddhist' refers perhaps as much to them as to all other Tibetan Buddhist schools. There has never been any test of orthodoxy, and if the yogin-sage *Padmasambhava* can fairly be acclaimed supreme buddha by the *rNying-ma-pas*, the *Bon-pos* might seem to have a right to an 'historical buddha' (*gShen-rab*) of their own creation. Despite the identity of doctrine and religious practice of *chos-pa* and *bon-po*, there exists, none the less, one fundamental difference between them. All *chos-pa*, whatever their favourite buddhas and gods, acknowledge the Indian origin of their doctrines and continue to hold the 'historical buddha' *Śākyamuni* in considerable respect, while the *Bon-pos* have persisted in their claim that the very same Buddhist teachings came from *sTag-gzigs* (Persia in a vague sense) and that the original buddha was *gShen-rab* and not *Śākyamuni*.

The chaotic period that followed upon the break-up of the old Tibetan kingdom gave free scope both to military adventurers and to religious improvisors, and little as we know about it from historical references, we may fairly assume that it was an extremely formative time for the kinds of doctrinal and ritual amalgamations referred to. Both *Bon* and the 'Old Order' (*rNying-ma*) emerge later with their doctrines and practices organized within frameworks of 'Nine Vehicles' (*theg-pa dgu*), yet arranged on entirely different bases. The 'Nine Vehicles' of *Bon* comprise both pre-Buddhist rites and beliefs together with all the main types of Buddhist practice such as had already entered Tibet during the earlier period. The 'Nine Vehicles' of the 'Old Order', however, are based mainly on the different categories of *tantras*.

Both *Bon* and the 'Old Order' developed sets of new temple-rituals, which paid honour both to the buddhas and the new Buddhist gods of Indian origin, as well as to selected indigenous gods, who from now on began to manifest themselves as 'protectors' of the new religion. A whole new category of divine beings came into existence, the 'oath-bound' (*dam-can*), who promised to defend Buddhism or *Bon*, as it may be, in return for the offerings (usually sacrificial cakes) and worship that they received. Other gods and demons who did not submit so easily were subjected to 'quelling rituals' of the old pre-Buddhist kind, which were performed in Buddhist and *Bon* temples with all the new sanctions that these 'higher religions' might claim to possess. Thus Buddhist monks and yogins were able to unleash against troublesome demons fierce gods such as 'Horse-Neck' (Sanskrit *Hayagriva*, Tibetan *rTa-mgrin*), who already belonged to the Indian Buddhist pantheon and so were purely foreign importations. Far less inventiveness was required of the *chos-pa* ('Tibetan Buddhists'), for Indian Buddhism of the eighth to twelfth centuries provided them with hosts of buddhas and gods of varying characteristics (all carefully listed in their rituals), while they were still surrounded by their old local Tibetan gods and demons, who clamoured for attention. The *Bon-pos* had to use far greater ingenuity, for although they were so concerned to adopt Indian Buddhist theories and practices, they could scarcely use the same names for their new buddhas and gods as the 'Buddhists', without losing their self-identity altogether. Thus they drew up sets of buddhas and gods corresponding to Buddhist ones, but with invented names. They produced a set of five supreme buddhas with distinct *Bon* names. They invented past-buddhas and a future one. They produced a 'Goddess of Wisdom' and 'Mother of All Buddhas', corresponding to the popular Indian Buddhist goddess *Tārā*, already introduced by the *chos-pa* with the name of *sGrol-ma*, 'Saviouress', a literal translation of the Sanskrit name. The *Bon-pos* called their new goddess *Byams-ma*, meaning 'Lady of Loving Kindness', and they clearly concocted this name simply by taking the name of the Indian Future Buddha *Maitreya*, as translated into Tibetan, namely *Byams-pa*, and by replacing the masculine ending by a feminine one. This complex and detailed process of borrowing and adaptation went on for several centuries, but we can be fairly sure from the actual choice of preferred buddhas and divinities that it took place quite early on. We have already referred to the Buddha *Vairocana* (page 90) whose image is the most usual one in the earliest Tibetan temples, and to the four other supreme buddhas who are his manifestations in the four directions. This set of Five Buddhas appears as a fundamental one in early *rNying-ma* and *Bon* rituals.

An interesting ritual, which deserves special mention, is that concerned with guiding the consciousness of the deceased through the 'Intermediate State' (*bar-do*) between death and rebirth. The older Buddhist orders and *Bon-pos* practise this rite, and while its 'theology' is based upon the Indian Buddhist 'Five Buddha' complex (in both gentle and fierce manifestations), the whole conception of guiding a departed consciousness, which to all intents and purposes is an erring soul (despite determined orthodox Buddhist arguments against any enduring principle of personality), through this 'Intermediate State' of forty-nine days duration is manifestly of non-Buddhist origin.

This early period of its history, when Tibet was open to all kinds of cultural influences from Central Asia, was clearly the most formative and creative of all the various periods into which, for convenience, we are dividing Tibetan history from the seventh to the twentieth century. Yet because of its distance in time and the comparative paucity of relevant documentation, it is the one of which we can write with least precision. At the same time there can be no doubt that the most extraordinary 'cultural connections' came about.

Both *rNying-ma* and *Bon-po* possess a special kind of ritual, known as the 'Consecration for Life' (*Tshe-dbang*), the main part of which is the distribution to all present of little pellets of barley-flour and sips of consecrated ale (*chang*). The receiving of these sacred items of food serves to strengthen the 'life-force' or 'soul' (*bla*) of the faithful. One may wonder whether such a ritual was copied from the Nestorians who had penetrated through Persia and Central Asia to China. But to prove this beyond doubt would be difficult.

We may presume that Tibetan temple chant has been strongly influenced by earlier (and now non-existent) Indian Buddhist styles, but nothing similar to the extraordinary Tibetan medley of sound survives in the temple-rituals of the Buddhist Newars of Nepal, who were likewise the inheritors of medieval Indian Buddhist traditions. Tibetan religious music, with its cymbals, drums, bells, shawms and trumpets, must be a synthesis of influences from China, India and Central Asia (representing trends from further west), but the Tibetans have certainly succeeded in creating a distinctive style of their own, whose weird and unearthly effects must be heard to be believed. Such styles of chant and temple music must again go back to the early period, when Tibet was open to cultural influences from all sides. These influences did not necessarily cease altogether with the break-up of the Tibetan kingdom in 842, for the Tibetans remained for quite a long time afterwards in active contact with the world around them.

PART TWO

The Middle Ages

Chapter 4

Foundations of
Monastic Life

The Break-up of the Kingdom The collapse of the kingdom put an end to two centuries of co-ordinated expansion of Tibetan military power and political influence throughout wide stretches of Central Asia. Never again was there any united Tibetan military and political activity outside what may be regarded as its general ethnic and geographical boundaries, that lofty region known poetically as the 'heart of great snow mountains, the source of mighty rivers'.* But despite the disappearance of central organized authority the vigour of the Tibetan people continued to manifest itself in many ways.

A forceful and determined general of the *dBa's* family harried the border regions of China from Tun-huang to Sining and the Yellow River, until in 866 he was defeated and killed by the Uighurs, called in as helpers of the dying T'ang dynasty.† As late as 960 the Tibetans were dominating the cosmopolitan border town of Liang Chou, and Tibetan chieftains from the Kokonor region and further south were in touch with the petty rulers of the 'Five Chinese Dynasties' (907-960), from whom they received titles of honour in return for presents construed conventionally as 'tribute'. One such Tibetan group discovered and invited to rule over them a descendant of the line of Tibetan kings.‡ There are traditions of Tibetan soldiers left behind at several border outposts, such as Cho-ne, where they established viable settlements, and of the remaining Tibetan conscript troops, called the Wun Mo, carving out a considerable territory for themselves until they were perhaps absorbed into that amalgam of people of Tibetan stock, which came to form the Hsi Hsia Kingdom (982-1224). These pockets of Tibetan peoples long held their own against the Uighurs and against the small city states, such as Tun-huang, which, once liberated from Tibetan rule, began to resume their Chinese characteristics. Further west, Tibetan encampments were to be found all the way to Khotan, and Khotan itself was still liable to Tibetan attacks until 950.

Another example of Tibetan enterprise was the migration westwards of the displaced descendants of the kings. In Central Tibet the rivalries and disturbances which followed immediately upon the death of the last king, *Glang-dar-ma*, resolved themselves for a time into a kind of armed neutrality with the land divided between the supporters of the two infant claimants to the succession. But about 866 civil war broke out on such a scale that the head of the branch claiming to be the senior descendant of the old royal line found it impossible to remain in Central Tibet. He took refuge in the far west, where he and his descendants gradually established throughout the Tibetan border lands from Ladakh to Mustang three closely linked kingdoms known as *Mar-yul*, *Gu-ge* and *sPu-hrangs*. Other lesser scions of the royal line continued to live as small local chiefs in many parts of Central Tibet. Their various fiefs are clearly described in Tibetan records and their descendants continue to figure in Tibetan history at least down to the sixteenth century, but only one, the *lHa-rgya-ri* family, survives to the present day.

Although the end of the kingdom was due in part to increasing opposition to Buddhism as a foreign religion, there is no good evidence to support later Buddhist traditions that it was accompanied by a thorough-going persecution of the new religion at the hands of the triumphant *Bon*. Certainly no *Bon* organization of any kind arose to take its place, and there is evidence in Tibetan records that Buddhism was kept alive in private houses in Central Tibet and that the more holy places, although allowed to fall into dilapidation, were at least preserved from desecration. Buddhism was now neglected, rather than persecuted, for the continuing civil strife exhausted and impoverished the leading families in Central Tibet, on whom organized religion of any sort always depended for patronage. But in the outlying regions, such as the small principalities of the east where Buddhism was the established religion, and later in the new kingdoms of the west, which bordered on the Buddhist lands of north-western India, Tibetans continued and developed their practice of the new faith.

The Restoration of Buddhism Tibetan chronology is reasonably precise about the date of the restoration of Buddhism in Central Tibet, namely sixty-four years before the Indian teacher *Atiśa* visited Tibet in 1042, that is to say about 978. It was in this year that some Tibetan teachers returned to Lhasa from their refuge in eastern Tibet. Their early endeavours and the temples they founded were on a small scale, but in 1012 a disciple of theirs, significantly descended from a once powerful noble family, founded in *'Phan-yul* the monastery of *rGyal-lug-*

lhas, which was to become famous for its great wealth. Thus after a century of recovery and consolidation, the leading families had now regained their lost ability to patronize religion.

An important part was played in eastern Tibet (*Khams*) by the Indian scholar Smriti who initiated the translation of new sets of tantric texts. From this time on all such works were classified as the 'New Tantras' thus distinguishing them from the 'Old Tantras' of the earlier period.

At the same time under a line of enthusiastic Buddhist kings, Western Tibet played a major part in the propagation of Buddhism. The great Tibetan figure of this time is the translator *Rin-chen bZang-po* (958-1055), under whose leadership numbers of *sūtras* and *tantras* with their voluminous commentaries were translated from Sanskrit. The Tibetans followed the *Mahāyāna* traditions as still prevalent in central and north-western India just before they were swept away for ever by the rising tide of Islam. The Indian regions bordering on Western Tibet, namely Kulu, Kashmir, Gilgit and Swat, could still provide Buddhist scholars and yogins, craftsmen and artists, and since the Tibetans were willing to pay generously for their help and their services, there was no shortage of foreign talent on which they might draw. *Rin-chen bZang-po* made three visits to India, where he spent a total of seventeen years, presumably progressing from one Indian Buddhist master to another, seeking initiations into various traditions, copies of texts and their interpretations, as well as the methods of religious practice. He is credited with the founding of a large number of temples and monasteries, and since several of these remain little changed (except for their inevitable dilapidation) since his times, it is possible for us to be precise for the first time about the actual styles of architecture and painting in a known period. The painting must have been carried out under the direction of Indian artists, who, in the manner still followed by Tibetan master-artists to this day, would sketch the divine images according to the conventionally fixed measurements, leaving their pupils to fill in the different colours. We may reasonably deduce that all the decorative motifs appearing on a ceiling in the old monastery of Tabo (page 82) follow tenth century styles of north-western India, the gods and goddesses, the peacocks and the conventionalized cloud-designs. Of the frescos those depicting local people as donors and as workers in the construction of temples are particularly interesting.

In these ancient temples of Western Tibet we come as near as we possibly can in time and place to the now almost totally lost cultural and artistic traditions of old Buddhist Kashmir. The most favoured divinity of the period, to whose importance both texts and paintings bear witness, is *Vairocana* (see page 90), the supreme central buddha of the set of Five Buddhas, who plays a major part in the symbolism of later Indian and Tibetan Buddhism (page 81). The main temple at Tabo preserves a complete set in stucco of the main divinities of his *maṇḍala* (mystic circle), namely *Vairocana* himself, the other four buddhas of the directions, each flanked by four attendant *bodhisattvas*, and then the eight goddesses of worship and the four fierce guardians of the four directions. In many of the texts which he translated, *Rin-chen bZang-po* was concerned with this same set of divinities. It is important to realize that the translated texts did not represent scholarly achievement for its own sake, and the temple murals were not just decoration. These kings of Western Tibet and the scholars and craftsmen who furthered their aims, were concerned in introducing a whole living culture, to which these interrelated collections of texts and paintings alone remain to bear witness ten centuries later. Another frequently recurring painting is that of *Vaishajyaguru*, Lord Buddha of Medicine, and his presence suggests immediately the importance of Indian medical texts and practices introduced into Tibet at this time. These tenth- and eleventh-century temples were constructed of large sun-dried clay bricks. The walls sloped inwards slightly and were seldom more than two storeys high. The roofs were flat, braced with wooden struts and supported by wooden pillars. There can have been little difference in style between these and the first temples of the seventh and eighth centuries built in Central Tibet (see pages 73–74), and buildings of similar style and design have been constructed throughout Tibet right up to the most recent times.

The many texts translated by *Rin-chen bZang-po* and his collaborators represented primarily the Buddhist traditions favoured in north-western India during his time. There was no recognized canon of *Mahāyāna* Buddhism, and traditions clearly varied greatly from one area to another. Only a few decades later we find very different religious traditions and cycles of texts being introduced by another famous Tibetan translator from Nepal and Bihar (see page 115). Buddhist religious life in north-western India was clearly still based on conventional monastic practice with its regular rules of discipline and ordered cenobitic life. Some writers, obsessed with the idea that all later Buddhism was debased and adulterated, fail to draw attention to the fact that the older conventional forms continued to exist side by side with those that are now often referred to generally as 'tantric', and moreover that the texts known as *tantras* often formed the basis both of ceremonies and forms of meditation, which could be practised quite properly within a monastic setting. Thus while the followers of the *Mahāyāna* produced whole new series of texts, known as *sūtras* and *tantras*, they kept the collections of books concerned with 'Monastic Discipline' (*Vinaya*) just as they received them. In north-western India the 'Monastic Discipline' in common use was preserved by the *Mūlasarvāstivāda* School ('the basic school of those who believe that all the elements of existence are real'), and so it was this particular set of texts that the Tibetans received from their Indian teachers, translated and eventually included in their own Buddhist canon. The study of Tibetan Buddhist developments is complicated by the haphazard manner in which Tibetans collected over a period of several centuries whatever Buddhist teachings they could gain from Indian and Nepalese teachers, and by the fact that these teachings were themselves the heterodox accumulation of centuries of Indian religious and philosophical speculation. However, one can usually distinguish two main trends, the one conservative (or at least comparatively so) in that it is based upon an ordered monastic life, and the other free and unorthodox in that it is based upon the experiments and experiences of non-monastic yogins, who practised and developed new styles of Buddhism, untrammelled by the conventions of an ordered monastic life.

The Buddhist developments of the tenth and eleventh centuries in the west are comparatively well documented; thus we might appear to underestimate the importance of developments in eastern Tibet (the Indian teacher Smriti was mentioned above) and in Central Tibet itself, where from the end of the tenth century religious practitioners and scholars had been quietly rebuilding Buddhist fortunes.

Tibetans from Central Tibet began to go in increasing numbers to the great Indian Buddhist centres, of which the great monastic universities of Nālandā, Vikramashīla, Bodhgayā and Odantapuri were the most famous, but they went too to smaller places, wherever religious masters could be found. Two famous Tibetan scholar-travellers of this period are *'Brog-mi* (992-1072) and *Mar-pa* (1012-96), who became respectively the spiritual fountainheads of the *Sa-skya* and the *bKa'-rgyud* Orders. *'Brog-mi* set out for India and Nepal with the financial assistance of the local Tibetan rulers of western *gTsang*, and having studied Sanskrit intensively for a year in Nepal, he pursued his textual and religious studies at Vikramashīla for eight years under the guidance of the 'Great Magician' (*Mahāsiddha*) *Śāntipa*. Here he was initiated into series of texts which have a very different character from those in which *Rin-chen bZang-po* was mainly interested. One such text is the *Hevajra-Tantra*, on which *Śāntipa* had written an important commentary, and it was *'Brog-mi* who later translated this *tantra* into Tibetan with the result that it subsequently became one of the basic texts of the *Sa-skya* Order.*

Tantric Divinities Buddhism in Bihar presumably succumbed to Hindu religious influences far more readily than in Kashmir. In both regions Buddhism had become generally 'tantric', that is to say its practice was mainly sacramental and ritualistic. The buddhas and their divine attendants with their stylized and symbolic names and postures were conceived as coherent units in a kind of divine pattern or mystic circle (*maṇḍala*). This pattern, usually drawn on the ground for the purposes of the rite, served as a means towards the psychological reintegration of a suitably instructed pupil, who received consecration from his master in the actual centre of the diagram. In some cases temples were built as *maṇḍalas*, thus serving as permanent places of consecration. As an architectural form of analogous religious significance, one might compare the separate baptistries, octagonal in shape, attached to some famous Christian churches (e.g. San Giovanni in Laterano, Rome). The final truth was a mystery, concealed rather than revealed by the texts which sought to describe it, and it could be gained only as a result of years of training under a master, who himself possessed that truth, and who would bestow it sacramentally upon his pupil, once he knew he was ripe to receive it. This was a very different kind of 'enlightenment' from that envisaged by the followers of the early *Mahāyāna*. They had conceived of a 'would-be buddha' striving throughout an interminate series of lives to perfect himself in all-resolving wisdom and all-saving compassion. He would quite properly have devotion to the buddhas of all ages and to his religious teachers, whoever they may be, but the *thought of enlightenment* that inspired him was set quite beyond the limits of all emotional and physical considerations. The *tantras*, those strange texts which were certainly sponsored to begin with by non-monastic yogins, introduced a very different conception of the goal of 'enlightenment' or 'buddhahood'. It was now something that could be gained in the course of a single life, if only one could find a qualified master able and willing to impart the truth. Being essentially secret, this form of Buddhism does not lend itself to literary disquisition. One can read the texts which formed the basis of a pupil's training and provided the substance of the ceremonies and rituals, and one may note that while these texts seem strange and even disconcerting to Western readers, many Tibetan men of religion, following their Indian masters, practised them in all good faith.

It is possible to distinguish two main groups of *tantras*, those which construct their basic set of divinities with the forms of the Five Buddhas, usually with *Vairocana* in the centre (see page 113), and those which make use of other divinities whose close relationship with the non-Buddhist gods of medieval India is clear to any student of Indian religion. Tantric practisers used with best effect those divinities to whom they felt through constant association the strongest feelings of devotion, and so wherever there was great devotion to a particular god, he became quite naturally the central divinity of a newly devised 'mystic circle'. One must always bear in mind that ninety-five per cent of those who called themselves Buddhists in India were not erudite philosophers seeking to maintain a logical Buddhist position *vis-à-vis* Brahmanical opponents, but simply those who revered Buddhist monks and Buddhist teachings while never questioning for one moment their allegiance to the gods of their fathers. Pan-Indian tantric notions would thus seem to have permeated organized Buddhism before Buddhist scholars had even bothered to take note of them. Soon put to practical use by experienced masters of *yoga*, they gained serious approval by the acknowledged effects they achieved, and as a final stage we find serious Buddhist scholars turning their attention from writing commentaries on the *sūtras* to writing commentaries on the *tantras*.

With the general equating of Buddhist and Hindu forms of ritual, Hindu devotion to the Great God Shiva, commonly referred to as *Lokeśvara*, 'Lord of the World', finds its parallel in Buddhist devotion to *Avalokiteśvara*, the 'lord who surveys (all living beings with compassion)'. *Avalokiteśvara*, like his opposite number also entitled *Lokeśvara*, 'Lord of the World', seems to have become the great god of late Indian (especially in Bihar) and Nepalese Buddhism. He becomes the supreme ideal of the divine *bodhisattva* (would-be buddha) who continually defers his entry into the tranquillity of final enlightenment, so that he may exert himself on behalf of living beings in all their various spheres of existence. He is saluted as 'Universal Saviour', as 'Great Compassionate One', as 'Stirrer of the Pit of Existence', as 'Stirrer of the Pit of Hell', and since each title implies a different manifestation, it involves a differing entourage of supporting divine forms and a different rite of invocation.

As chief of yogins Shiva had his macabre form as 'Lord of the Cemetery', and this too is paralleled in Buddhist usage, once again with a plurality of names. Of macabre Shiva type are the great Buddhist gods *Heruka* and *Hevajra*, gruesome in appearance, garlanded with bones and skulls, and surrounded by an entourage of wild goddesses in the form of low-caste women. They signify before all else the yogin's rejection of ordinary human life and its conventional values, and arranged figuratively as a symmetrical set for the purposes of consecration in the mystic circle, they are as effective as the set of Five Buddhas with their divine attendants. Of all the Buddhist teachings available in India during this last Indian Buddhist period (tenth to twelfth centuries), those most attractive to the Tibetan character seem to have been the mystical and magical, the awe-inspiring and the terrible. Like their Indian teachers they believed in these strange gods as perfectly valid channels of divine grace, and terrible as some of them certainly were in appearance, nothing was more terrible to a sincere Buddhist intent on salvation than the endless ocean of the miseries of phenomenal existence. Those of weak intent might invoke the mercies of the 'Lord of the World' in his gentler aspects, but those of stronger disposition would resolutely take the bull by the horns (page 252). Abandoning the conventions and make-believe of ordinary human life, they fearlessly accept existence in its most fearful and repulsive forms, and so reach the stage where there is nothing to reject or accept. It is interesting to observe that Indian and Tibetan society have never abandoned those who reject their social norms. A place of honour and respect is accorded to the mendicant and the yogin, once it is judged that his intentions are sincere, and if he has teachings to impart, he will soon have disciples. But possessing supreme value, special religious teachings are not just given away for the mere asking.

A Famous Tibetan Translator   *Mar-pa* (1012-96), the spiritual head of the *bKa'-rgyud* Order, spent some while with *'Brog-mi*, another famous Tibetan scholar-traveller, at his hermitage at *Nyu-gu-lung*, but finding the fees demanded of him far too high, he embarked on his own expeditions to Nepal and India, where the same teachings could be obtained much more cheaply. His chief Indian teacher was the 'Great Magician' *Nāropa*, with whom he stayed for more than sixteen years in his hermitage at *Phullahari* in Bihar. *Mar-pa* was an extraordinary figure; a translator and great collector of texts, he settled down to the life, at least in appearance, of an ordinary married householder. He arranged to be found ploughing his fields when his famous disciple *Mi-la Ras-pa* first came looking for him, and it is made clear from *Mi-la Ras-pa*'s biography that only a small inner circle of initiates knew *Mar-pa* for the great teacher that he really was.

Mar-pa and those of his succession introduced a new kind of Tibetan poetry, often religious and didactic on the Indian model, but also expressive of their personal feelings and observations. As with the pre-Buddhist Tibetan poetry quoted in Chapter 1, the verses simply consist of lines of equal numbers of syllables with alternating heavy and light stress. An overall pattern is sometimes given to the complete set of verses by arranging the contents on a numerical basis. *Mar-pa*'s song on the completion of his studies in India serves as a good example:

> We met thanks to the same prayer we both used to use,
> the great Indian scholar, *Nāropa*, and I, *Mar-pa*, Tibetan translator.
>
> I have stayed with him for sixteen years and seven months,
> and staying together without a moment's separation,
> there has been no occasion he has not had me in mind.
> In this noble hermitage of *Phullahari*
> he has baptised me with the water of the four consecrations
> and given me in full the precepts of the Oral Tradition.
> I have practised contemplation, single-minded, one-pointed,
> on the essence of the supreme, the highest way,
> thus comprehending the total vacuity of thought.
>
> But since I am appointed the religious teacher,
> as ordained for our northern snowy land,
> I, religious junior, will go to Tibet.

As I, religious junior, set out for Tibet,
I have three regrets and three attachments,
three fears for the journey, three anxieties for the way,
three joys ahead and three great matters for wonder.
Now if I fail to recite the last part of my song,
the sense of these words will remain unexplained.

As for my three regrets,
First I regret my 101 accomplished teachers
of whom *Nāropa* and *Maitripa* are foremost.
Leaving them behind, I yearn for them more than a mother yearns for
  her son.
Secondly I regret my 101 men and women companions
of whom *Abhayakīrti* is foremost.
Leaving them behind I yearn for them more than a mother yearns for
  her son.
Thirdly I regret the 101 places of religious practice,
of which *Phullahari* is the chief.
Leaving them behind, I yearn for them more than a mother yearns for
  her son.

As for my three attachments,
first *Deva-Dharma-Bodhi-Ashoka*, my kind host and his wife,
not bearing to part with them, I cleave to them mentally.
Secondly the Brahman boy named 'Golden Rosary',
who is my friend linked in life and death,
not bearing to part with him, I cleave to him mentally.
Thirdly the captain's daughter named 'Clear Blue Sky',
whose company I kept as my valid religious partner,
not bearing to part with her, I cleave to her mentally.

As for my three fears for the journey,
first there are the vile surging waters,
for I must now cross the eastern stretches of the Ganges.
Before I see them, how frightened I am!
On the forest-edge of the *U-shi-ri* Hills
thieves and robbers lie in wait by the way.
Before I see them, how frightened I am!
The toll-gatherers in Tirhut's city

fall upon one like rain.
Before I see them, how frightened I am!

As for my three anxieties for the way,
there are 101 swaying rope-bridges
quite apart from the *La-ha-ti* Gorge.
Alas, I tremble more than quicksilver!
There are 101 large and small passes
quite apart from the *Kha-la-bye-la.*
Alas, I tremble more than quick-silver!
There are 101 small and large plains
quite apart from the *dPal-mo-dpal* Plain.
Alas I tremble more than quicksilver!

As for my three joys ahead,
I know 108 linguistic works
of which *Kalacandra's* is chief,
and I think joyfully of the society of fellow-translators.
I know 108 tantric commentaries of which *Hevajra*'s 'Four Thrones' is
    chief,
and I think joyfully of the society of my fellow-teachers.
I know 108 oral traditions of which the 'Four Word Precepts' is chief,
and I think joyfully of the society of fellow mystics.

As for the three matters of wonder,
I have 108 special teachings quite apart from the mingling and transfer
    of consciousness.
If there is any great wonder, it is certainly that!
I have 108 religious defenders quite apart from the Goddess *Hariti.*
If there is any great wonder, it is certainly that!
I have 108 processes of realization quite apart from the 'Sure Instructions
    in the Fivefold Series'.
If there is any great wonder, it is certainly that!

This is all by the kindness of my lord and lama,
whose favour, I your subject, can never repay.
O Lord, remain as my head-ornament, inseparable from me!
Next I beg my men and women companions
to pray that as I go to Tibet,

Religious activities   Ceremony in the courtyard in front of the *Jo-khang*, the 'Cathedral' of Lhasa. The despatching of 'scapegoats' at the time of the New Year

(*above*) Monk dignitaries at *bKra-shis-lhun-po*

(*below*) Traditional postures adopted during a monastic debate (see page 239)

(*above*) Simple monks photographed after serving tea to the whole community at *bKra-shis-lhun-po* (Tashilhunpo)

(*below*) Annual parade of horsemen in traditional armour. Each aristocratic family in Lhasa used to provide one officer with six or seven retainers from their estates for ceremonial 'call-up' at the time of the New Year festival (see page 197)

Nying-ma-pa
lama of Tarap (Dolpo)
reciting the daily office. He
holds a bell and a small
drum (*damaru*) and before
him are a butter-lamp, a
miniature skull cup
containing consecrated
chang and a silver-lined
wooden tea-bowl with lid
(see page 257)

Bon-po lama
reading in his chapel in
Tarap (Dolpo). The fresco
behind him illustrates
Shen-rab as Buddha.
Books are arranged in
special racks around the
images (see page 257)

(*overleaf*) Villagers on
pilgrimage in Dolpo (see
page 257)

(*opposite*) Village festival on the occasion of erecting new prayer-flags on the shrine *Ri-bo bum-pa* above Tarap, Dolpo (see page 248)

(*above*) Ceremony in a nomad's tent performed by laymen led by a married lama (see page 248)

(*above*) A nun on pilgrimage
with her staff and prayer-wheel

(*upper right*) A meditating yogin,
probably *rNying-ma-pa*. A
string of 108 beads for counting
invocations hangs round his neck

(*lower right*) A beggar making
the rounds of a sacred site by a
continual series of prostrations,
thus inviting alms. His hands
are protected by wooden pads

I, religious junior, may meet no obstructions.
As there is no chance of our meeting again in this life,
I pray that at all costs we shall meet later on
in the Land of *U-rgyan* or some heavenly sphere!*

Atiśa Perhaps the greatest stimulus to religious developments in Tibet in the eleventh century was the mission of the great Indian Teacher *Atiśa*, who arrived in *Gu-ge* in 1042 at the age of sixty after repeated invitations from the religious kings of Western Tibet. He had studied and taught at the Indian monastic universities of Bodhgayā, Odantapuri and Vikramashīla, and he was probably the most famous and revered religious teacher in India at the time. He came intending to stay only three years, but from *Gu-ge* he went on to Central Tibet, finally settling in *Nye-thang*, where he remained until his death in 1054. In accordance with custom he received vast quantities of gold as a fee for his trouble in travelling so far and imparting his learning, and he sent nearly all of it back to Vikramashīla. One imagines that the Indians must have been really impressed with the Tibetans' willingness to pay such large sums for the teachings that they coveted so much. One is reminded of the biblical parable (Matthew XIII, 45–6) of the merchant who having discovered a pearl of great value, sold all his possessions so that he might buy it. From this time on the Tibetans clearly began to subordinate everything else to the propagation of their holy religion, even though their practice of it might not always be particularly holy. At all events *Atiśa*'s authority and prestige gave a new direction to the thinking and practice of other religious teachers in Tibet, and he certainly attracted the attention and devotion of ordinary people to such an extent that the dominance of Buddhism over the whole range of Tibetan social life was never thereafter seriously challenged. The religious kings of Western Tibet were anxious to invite renowned Indian teachers not only to benefit from their special learning, but also to use their authority to combat the freer and coarser interpretations of tantric theories, to which the Tibetans seem to have been particularly drawn. The *tantras* provided limitless materials for colourful and enjoyable (dare we say licentious? – this is the usual charge) rites and for magical arts of all kinds, and many Tibetans, like most people everywhere, found such matters more diverting and even more useful than the hard single-minded practice of serious religion. Simple villagers are likely to be far more interested in a lama's ability to produce rain or to keep off hail than in the progress of his meditation and the moral teachings that he might have to give them. Great as *Atiśa*'s influence certainly was (probably due largely to his mastery of Tibetan, a rare feat among visiting Indian scholars), it would be a mistake to regard him simply as a reformer of debased tantric theories and practices. He was himself widely read in tantric texts and the master of their consecrations, and he was not above the performance of magical rites on occasions. However, he seems to have been much influenced by his chosen disciple '*Brom-ston*, who was six years his senior. It was mainly on his account that he stayed on in Tibet, and the austere, almost puritanical, attitude of his chief disciple seems to have restrained the master from laying too much stress on mystical and tantric teachings, with the result that the main basis of his teachings was the more philosophical 'Perfection of Wisdom' literature. He appears therefore somewhat at variance with such established Tibetan masters as '*Brog-mi* and *Mar-pa*, who seem to have avoided meeting him; even *Rin-chen bZang-po*, who had played an important part in finally getting him to come to Tibet and who had been studying Buddhist religion almost before the Master was born, appears not to have been always in accord with him. In return *Atīśa* treated him and other Tibetan scholars with sympathetic respect, praising the country that could produce so many learned men and tactfully commenting upon the excellence of Tibetan tea, but beneath such diplomatic politeness there was at times a sharp magisterial attitude.

From the time of *Atīśa* there was no less diversity in the manner and matter of Buddhist teaching in Tibet, but few Tibetan teachers could remain unaffected by the new influence, even if they were not in complete agreement. Two important cults date from this time, the Indian mystical cosmological and astronomical system, known as the 'Wheel of Time' (*Kālacakra*), and a new development in the cult of *Avalokiteśvara* (Tibetan *sPyan-ras-gzigs* 'Glancing Eye') in his various forms. It is significant that while *Atīśa* was staying in *Gu-ge* he devised a special version of the *Guhyasamāja-Tantra* ('*Tantra* of the Secret Unity'), which normally concentrates on the set of Five Buddhas, making instead *Lokeśvara* ('Lord of the World' *alias Avalokiteśvara*, see page 117) its central divinity, a subtle change from dependence on an accepted Buddhist symbolic arrangement to devotional allegiance to a divine being conceived as a god in the Hindu pattern. From now on this change begins to characterize all Tibetan Buddhist practice, as expressed in private meditation upon tutelary divinities and public worship of the great gods of later Buddhism in temples and monasteries. More on this matter will be written below, for in this respect *Atīśa* merely represented the trends which must have been typical of Buddhist practice in Bihar in these last centuries of Indian Buddhism.

Perhaps the most potent effects of his mission derived from his insistence on the need for a restoration of monastic order and discipline and on the necessity for a pupil to choose and be accepted by one teacher, and then to follow him with complete obedience and devotion. But in this last respect his views were in no way different from those of other masters of the higher tantric practices. In all these secret doctrines associated with the aspiration towards buddhahood in the course of a single human life, only a master who was himself already constituted in this kind of buddhahood had the power to bestow it, and he would grant it to no disciple whose worthiness was not proved by his total devotion to his master. Nothing in this world or any other could break the bond between such a master and pupil. In adhering to such views *Atiśa* by his great prestige gave them a kind of formal sanction, and far from being an innovator or reformer, he helped rather to bring together into a united stream the practices of monk and yogin, for the higher tantric practices aiming at buddhahood here and now certainly had their followers from this time on within the monasteries.

Religious Orders In spite of *Atiśa's* unparalleled prestige, the direct transmission of his personal teachings played only a small part in the development of the various Tibetan religious orders after his day. The reason lies mainly in the strict austerity which characterized his disciples, especially his favourite '*Brom-ston* (1008–64), who avoided publicity of all kinds, even refraining from giving religious instruction. Having founded the monastery of *Rva-sgreng* in 1056, he continued to lead a life of secluded meditation there until his death. His tradition of teaching, small and without wealthy patronage, became known as the *bKa'-gdams-pa*, literally 'Bound by Command'. The four laws to which its followers were subjected, abstention from marriage, intoxicants, travel and the possession of money, had small appeal for the majority of Tibetans, who though ready to accord admiration and alms to an ascetic, were far more attracted by the emotional and magical aspects of Buddhism. In their zeal for religious truth a few would endure considerable privations for limited periods at the command of a chosen master, but this is rather different from enduring privations for their own sake as part of normal monastic rules. Tibetan monks have always enjoyed a degree of personal freedom, which despite certain shared characteristics of a very general nature, makes their monastic life radically different from Western monasticism.

bSam-yas, Tibet's first monastery, continued still, enjoying wealthy patronage and regarded with respect by new generations of teachers, who none the less developed rather different lines of thought, derived from their contacts with Indian masters and such Tibetan scholars as '*Brog-mi* and *Mar-pa*, who returned from study in India and Nepal. Groups of disciples gathered around these new masters, and it was in their centres of teaching that the various subsequent 'orders' of Tibetan Buddhism had their origin. As in most human affairs, these 'orders' were those which achieved success in a worldly sense, attracting wealthy patronage without which there could be no religious foundation worth the name, and attracting novices, often with noble and wealthy connections, without whom there would be no assured continuity for the 'order'. In this creative period there must have been scores of worthy teachers, whose lines of teaching simply came to an end with their death, their few followers wandering off possibly to join foundations with a more secure future.

The first of the great new schools or 'orders' was the *Sa-skya-pa*, which takes its name from the monastery of *Sa-skya*, founded in 1073 by *dKon-mchog-rgyal-po* of the *'Khon* family, who was a disciple of *'Brog-mi*, that rather eccentric mystical wonder-worker, a type much admired in Tibet, who had studied and collected tantric traditions in India (see page 115). It was the son and successor of *dKon-mchog-rgyal-po*, the Great *Sa-skya-pa Kun-dga'-snying-po* (1092-1158) who consciously formulated these received teachings, and it is only from his time onwards that it is possible to refer to a specifically *Sa-skya* school. *Sa-skya* (pages 40–1) was established on a site recognized as auspicious by the founder, *dKon-mchog-rgyal-po*. He managed to acquire it from the local ruler, who was a descendant of the line of Yarlung kings and perhaps overlord of the *'Khon* family. After *Sa-skya*'s rise to greatness a genealogy was constructed linking the *'Khon* family with a noble house at the time of the Kings, but although they may have been wealthy landholders in *gTsang*, the extended genealogy is probably a pious fiction. The site indeed proved auspicious, for it was on a trade-route linking the Nepal Valley and the rich agricultural area around Shigatse, as well as being on the edge of nomad lands with their supplies of butter and wool. Thus with local patronage and the keen organizing powers of *Kun-dga'-snying-po*, the wealth and fame of *Sa-skya* grew rapidly.

Other monasteries, owing something to the influence of *'Brog-mi*, came into being in various parts of Tibet. *Mar-pa*, once a pupil of *'Brog-mi*, is regarded in retrospect as the Tibetan founder of another 'order', that of the *bKa'-rgyud-pa*, the 'transmitted command'. Chief among his disciples was the great ascetic *Mi-la Ras-pa*, the most famous and popular of Tibetan yogins, renowned both for his magical powers and his songs. Having been translated both into English and French, his biography is well known in the West.* It represents a quite distinct type of Tibetan literature, religious and didactic in content, yet generally quite historical, and often precise in its descriptions of local characters and situations. Taking note of Tibetan predilections for the monstrous and fantastic, which is so evident in the *Padmasambhava* literature (see page 97), in the *Ge-sar* Epic and the 'life-story' of *gShen-rab*, founder of *Bon*, one is tempted to inquire into the origins of this more sober kind of religious writing. It develops, we would suggest, under the influence of the very serious scholarly work in which Tibetan teachers, even those whose main interest lay in the pursuit of mystical truths, were now continually engaged. Tibetans were no longer concerned with religious notions of a mythical nature, as certainly seems to have been the case with the ancient *bon* traditions, originally learned by heart and repeated as part of almost mechanical ritual by priests who were necessarily illiterate in those early days when Tibet had not yet developed a literary language. By contrast Tibetan men of religion were now operating within the entirely new sphere of conscious historical development. They knew that their circle of knowledge and teaching could only be extended by determined academic endeavour, and so they acted accordingly. This historical attitude clearly affects the whole manner of their biographical writing, and the *bKa'-rgyud-pa* seem to have taken the lead in this new kind of literature. The following extract about an incident in *Mi-la Ras-pa*'s life is taken from a *bKa'-rgyud-pa* anthology:

> While *Mi-la* continued with his meditation, an old man named *gShen-rdor-mo* who used to take him *tsam-pa*, spoke about him at a local feast, saying: 'At the head of that gorge there is someone named "*Mi-la* Delighting in Learning", and he thinks of nothing but religion. It would be good if we all collected things for him. He has one relative here, an aunt. Let her take him some supplies of food'. The aunt was ashamed. 'I will take him some food,' she said. So she and her servant took a piece of meat and a lump of butter, and reached the place. However *Mi-la* did not interrupt his meditation, and becoming impatient, she threw the things down on the grass and went off in a temper. As *Mi-la* did not see them, a fox or a wolf carried them off. Then *Mi-la*'s sister heard something (about this visit), and wondering if it was true about her aunt, she asked her about the matter. 'Although I collected some things together and took them to him on one occasion, he paid no attention,' she said. 'As you are his sister, it is likely he will respond to you.' Then she showed his sister the way and sent her off. The young woman came up to the place and called out from underneath the door of his shelter. When *Mi-la* looked at her, she thought: 'That is an emaciated fellow. He is not my brother.' Then he said: 'Come in,' and she was so distraught that she did not ask him how he was. She looked at him, and his body was grey, fusty, emaciated; as a result of eating nettles, the hair on his head and his body was grey and rotten, and his body was like a skeleton; his nose was hooked, his eyes sunken and his mouth and tongue quivered. She had an involuntary feeling of sadness, and thought: 'There is no one more wretched than we two.' She bowed her head between her knees and wept bitterly. Of the clothes that his aunt had given him only the rags of a cloak remained, and with these he covered his private parts. Then taking his sister's hand, he sang this song:
> Salutations to my lordly lamas,

And may they bless this hermit!
O sister, your affection leaves only sadness.
Since neither joy nor sorrow are permanent,
I beg you listen a while to my song.
If you consider my lair, I seem a wild beast.
At the sight of it, others would feel aversion.
If you consider my food, I seem a mere animal.
At the sight of it, others would just feel sick.
If you consider my body, I seem a skeleton.
At the sight of it, even an enemy would weep.
If you consider my conduct, I seem a madman.
At the sight of it, you my sister are sad.
But if you consider my mind, it is really enlightened.
At the sight of it my former lamas rejoice.
The gritty gravel beneath me
persistently pricks my skin and my flesh.
Inside and out my body has the nature of nettles
And is changeless in its greyish colour.
High in this lonely rock gorge
Nothing eases my constant melancholy,
And such melancholy is inseparable
From the enlightenment of holy lamas.
As a result of my great effort
There is no doubt my spiritual understanding grows.
O *Pe-ta*, do not be sad, but cook some nettles!*

As a 'biography' of a rather different kind, which exists halfway between the historical and the fantastic, one may refer to that of *Mar-pa*'s teacher, *Nāropa* of *Phullahari*, who was a disciple of the 'Great Magician' *Tilopa*.† *Tilopa* proved the worthiness of his disciple by subjecting him to twelve tests of physical endurance which by any human standards can only be described as vicious. However, one is left in no doubt of their unhistorical character: *Nāropa* throws himself from the top of a three-tiered temple roof; he jumps into a blazing fire; he is beaten near to death on several occasions by villagers, courtiers and soldiers, whom he deliberately provokes to fury on his master's command; he feeds his body to leeches; he is tortured with burning pointed sticks; he exhausts himself totally by chasing phantom figures; he batters his own sexual organ with a stone, and finally he cuts his own head and limbs off and makes an offering of them in a mystic circle (*maṇḍala*) to his master. The main lesson to be learned from all this is that of absolute devotion to one's chosen religious master, whatever he may command, and complete faith in his ability to bestow the coveted truths. *Tilopa* restores *Nāropa*'s well-being after each of the tests and rewards him with the next phase of teaching. Although told as a Tibetan tale, the deliberate and excessive cruelty is quite non-Tibetan. In its exaggerations of the sufferings endured for the sake of religious truth it belongs to the Indian Buddhist traditional literature of stories of heroic 'would-be buddhas', whose actions by any religious standards, whether Buddhist or Christian, are often quite fantastic. The notion of 'initiation by suffering' is a well-known social phenomenon, as common in the highly cultured civilizations of both East and West as amongst pre-literate peoples. It is thus not at all surprising to find that it plays its part, usually on a limited scale, in both Indian and Tibetan Buddhism, and we are far from expressing any shocked surprise. *Mar-pa* subjected *Mi-la Ras-pa* to such continual hardships, real, not fantastic ones in his case, that the youth even ran away in search of another teacher. As his chief labour on his master's behalf, he built a nine-storey dwelling, building it not once but several times, for in the process of building his master made him frequently destroy what he had built. However, his sufferings were mitigated to some extent by the sympathy and kindness of *Mar-pa*'s wife, *bDag-med-ma*. The tower he built still stands (page 40), and from internal literary evidence there is no doubt of the general historical validity of his biography, and those of his successors.

Mi-la Ras-pa lived all his life as a strict ascetic, and he was not a master who encouraged or readily accepted disciples. Nevertheless to one persistent follower, *sGam-po-pa* (1079-1153), he transmitted the teachings and religious practices of his master *Mar-pa*, which were derived from a whole series of great Indian sages and yogins. The influence of *sGam-po-pa* was very far-reaching indeed. He was born of a noble family, first studied medicine, and then with that kind of creative religious discontent which was so typical of this period, he turned to the practice of mystical contemplation, seeking a master who would initiate him in these special arts. His persistent seeking for guidance was eventually rewarded by his acceptance by *Mi-la Ras-pa* himself. After years of study, meditation and teaching, he founded a monastery in *Dvags-po*, where he gave guidance and instruction to some of the most learned and holy men that Tibet has produced. This monastery of *Dvags-lha-sgam-po* continued to transmit his teachings, and although it never became the centre of a separate religious order, *sGam-po-pa*'s direct disciples established no less than six famous schools, all based on his teachings.

The three greatest of his immediate successors were Lama *Phag-mo-gru* (1110-70), *Dus-gsum-mkhyen-pa* (1110-93) and *sGom-pa* (1116-69). The first named, who came to *sGam-po-pa* late in life after studying with lamas of all persuasions including the *bKa'-gdams-pa*, has the credit of founding the first great *bKa'-rgyud-pa* monastery, that of *gDan-sa-mthil*. He himself lived in a simple grass hut, around which the monastery first developed in a simple way, consisting of the huts of his followers. Then after his death it rapidly became a great and wealthy monastery with the original hut still enshrined in the centre. This transformation was made possible thanks to the patronage of the noble family of *Rlangs*, which like the *'Khon* family who supported *Sa-skya*, sought to trace its origins back to the days of the Kings. Thereafter this noble family provided the religious head of the monastery and the chief lay administrative officer. The latter was responsible for continuing the family line, from which the next celibate abbot would come in a continual sequence of uncles and nephews. Such a close association of religious and secular interests marks the beginning of the process leading eventually to that peculiar form of all-embracing 'church' government which has become so typical of Tibet right up to 1959. Likewise the political preoccupations of some of the great Tibetan monasteries throughout the rest of our story become all the more understandable, when one realizes how close were their family connections with noble families, who were so often concerned to extend their influence at the expense of their neighbours. From now on success in religion begins to spell success in the world. However this particular *Phag-mo-gru* branch of the *bKa'-rgyud-pa* was one of those which despite its great influence and authority in Tibetan religious and civil affairs, failed to establish a definite line of teaching and practice sufficiently distinguished to survive until the present day.

Dus-gsum-mkhyen-pa, the second of the three successors of *sGam-po-pa* listed above, was one of the earliest and most devoted of his disciples. He was born in *Khams* (eastern Tibet), and although the principal monastery of his school was at *mTshur-phu* in Central Tibet (founded by him in 1185), the *Karma-pa* connection with *Khams* has continued strongly down to the twentieth century.* These lamas in fact became renowned for the amount of time they spent travelling between their monasteries in central and eastern Tibet. The succession of the abbots of this school, as also of the *'Bri-khung-pa* (see page 137), operated by means of reincarnation and not by heredity as in the other four *bKa'-rgyud-pa* schools. The successor came to be regularly sought in an infant showing signs which indicated that he was the reincarnation of the deceased head-lama. The origin of this unusual idea, later developed by the 'Yellow Hats' in the Dalai Lama succession, is probably to be found in the series of Indian yogins, known as the 'Eighty-Four Great Magicians' (*mahāsiddha*), amongst whom are numbered many founder-teachers, on the Indian side of transmission, of the whole *bKa'-rgyud-pa* Order. It is noteworthy that succession by reincarnation seems to have been adopted where there was no one dominant family line which might not have liked the risk of a reincarnated successor being found outside the family. It has already been mentioned that in the case of the *Phag-mo-gru* branch, a powerful noble family had secured the rights of succession for itself. Nevertheless reincarnation of a kind may still operate. In *Sa-skya* every child of *'Khon* descent has been regarded as the incarnation of some holy person, but the identification has to be made later (see page 200).

It is significant that unlike the *Phag-mo-gru* branch, the *Karma-pa* had no wealthy patron, but drew their support from a wide range of landed and nomad families in the neighbourhood of their monasteries, some of whom provided a special travelling guard, known as the *sGar-pa*, whenever these lamas went on tour. Several lines of reincarnating lamas developed within the *Karma-pa* fold, first the *Zhva-nag* (Black Hat), then the *Zhva-dmar* (Red Hat), the Precious *Si-tu* Incarnation of *dPal-spungs* near *sDe-dge* in *Khams*, and the Precious *dPa'-bo* Incarnation of *gNas-nang* in Central Tibet.

sGom-pa, the third of *sGam-po-pa*'s successors listed, was instrumental in establishing a third *bKa'-rgyud-pa* school through his disciple *Lama Zhang* (1123-93), who founded *Gung-thang* Monastery near Lhasa in 1175 in the district known as *mTshal*, after which this school was named. This branch gained substantial patronage and importance in political affairs. *Lama Zhang* himself claimed descent from an ancient family, and succession to the abbacy was either hereditary or by appointment. It was a Lama of *mTshal* who later negotiated Tibetan submission to Genghiz Khan. But despite its earlier importance, this *bKa'-rgyud-pa* branch has ceased to have any independent existence.

The other three *bKa'-rgyud-pa* schools were all founded by disciples of Lama *Phag-mo-gru*. The most important was the *'Bri-khung-pa* school, named after the monastery of *'Bri-khung*, which was founded by *'Jig-rten mGon-po* (1143-1212), who gained a great reputation for the excellence of his teaching and holiness of life. Like the *Karma-pa*, the head-lamas of this school succeeded by reincarnation, developing the system to a very great extent, for each head-lama often had three incarnations, one of 'body', one of 'speech' and one of 'mind'. Meanwhile the administration of *'Bri-khung* remained in the hands of a powerful lay official, known as the *sGom-pa*. Although we do not wish to include too many small details of this kind, it is important to emphasize from the start that each school and often each monastery began to develop its own special traditions and customs very early on. This is exactly as one would expect, and one could easily find many analogies within our European universities and religious orders.

The two remaining *bKa'-rgyud-pa* schools are the *sTag-lung-pa*, based on the monastery of *sTag-lung* (p. 40), founded by *sTag-lung Thang-pa* in 1185, and the *'Brug-pa*, based on the monastery of *Rva-lung*, founded by *Ye-shes rDo-rje* c. 1180. This last school is named after the monastery of *'Brug* in *dBus*. Nowadays it is chiefly important in Bhutan (*'Brug-yul*) and to some extent in Ladakh (*La-dvags*).

Monastic Culture Thus by the beginning of the thirteenth century there were seven powerful centres of religious teaching in Tibet, all conscious of the strength which came from the freshness of their doctrines and traditions. They were mostly situated in quiet valleys on the borders of upland grazing grounds but also close enough to frequented trade-routes, or in the case of *mTshal Gung-thang* and *gDan-sa-mthil*, in prosperous agricultural areas. From each of these main centres branch monasteries developed all over Tibet, but especially in the eastern parts of the country. It was an age of ebullient religious zeal, almost as though all the expansionist energy of the Tibetans, which had caused their neighbours so much trouble in the past, was now going into religious developments. It has been suggested by some writers that the gentle teachings of Buddhism had a taming effect upon the wild nature of the Tibetans, but this is perhaps only a partial truth, for within the new religious context they remained capable of being quite as determined and aggressive as they had shown themselves in pre-Buddhist times. Nevertheless all this remarkable energy was often tempered by the profound piety of quite a number of distinguished lamas, turning it towards creative development of the highest moral and cultural worth. Many Tibetans practised their religion with simple faith and devotion, and the long labours of translating Indian Buddhist works from Sanskrit continued unabated.

Moreover *Atiśa* was by no means the last renowned Indian teacher to visit Tibet. As a complete contrast to him we might mention the strange yogin *Dampa Sangs-rgyas*, who came of a Brahman family from South India. He is said to have spent a total of sixty-five years practising meditation in various sacred spots in India and Nepal, and to have made no less than five visits to Tibet, gaining many disciples throughout the length and breadth of the country; on his last visit he went on to China, where he spent twelve years. He is reputed to have been a 'swift runner' (*rkang-mgyogs*) in the special tantric sense; this was a special accomplishment of a trained yogin, enabling him to travel large distances at high speed in a kind of trance. No dates attach to him and he is said to have lived to an enormous age, but this would not be surprising in the case of such a kind of religious practitioner.* He must have been active in Tibet during the second half of the eleventh century. He wrote nothing, but bestowed tantric initiations upon suitable disciples, producing spontaneous enlightenment in some of them. One of his followers was a woman, named *Labs-kyi sgron-ma* (Lab-kyi Dron-ma), who lived sometimes as a nun and sometimes as a married woman. Accepted as a repository of the highest tantric truths, she was identified as a *ḍākinī*, a kind of attendant goddess, and later became deified as the centre of a tantric ritual under the name of the 'One Mother' (*Ma-gcig*). This is still used by the older Tibetan religious orders.

Of Indian scholars who followed *Atiśa* the greatest was probably the 'Kashmir

Scholar' *Śākya Śrī* (1127-1225), who travelled around Tibet from 1204 to 1213, visiting all the principal holy places, including Lhasa, *bSam-yas*, *Sa-skya* and *Rva-sgreng*. He himself founded four new monasteries, known as the Four *Tshogs-pa*, and nearly all the leading figures in Tibet from every school of teaching seem to have been his pupils.

There were no essential differences in doctrine between all these various orders. Their main differences consisted in their traditional attachments to different lines of teachers and particular tutelary divinities. We have already referred to '*Brog-mi*'s preoccupation with the *Hevajra-Tantra*, and as a result this became one of the fundamental texts of the *Sa-skya* Order. The *Sa-skya-pa* were for the same traditional reasons attached to a set of teachings known as 'The Way and its Fruit' (*lam-'bras*), a concise title referring to the whole process of training for enlightenment in a single life, which may be subdivided into training in right views (*lta-ba*), meditation (*sgom-pa*), informed ritual action (*spyod-pa*) and finally the fruit or fulfilment (*'bras-bu*). Other schools had similar teachings, but they were known as 'The Way and its Fruit' at *Sa-skya*, because it was under this term that '*Brog-mi* received them from the Indian yogin *Ḍombhi-Heruka*. Similarly in *bKa'-rgyud-pa* tradition there is frequent reference to the 'Six Teachings' (*chos-drug*) of *Nāropa*. These teachings are concerned with the gaining of enlightenment here and now, or at least at the moment of death, and thus they represent special techniques of *yoga* as transmitted by *Nāropa* to *Mar-pa* and through him to the whole *bKa'-rgyud-pa* Order. While these zealous Tibetan religious practisers were clearly willing to learn wherever and from whomever they could, they naturally retained a special pride in their own received traditions, and thus although they all tended to practice much the same kind of religion, depending on the varying interests and capacities within the different orders, they retained their attachments to their traditional tutelary divinities (any divinity of buddha-rank, commonly referred to as 'god of knowledge', served the same purpose once one had established a bond with him through concentrated meditation), and to the names used traditionally for their religious practices.

We are probably right in assuming that from the start only a minority of monks were concerned to gain the higher truths here and now. Others were concerned with academic work, translating, editing and copying manuscripts, and eventually printing. It is not impossible that the technique for carving wooden printing blocks reached Tibet from China before the fifteenth century, although there is no evidence of any Tibetan book being produced by that method before the printing of the Canon (*bKa'-'gyur*) in China in 1411. All monks were involved in the temple-ceremonies, the ritual and the chanting and the music. A few, practising under the direction of a qualified master, would be intent on establishing a special relationship with a particular tutelary divinity, while the great majority of monks would be content with the 'external' temple worship of the same great gods. All monks were concerned, more or less, in the practicalities of their daily life, and as the monasteries grew in size and wealth, so the work of administration and maintenance became ever more time-consuming. Some might still join the monasteries because of a special interest in religion, but others simply because there was work to be done there and they would be assured of means of livelihood.

The fame and wealth of the monasteries certainly grew fast. Within only a few years of its foundation there were 800 monks at '*Bri-khung*. From his cave the ascetic *Mi-la Ras-pa* gently mocked the silks and furs, the jewelled rosaries and lavish tea-drinking of the great ecclesiastical dignitaries, but Tibetan religion has found as much room for the display of wealth as the practice of poverty, and once again we could easily point to parallels in Western religion. The abundant gold, turquoise and other precious stones, of which there is frequent mention, are a sign of the recovery of the Tibetan economy, and besides barley, mutton and butter, the staple foods of the country, we note also the existence of molasses and cotton cloth, which, together with iron and copper, presumably came from India in return for the musk, gold-dust, wool, chowries (yak tails), which were for a long time the main exports of Tibet.

Despite certain foreign influences the basic architecture of the monasteries remained Tibetan, *viz.* solid construction of stones or sometimes large sun-dried bricks, inward sloping walls with flat roofs supported by wooden pillars. Only the finishing decoration and equipping of the temples were modelled upon Indian and Nepalese styles of the period. Chinese influences, which becomes marked in later centuries, remains equally superficial. Important collections of photographs of temples constructed from the tenth and eleventh centuries onwards are available in *Indo-Tibetica*, vols. III and IV, by Professor Giuseppe Tucci, who was the first to draw attention, as a result of his expeditions in Western Tibet in 1933 and 1935 and in the Gyantse area in 1937, to the vast amount of early architectural motifs and religious imagery still surviving in Tibet. There are frescos and stucco-decorations, images, carved pillars and doorways, all illustrated in detail (pages 81–88). The old Indian styles of decoration, on which these Tibetan developments were based, have almost completely disappeared in India. In Kashmir, which was the main centre of Buddhist civilization accessible to Western Tibet in *Rin-chen bZang-po*'s time, nothing relevant now remains.

On the other hand the contacts with Nepal are still easily discernible, for whole groups of ancient Buddhist monasteries have survived in Nepal to this day. One should note that in this particular context 'Nepal' refers specifically to the Nepal Valley, for until the end of the eighteenth century this represented the limits of

Nepalese (*viz.* Newar) civilization.* Its chief city was then Pātan, well known to Tibetan travelling scholars, merchants and pilgrims as *Ye-rang* (corresponding to the Newar name *Ye-la*), and Pātan still exists, not as the capital (for it has been displaced by Kathmandu), but as the chief Buddhist city of Nepal. It has suffered much neglect, but having escaped modern development, it looks very much as it must always have done to Tibetan visitors from the eleventh century onwards, so slight have been the changes in architectural style. The highway that leads down from the surrounding mountains and into Pātan from the north is still the same wide earth track buttressed high above the rice-fields, which Tibetan feet must have trod for centuries.

The lay-out of Nepalese monasteries, two-storey buildings around three sides of a courtyard, with the main temple, adorned with tiered roofs on the fourth side, has been repeated to some extent in Tibet. But the basic structure is different, for the Nepalese built with small baked bricks and with tiled sloping roofs, whereas the Tibetans, following their own usage, built with stones or sun-dried bricks and used flat roofs. Thus the tiered 'pagoda-roof' which often covers the shrine or some other specially holy object, is a deliberate addition as pure religious ornament to a roof which is otherwise flat. These tiered roofs with their ornamental edging and dragon-gargoyles are commonly associated with China, but although China has certainly been the direct source in recent centuries, one must bear in mind that China herself received this architectural style from India in the early centuries A D. It was still the normal type of roof in India long after the Muslim conquest, and it has survived in Nepal to this day. Thus the earlier Tibetan prototypes were presumably Indian and Nepalese.

There is a close cultural and religious connection between tiered-roof temples and those built in the form of a *maṇḍala*, the mystic circle or divine palace, representing the centre of existence dominating the four quarters of the compass (see page 70). A particularly fine example of this exists as the *gSer-khang* (Golden Temple) at *sTod-gling* in Western Tibet, first described by Tucci. We have already mentioned that *bSam-yas* was constructed in the form of a *maṇḍala* (page 78). Another example of the same cultural motif is the Great Great Stūpa (*sku-'bum*) of Gyantse, built in the fifteenth century (page 43).

As for carving and metal work, although once again these traditions as applied to Buddhist buildings have disappeared from Kashmir, the connections with Nepal are still evident. Superb examples of early Tibetan decorative wood-carving, probably carried out under the guidance of, if not actually by Kashmiri craftsmen, still exist in the old neglected temples of Western Tibet, and the Tibetans clearly continued this tradition themselves. As for the cast images and ritual articles in the temples, these are often of exactly similar workmanship, whether we call it Tibetan or Nepalese, for until only a few years ago Nepalese craftsmen, settled in Lhasa itself, were still helping to produce such things for Tibetan use, while some of the best craftsmen for Tibetan ritual and domestic silverware are still to be found amongst the Newars of Pātan.

As for the murals and frescos, again nothing remains in Kashmir, and surprisingly little in Nepal. It seems likely that however much the Tibetans learned in the early stages from their Indian and Nepalese masters, they rapidly became master-painters in their own right. Of all their religious arts, even in spite of some later Chinese influence, this is the one which may be considered the most typically Tibetan. The subject-matter and stylized symbolic arrangements were completely Indian in origin, and Tibet received these as part of a general Buddhist heritage, just as every other Buddhist country in Asia received them. But no other Buddhist country now possesses the wealth and variety of religious paintings, which completely cover temple-walls and appear in the form of temple-banners (*thang-ka*) in monasteries and lay dwellings throughout the length and breadth of the land.

The *stūpa* continued its development (see page 80) as the most ubiquitous and popular of Buddhist religious symbols. They were constructed in great clusters around the temples and wherever there might be any excuse for founding them (page 41). There is little doubt that they were just as popular in Buddhist centres in India, and the same tradition has certainly continued in Nepal, where large numbers of small *stūpas* often surround a major one. One particular example of direct Indian influence is the prevalence in *bKa'-gdams-pa* foundations of large *stūpas* of bronze or bell metal, often as much as five feet high, and usually connected by tradition with *Atiśa* himself or one of his disciples.

Tibetan monasteries continued to grow in size, duplicating and reduplicating the basic Tibetan and foreign components, until they appear as a vast coherent, but no longer symmetrically arranged, complex of buildings. The great new foundations were mostly established in sheltered and secluded valleys, while the houses of the local nobility rose as massive fortresses, entirely in Tibetan style, on the side of a hill, or as solid mansions, sometimes as many as nine storeys high, surrounded by a protective enclosure.

In literature the Tibetans established very rapidly their own traditions, although some lines of scholars have turned again and again to Indian models. From the seventh to the thirteenth centuries Tibetan scholars were primarily engaged in the enormous task of translating every available Indian Buddhist work from Sanskrit into Tibetan, and the scale of this work is indicated by the 108 massive volumes of canonical texts and the 225 volumes of translated works by Indian masters, which go to make up the basic set of Tibetan Buddhist scriptures common to all religious orders. But already before this work was finished other scholars found the time to record the biographies, sayings and songs of revered lamas, even to risk writing a few more or less original commentaries on the sacred translated texts, and also to record the pre-Buddhist traditions which we have already referred to in earlier chapters.

Chapter 5

Mongol Overlordship

Tibetan Submission While the Tibetans were engaged in all this creative endeavour, forces beyond their control were beginning to transform the world around them. They were curiously indifferent to these great events, simply making the best of suddenly changed circumstances and continuing to develop their newly acquired accomplishments, unaware of the consequences of the cultural isolation in which they were soon to be enclosed. One of these 'great events' was the Moslem advance across northern India, resulting in the total destruction of all the great Buddhist centres, the last to disappear in the early years of the thirteenth century being Vikramashīla, once so much frequented by Tibetan scholars. Its destruction was so deliberate and so complete, even its foundation stones being thrown into the Ganges, that to this day its site remains unidentified. The monks were put to the sword. About the same time the other 'great event' began to unfold on Tibet's northern and eastern frontiers. Genghiz Khan, who had been chief of the Mongols since 1206, attacked the Kin Empire of northern China in 1210, burning Peking, its capital, and slaughtering its inhabitants. A few years later the Hsi Hsia kingdom was totally destroyed together with almost its whole population. China was gradually conquered, and with the accession of Kublai Khan in 1263 and the foundation of a new capital at Peking, the Mongols became its acknowledged rulers. Despite all their internal feuds since the break-up of the kingdom in 842, the Tibetans had remained independent. They had channelled their energies into their various religious activities, and so long as there was no active intervention from outside, their internal differences were mainly confined to such manifestations as the rather aggressive competition for prestige between the monasteries of *Sa-skya* and *'Bri-khung*, or the dispute between *'Bri-khung* and *sTag-lung* which started when the chief lama of *'Bri-khung* carried off the library of the late Lama *Phag-mo-gru*. Then there developed the standing quarrel between these two monasteries about the right to cut timber, so necessary for the great building operations, in the *Nags-shod* region north of Po. In this small world there suddenly arrived in 1207 envoys of Genghiz Khan, who had just embarked upon the most barbaric and murderous course of conquest that the world has ever seen. These envoys demanded Tibetan submission under threat of invasion and consequent extermination, for such was the Mongol rule of war. Doubtless it was their preoccupation with their own internal affairs and local feuds which saved the Tibetans. A united kingdom of resolute Tibetans, such as the country had once been, would almost certainly have attempted to resist the Mongols – with disastrous consequences. But as matters then were, they hastened to yield gracefully, almost unconcernedly, to the envoys' demands. As their spokesmen they had a descendant of the former kings, named *sDe-srid Jo-dga'*, as well as the Abbot of *mTshal Gung-thang*, who was known amongst the *Mi-nyag* of the Hsi Hsia kingdom and had possibly already been in touch with Mongol leaders. According to Tibetan pietistic accounts, Genghiz himself was interested from the start in learning something of Buddhism from Tibetan lamas, and it was for that reason he spared the country. This would seem to be doubtful, but in any case the Tibetans in their innocence of the world around them succeeded in remaining the only country in central and northern Asia to escape the merciless scourge of the Mongols. However, the effects of their relationship as it subsequently developed with their overlords, on the rather unusual terms of religious guidance in return for political protection, have pursued them with a strange vengeance right through to the twentieth century. Only monks, whose main interest was the prosperity of their monasteries, would have devised a compact of this kind, and it was probably not the original intention of the Mongols to initiate such unusual arrangements. Later on they realized the peculiar advantages of such an understanding, and thus the main pattern was fixed for Tibetan political relations with her eastern neighbours (see page 149).

Tibetan Relationship with India But before describing events in the east, we must consider the effects on Tibet of the great changes that were taking place in India. For six centuries the Tibetans had been absorbing all they could of Indian culture, and they had developed with their southern neighbours an extraordinary relationship. Unless we count the Tibetans' military incursion into India in the seventh century, there was no government contact. The two countries were certainly linked by trade-routes, of which the most important passed through Nepal, but there were so many changes of dealer on the long and difficult tracks that it is hardly possible to write of trade-relations between India and Tibet during this whole period. As for cultural influences, they seem to have been all one way, and the Tibetans clearly limited their interests to those things that might be called Buddhist. They went to get Buddhist texts and everything that would help to create a viable Buddhist culture back home, and there their interest in India seems to have stopped. Despite the vast numbers of Tibetans who visited all parts of northern India, very few bothered even to describe the holy places of Buddhism which they visited, and as for descriptions of the other manifold aspects of Indian life, one usually scans their writings in vain.* They seem to have been chiefly interested, as pilgrims of other religions still are, in hearing and retelling the various pious legends, usually complete fabrications, attached to the many holy places they visited. If one had only their accounts to go on, one would assume that both India and Nepal (and with the latter they have had much longer contacts) were mainly Buddhist countries, so little are they concerned with anything unconnected with their holy religion.

Fortunately the great Buddhist monastic universities of India taught in accordance with a fairly wide syllabus, not only philosophy and logic, but also astronomy and medicine, ritual and liturgy, grammar and poetics, even arts and crafts. Tibetan students and scholars equipped themselves linguistically to follow the texts and the courses, and this entailed learning both Sanskrit and the locally spoken language, whether north-west Indian *prākrit*, or early Bengali. Thereafter they had to immerse themselves in a culture which to begin with was totally alien to their indigenous Tibetan ways of thought and expression. As more and more monastic centres developed in Tibet itself, some initial training with Tibetan teachers, who had already studied in India, would render the task of cultural accommodation progressively easier. Likewise as more and more texts were translated and more and more Tibetan teachers became competent in the theories and practices connected with them, so it became an ever more practicable proposition to become a well-instructed Buddhist without knowledge of a foreign language. Moreover whole generations of trained Tibetan translators were so skilfully consistent in their translations of Sanskrit Buddhist literature that later generations of teachers and students, who knew no Sanskrit and had never been to India, could overlook the fact that the doctrines they were studying were at all foreign in origin. By the twelfth century a skilled minority of Tibetans had transferred to Tibetan soil not only the texts, but the whole way of life of Indian Buddhist monks and yogins.

The great majority of Tibetans remained quite as ignorant of Buddhist philosophy and logic, Indian astronomy and medicine and all the rest, as they always had been. But they became ever more and more willing to accept Buddhist priests to act on their behalf in place of their old indigenous priests, especially when they saw the splendours of the new establishments with their impressive stacks of sacred literature (even though they could not read it), the gods cast in metal, often gilded, and gorgeously adorned, the wonderful murals illustrating the heavens and hells, and other spheres of existence, not to mention the terrible defenders of the new doctrine, who must surely be so much more powerful than the old local gods. We shall say more of the old indigenous priests, the followers of *Bon*, later on, but we observe now that they were already busy equipping themselves with all the paraphernalia of the new religion. Otherwise they would have had no hope of surviving.

Even for serious practisers of the doctrine, the Indian connection became ever less important, and probably by the twelfth century most Tibetans had come to regard Buddhism as their own Tibetan religion without any further thoughts on the matter. There was still a minority of scholars who studied Sanskrit seriously and worked on translations, but they were no longer the prime movers of Buddhist developments, as they had been in the early centuries, for Buddhism now existed in its own established right in Tibet. There seems to be no sign of dismay in Tibetan records at the catastrophic disappearance of the whole Buddhist culture in the land where they had spent so many centuries in continual quest of whatever Buddhist materials they could find. In fact they seem to have acquired almost everything that was available just in time. Nepal still had something to offer them, and during these fierce Moslem onslaughts many Indians, Buddhist scholars amongst them, took refuge in the Himalayas. But the Buddhist centres in Nepal proved themselves now to be little more than outposts of the great Indian settlements, and Nepalese Buddhism, which was almost entirely a Sanskrit tradition, began to decline very rapidly from the thirteenth century onwards. Celibacy gradually disappeared in the monasteries; textual scholars and competent masters of *yoga* became increasingly rare. The Buddhism which had once been practised by all Tibet's neighbours (unless we count China, which during the first half of the thirteenth century was in the throes of the most terrible invasions of all time) was now practised by the Tibetans alone. Tibet was entering upon a new period of cultural isolation. All it had now in common with its neighbours were: first, medical theories, based partly on Indian psychophysical notions connected with the practice of *yoga* and partly on Chinese anatomical observations, together with a whole literature, Indian in origin, of diseases arranged in numerically significant groups, and the means of their cure, more observed in theory than in practice; secondly, the theories and arts of astronomy and a calendar based on a lunar month and a week of seven days, named like ours after the sun and moon and five planets; thirdly, styles of architecture, iconography and painting, which from now on became more and more specifically Tibetan preserves. Of supreme importance, however, to the Tibetans was their religion, and very few of their neighbours were now interested in Buddhism of any kind.

The Mongols and Sa-skya It is somehow typical of Tibetan religious pre-occupations that they should have assumed that the Mongols, murderous hordes that they then were, were primarily interested in learning something about Buddhism. There is in fact nothing to substantiate *Sa-skya-pa* claims that their chief abbot was asked to send his blessing and religious books to Genghiz. It is likely that he offered these gifts, and the Mongol envoys, interested in more practical matters, did not bother to refuse them. It was not until the reign of Genghiz' successor, Ogodai, who became Khan in 1227, that the Mongols gave serious attention to Tibet. It seems to have fallen, as a very small part of his heritage, to Godan, the second son of the new Khan, who, far from seeking religious instruction, sent raiding parties into the country in 1239. One of them attacked and looted *'Brom-ston*'s monastery of *Rva-sgreng*, as well as the early wealthy chapel of *rGyal-lug-lhas*. Another reached *'Bri-khung*, but there, according to Tibetan accounts, the personality and magical powers of the hierarch *sPyan-snga* so overawed the Mongol commander that the monastery escaped harm. It is also stated that the commander who had raided the other two holy places repented of his evil deeds and paid for their restoration. Whatever truth there may be in these stories, there is evidence of continuing friendly relations between *'Bri-khung* and one section of the Mongols.

As a result of these raids, possibly impressed by what he was told of the influence of the grand lamas, Godan summoned a Tibetan representative to his court. The effective choice lay between the grand lamas of *'Bri-khung*, *sTag-lung* and *Sa-skya*, and in 1244 the Lama of *Sa-skya* set out accompanied by two young nephews. It was a dubious honour, which the others were not over-anxious to accept, for no one yet knew what might be in store for Tibet's representative. However, he made full submission to Godan on behalf of Tibet, and wrote a letter to the lamas, lords and people of the whole country, praising the Khan and explaining that in return they would be given peace and religious freedom. He also held out the hope that Mongolia would become a mission field. He himself was appointed Regent with the duty of residing at the Khan's court and transmitting orders to officials in Tibet. His act of submission, already disliked by many Tibetans, became even more significant in its consequences when his nephew and successor *'Phags-pa* (1235-80) so won the confidence of Kublai Khan (soon to be chief of all the Mongols and Emperor of China), that he became in effect the Mongol's vassal-ruler of Tibet, while Kublai himself became, if not a convert, at least a powerful and devoted patron of Buddhism. From this time dates that peculiar relationship between Tibet and China, known as *Yon-mChod*, 'Patron and Priest', by which the ruler of Tibet in the person of the predominant grand lama was regarded as the religious adviser and priest of the Emperor, who in return acted as patron and protector. No written bond sealed this relationship and no other basis was recognized for the connection between the two countries. One may find some kind of Western analogy in the one-time relationship of Pope and Holy Roman Emperor. It was and continued to be a flexible and variable relationship, depending on the relative power and interests of the parties at any given time.

The Mongols made no attempt to administer Tibet with their own people, but they arranged a broad survey of the country for the purposes of taxation, created an efficient system of communications with well-placed staging posts, and established an overall organization of 'thousand-districts', probably based upon old Tibetan administrative arrangements. Over this administratively reunited Tibet the grand lamas of *Sa-skya* may justly claim, at least from 1261 and possibly from 1254 to have had the authority of 'Kings of Tibet' (they received the title of *Ti Shih* from the Mongols), but they were bound to reside at the Mongol court and their position was by no means willingly accepted by all 'lamas and lords' of Tibet.

The grand lamas of other great monasteries, seeing how greatly the original act of submission and residence at the Mongol court had turned to the advantage of *Sa-skya*, now set about trying to secure a share of the patronage for themselves. The *Karma-pa*, the *mTshal-pa* and the *'Bri-khung-pa* all found patrons among the great Mongol chiefs, and the support of different monasteries by different members of Genghiz' relatives and descendants infected Tibetan affairs with a new bitterness derived from involvement in the endless and internecine factions of the Mongols. Tibetan rivalries were intensified by the thought, introduced by the Mongols, that a single ruler of Tibet was again a possibility, and by the new weapon of armed foreign allies now at the disposal of the competitors. Between 1267 and 1290 *Sa-skya* and *'Bri-khung* waged intermittent war with the help of their Mongol supporters, and in these and like struggles there was no room for Tibetan patriotism or thoughts of nationhood. It was now a matter of powerful monastic orders in close association with landed aristocratic interests seeking their own predominance by whatever available means and without any seeming feeling for their fellow-countrymen and co-religionists. The influence of the nobles was far from over, but it could hardly again be effective without co-operation with the leading religious figures. The 'church' had already established its monopoly in the sphere of learning and culture, and was now well on the way to gaining political supremacy, although to the greater tragedy of the country it still remained undecided which great prelate would be supreme. It was a period of bitter, bloody deeds and unscrupulous intrigue, in which men of religion played the leading parts and monks fought in the battles, for fighting seemed already to have become the responsibility of one class of monastic inmates. But we must remember that this was only one aspect of the Tibetan scene. Even this age produced scholars, teachers, contemplatives and poets, whose devout and benevolent lives would seem to have been unaffected by the turbulent times in which they lived.

Men of Religion The *sTag-lung-pa* Lama exemplifies the disciplined and pious existence of a founder of a great monastery. The *Blue Annals* (pp. 610–21) describes the simple austerity of his life, which was a continual process of silent meditation, preaching, ceremonies and rites. No wine or meat was allowed in his monastery, and no woman might enter his house. He never went for a walk beyond the limits of his monastery, and he never failed to attend to rites and teachings given by his own lama, the Lama *Phag-mo-gru*. His advice was constantly sought, and he was frequently called upon to mediate in the disputes of his contemporaries.

The same strictness of monastic discipline was shown by the grand lama of *'Bri-khung* (1143–1212, *BA*, p. 641) and by the *Karma-pa* Lama *Rol-pa'i rDo-rje* (1340-83, *BA*, pp. 499-506) who became the spiritual adviser of the Emperor of China, and by many other lamas whose lives are recounted in the *Blue Annals*. Others, having first acquired a deep knowledge of religious texts, withdrew to lonely meditation, acquiring the height of spiritual power by means of special techniques of *yoga*. The founder of the *Karma-pa* Order, *Dus-gsum-mkhyen-pa* (*BA*, pp. 473-80) and *Sangs-rgyas Rin-chen* (*BA*, pp. 779-80) who lived some two centuries later are examples of this kind. Others can be described as visionaries, and the details of the signs and portents they used to see, and the miracles performed during and at the close of their lives, abound in the *Blue Annals* and throughout Tibetan literature.* Others described their experiences and their teachings in poetry, and all of them were keen to transmit their doctrines to chosen disciples. Whatever one's reactions to the many pious tales of their extraordinary spiritual and miraculous powers, one can scarcely avoid the conviction that many of these sincere seekers of religious truth really did experience for themselves the fundamental Buddhist truths. The greatest of them manifestly teach not on the basis of texts, but from their own personal knowledge and experience.

As well as those devoted to calm and holy living and dying, there were many who were inclined to more extreme and violent asceticism, living naked in snow and ice, haunting graveyards and eating vile substance, licking lepers' sores, beating their heads on rocks, and enduring all kinds of self-inflicted hardships. It may seem strange to us, though in no way to Tibetans, that some of these ascetics acquired great wealth from the offerings of those who were impressed by such austerities. *sGrub-che* (*BA*, p. 987), for example, was the master of a thousand shepherds, who offered him their ewes, which he accepted so that their lives might be sacrosanct. With these extremists may be classed the holy madmen and mad women who abound as popular figures in Tibetan literature, and whose eccentricities were intended, or at least interpreted as pointing some moral or spiritual lesson. Eccentricity, short of madness, was frequently used by some lamas to impress their teaching on ordinary people, and displays of violence, of irascibility, or of wild and furious dancing are often recorded (e.g. *BA*, pp. 187, 480, 957 and 1066). Even practical joking and horseplay had their place, such as the story of '*Jam-dbyangs*, who put on the dancing mask of the *Lord of Death* and chased his terrified teacher round the monastery by moonlight (*BA*, p. 337). Serious magical practices played an important part in this Tibetan world. One of the greatest of such practitioners was Lama *sPyan-snga* of '*Bri-khung* (1175-1255). A magician sought to transfer upon him certain evils which were threatening the son of a local prince. *sPyan-snga*'s superior powers turned back upon the magician the whole strange complex of spells which had been prepared for his destruction (*BA*, pp. 575-7).

Tibetan Relations with the Mongols Tibetan lamas certainly made an extraordinary impression upon the Mongol Emperors of China, and the maudlin admiration of these 'patrons' for their 'priests' may have contributed in no small way to the swift decadence and fall of the Yüan (Mongol) dynasty. That the Tibetans should have been able to make such a rapid spiritual conquest is evidence of the personal authority and extraordinary ability of the great lamas of the day, who had to compete with the champions of many other creeds and cults, Christian, both Nestorian and Roman Catholic, Muslim and Taoist, as well as the Shamanism of the Mongols themselves. The early Khans were glad to try every form of religious prophylaxis and to employ the practitioners of every kind of religion to offer prayers and ceremonies on their behalf. They deliberately compared the results, and instituted special tests by means of religious debates and magical displays. The Tibetans had to debate with Taoists and with Franciscan monks, and by their own account they carried the day. As for their magic, Marco Polo records that the arts of the Tibetan lamas, who could cause the Khan's cup to rise from the ground to his mouth, convinced him that their Buddhism was superior to Christianity.

This success brought Tibetans once more into close contact with the people of China. Monks and lamas swarmed in the capital, where many of them, by arrogant abuse of their new authority and privileges, aroused intense dislike amongst the Chinese. So long as the strong hand of Kublai (died 1265) and his successor Timur (died 1307) was in control, the *Sa-skya* Viceroys (*Ti-Shih*) had the backing of firm authority. But thereafter the Emperors, while inviting leading lamas from all over Tibet, paid little attention to affairs in the country. Thus with the declining power of the Yüan dynasty the power of *Sa-skya* also declined, hastened by internal dissensions resulting from the system of succession by birth and by the great productiveness of the *Sa-skya* hierarchs, which resulted in large numbers of expectant heirs, not all of whom could be satisfied.

In the cultural field contact between Tibet and Mongolia had two principal effects: the strengthening and reorganization of the administrative framework, involving the importation of some Mongolian words and titles, and the great increase in the wealth of the monasteries from the vast gifts of their Mongol patrons. There can scarcely be anything in the sphere of the arts which can be attributed to Mongol influence, and although a careful search at *Sa-skya* and *mTshur-phu* might reveal objects of the Yüan period, they would be Chinese rather than Mongolian. The extraordinary relationship between the Mongols and the Tibetans was important mainly for its political implications. For about a century Tibet was dominated by a foreign power, which having first asserted authority over Tibet, afterwards gained mastery of China. Later Chinese dynasties inherited or claimed to inherit the responsibility for maintaining the special relationship of 'priest and patron', which Tibetan lamas had instituted, to their great advantage, with the Mongol overlords. Such an understanding was of obvious advantage to the religious order or the particular monastery that enjoyed patronage at any particular time, but it was of doubtful benefit to Tibetans generally, for this more than anything else prevented the development of national consciousness. During this Mongol period of domination all the evils and disadvantages of such a system became apparent, and soon a determined effort was made to rid Tibet of this subtle kind of foreign interference.

Apart from their special favourites, the rule of the Mongols was disliked as much by Chinese as by Tibetans, and both peoples threw it off about the same time, the Tibetans being rather the earlier. With the gradual weakening of the Yüan dynasty, the first moves towards a reassertion of Tibetan independence involved the unseating of the *Sa-skya* grand lamas as viceroys. We have already referred (see page 144) to the long intermittent war between *Sa-skya* and *'Bri-khung*. This resulted in the destruction of *'Bri-khung* by fire in 1290 together with the loss of many of its fighting monks. After this a new lead in opposition to *Sa-skya* was taken by a man of quite remarkable character and ability, *Byang-chub rGyal-mtshan* of *Phag-mo-gru*.

Tibetan Independence *Byang-chub rGyal-mtshan* (Chang-chub Gyal-tsen) was a member of the great *Rlangs* family, who were masters of *gDan-sa-mthil* and held in a virtually independent manner the 'thousand-districts' of Yarlung and

Ne-gdong. He was first trained as a monk at *Sa-skya*, where he came to be employed in a minor official capacity. Then about 1332 he became the 'myriarch' of his home district, and began immediately to assert himself to the discomfiture of his neighbours. They appealed to *Sa-skya* and for many years *Byang-chub rGyal-mtshan* struggled against his rivals, singly or in alliance. He was the victim of intrigue and treachery; he was arrested and tortured; but eventually, by his resoluteness and courage and by playing on the factions at *Sa-skya*, in 1354 he triumphed over all his enemies, even attacking and occupying *Sa-skya* itself*. In all this warfare the weakening Mongol emperors of China took no interest, and simply handed out seals of office to whomsoever came out on top. Already by 1351 *Byang-chub rGyal-mtshan* had established himself so firmly that he was granted a special seal and the title of *Tai Situ* which he preferred to the discredited *Sa-skya* title of *Ti Shih*. The Yüan (Mongol) dynasty in China was in its last throes, but so long as it lasted he maintained what was little more than the fiction of a relationship in order to ensure his acceptance as legitimate successor of *Sa-skya*. In 1368 the last Mongol emperor of the Yüan dynasty was driven out of China by a nationalist Chinese revival under Chu Yuan Chang, the founder of the Ming dynasty. Tibet silently closed the period of nominal subjection to China under the Mongol emperors, and made no move to take up any new relationship with the next Chinese dynasty.

Although the divorce from the Mongols was carried out so quietly, *Byang-chub rGyal-mtshan* undertook an active policy of removing the traces of Mongol influence and of deliberately restoring the glories of the old Tibet of the Religious Kings. He himself took the Tibetan title of *sDe-srid* ('Ruler') in place of the former foreign titles. His successors emphasized their Tibetanness still further in this respect by using the title *Lha-btsun* ('Divine Lord'), and later emphasized their total independence of China by adopting the imperial title *Gong-ma* ('Most High'). In many other ways *Byang-chub rGyal-mtshan* urged the claim that he was restoring a real Tibetan kingship and putting an end to the inferior connection with China through the Mongols. He instituted civil celebrations at the New Year according to ancient royal traditions, ordaining that officials should wear the dress and ornaments of the former royal court. He revived and amended the old code of laws going back to King *Srong-brtsan-sgam-po*. He is credited with the revision of the revenue system by which one sixth of the produce was to be paid as tax. He built bridges and established guard-posts on the frontiers, especially those with China. Also during his time there were produced a famous set of literary works, known as the *bKa'-thang sde-lnga* (Fivefold Set of Scrolls), which were supposed to have been composed in the ancient royal period, concealed during the subsequent troubled times, and rediscovered now that a new age ready to receive them had arrived. These books glorify the achievements of the ancient kings, telling how the demons of Tibet had been quelled by the power of the new Buddhist law, how the great monastery of *bSam-yas* had been founded, and generally reviving the themes of ancient royal greatness. They are written in archaic language, and many passages undoubtedly represent genuinely archaic traditions, such as the description of how *Srong-brtsan-sgam-po*'s tomb was worshipped, quoted on (page 52). There was soon a great spate of 'rediscovered texts' of all kinds, for it enabled some religious groups, especially the *rNying-ma-pa* and the *Bon-po*, who were now reconstituting their doctrines, to endow their refurbished literary works with the sanctity properly due to genuinely early religious traditions. Such 'rediscovered texts' were known technically as 'treasure' (*gter-ma*) and lamas renowned for discovering them were known as 'revealers of treasure' (*gter-ston*). But apart from these special religious interests, of which we shall say more later, all this strange literature has one main motive in common, the creation of a national sentiment whether in state affairs or in matters of religion. Probably to this same period belong the archaic images of the Religious Kings and their Queens (page 88) which are still preserved in Lhasa *Jokhang* (Cathedral) and the *Potala* (Royal Palace). All this served to efface the memory of Mongolized dress, laws, customs and authority, but *Byang-chub rGyal-mtshan* still made use of the Mongol administrative framework, and he developed still further the concept of one universally accepted ruler for all Tibet. Although some of his successors were vigorous and relatively successful, they could not maintain the impetus that he had given to the ancient royal ideal, and after some 130 years these *Phag-mo-gru* rulers were displaced by their own powerful ministers, the princes of *Rin-spungs*, who in turn were displaced by their ministers, the governors of *gTsang*, who by 1565 had consolidated their hold on the greater part of Tibet to the extent that they may reasonably be referred to as the *gTsang* line of kings.

The supremacy of the *Phag-mo-gru* was in effect a continuation of the rule of a religious leader, whereas *Rin-spungs* and *gTsang* represented a return to lay rule. Both the latter, however, were in close association with a great monastery, the religious power of the day being that of the *Karma-pa*.

Throughout this whole period there was continual interplay of alliances between the lay successors of the once powerful noble families and the prelates of the growing network of Buddhist monastic centres. Each used the other as an ally for its own ends, but what helped to tip the balance in the favour of the 'church' was clearly the strenuous patronage of the *Sa-skya* grand lamas by the Mongols, and the manner in which they intervened at will in the internal disputes of the country, thus inevitably reducing the position of the lay nobles. All this must have increased the prestige of the 'church' in the minds of a people whose need for spiritual leadership during the aimless confusion that prevailed after the fall of the old kingdom, had provided a ready field for the propagation of Buddhist teachings.

Chapter 6

Religious Preoccupations

Arts and Crafts From the end of the Yüan dynasty (1368) there was no fixed relationship, certainly not one of subordination, between the rulers of Tibet and the emperors of the Ming dynasty, but contact was maintained by the frequent visits to China of monks and lamas of the great Tibetan monasteries. Although Chinese diplomatic fiction describes these as 'tribute missions', the participants, who represented no authority but their own monastery, went solely for the valuable commercial concessions they received. These business ventures added greatly to the wealth of the Tibetan 'church' and also provided a channel through which cultural and artistic influences might enrich Tibetan life and thought. Pearls and other precious stones, brocades and richly worked robes, incense-burners and ritual vessels, gilded bronze and copper images found their way into the monasteries. A small lead tablet on a pillar in the Cathedral at Lhasa records the offering of such presents in this period. One remarkable survival from the period was a great scroll, fifty feet long by two and a half feet wide, describing in five languages, beautifully written in gold, the miraculous events of a visit to the emperor by the fifth *Karma-pa* hierarch. The events are illustrated by panels delicately painted by a Chinese artist.

The effect of Chinese art on Tibetan painting, especially in the *Karma-pa* and *Sa-skya-pa* monasteries of east Tibet, may also be seen at this time. Tibetan painting, always religious in content apart from conventional decorative motifs, began by following Indian Buddhist painting in the portrayal of the great Buddhist gods. Such a painting normally consists of a symmetrical arrangement of divine figures with the main divinity, usually painted on a larger scale, in the centre. Above the central figure there sometimes appears the supreme buddha-figure, of which the central divinity is considered to be the emanation. For instance above the head of *Avalokiteśvara* there regularly appears a small figure of *Amitābha*, Buddha of Boundless Light, the 'absolute buddha-body' (*dharmakāya*) of which *Avalokiteśvara* represents the 'glorious buddha-body' (*sambhogakāya*). Such a painting often corresponds to a particular ritual, and its forms are stereotyped. Quite early it became common to represent right along the top of such a painting the tradition of lamas and teachers, through whom a particular ritual had passed up to the time of the painting's execution. It then became the custom, and this seems to have been an entirely Tibetan development, to portray a revered lama as the central figure, the more so as lamas occupied the central position by divine right in the eyes of their disciples. It became common to represent a particular lama as the manifestation of a particular divinity, indicated by the gestures he adopted and the implements he was holding. Now under Chinese influence a far freer arrangement of the main figures became acceptable. The main figure may be no longer in the centre, but arranged with other figures in the kind of balanced way that we in the West now expect (page 251). The painting of landscape begins to develop, never as the main feature as in Chinese painting, but as decorative motifs, which combined with the religious figures of the painting further assists towards the production of an altogether freer style, especially in paintings from eastern Tibet. The individual painter, while still bound to follow the prescribed model and measurements for each major figure, has a new scope to produce a religious work of art which he himself conceives of as pleasing, whereas earlier generations of Tibetan painters, tended to be craftsmen, who produced rather diagrammatical, although often extremely beautiful, groups of figures.

But it must not be thought that a new style of painting now entirely displaced the older ones. As happened in other spheres of Tibetan culture, all the various traditions continued to exist and develop side by side, some preferred by one line of painters, some by another. Styles of painting were transmitted from master to pupil in exactly the same way as religious teachings were passed on, and just as a brilliant religious teacher might give a new form to the teachings he had received, so a brilliant painter, nearly always however anonymous, might develop a new style in his school. A very old style of Indian religious painting is represented by a scroll depicting a main divinity in the centre of a whole set of small scenes portraying the events for which he is famous. Thus a painting of the historical Buddha *Śākyamuni* might comprise a main buddha-figure drawn conventionally to represent the Great Sage surrounded by inset pictures illustrating the twelve great events of his life, his birth, his leaving home, his realization of enlightenment under the pipula tree, etc. etc. Any revered lama might be represented in a similar style, and this tradition of 'didactic painting' continues right up to the present time (see page 253) remaining very different in style from a religious painting produced under Chinese artistic influence.

Chinese tastes also began to have the effect of raising domestic standards of furnishings and cuisine, but even to this day it has been mainly the noble families and great 'church' dignitaries who have benefited from such cultural influences. But it must be remembered that the same might be said of Western Europe until the nineteenth century. Chairs have been as little known in Tibet as elsewhere in Asia until very modern times, and for seats a raised platform is used, covered by a small mattress and a carpet. The weaving of carpets for Tibetan domestic use must have been a quite ancient Tibetan craft, just as was the weaving of woollen homespun for everyday clothes. But during the Ming period and probably even earlier Chinese carpets arrived in small quantities in Tibetan monasteries and great noble houses, with the result that Tibetan weavers noted and adopted the new designs. Floral designs often reveal their Chinese influence, but one very common design on Tibetan carpets, that of 'dragon and peacock', although quite possibly transmitted through China, presumably derives from Persia, where it occurs as the 'dragon and phoenix' design. The Tibetans know the peacock very well, as it has been introduced into Tibet from India, but the ancient design of the bird which Tibetans regularly refer to as a peacock is originally the phoenix, which like other odd cultural motifs referred to (page 27) reached Tibet through Central Asia and China (page 256).

Carved wooden tables and cabinets also began to appear in Tibet. Once again wood-carving was a well established Tibetan craft owing much to early Indian and Nepalese influence, but these new articles of furniture were clearly produced under Chinese influence, for cultured and wealthy Tibetans began to adopt the furnishing styles of their eastern neighbours. Yet it must be stressed that a well-furnished Tibetan room remains decidedly Tibetan in style, and no one at all familiar with the culture of the country would imagine he was in China, if suddenly placed in such a kind of room. A very noticeable difference is the Tibetan predilection for bright colours, especially the religious colours of yellow and dark red. Moreover, whatever the Chinese influences in certain motifs, no one who is at all familiar with Tibetan painting, its religious preoccupations and its whole general format related to early Indian styles, would mistake a Tibetan painting for a Chinese one.

The Tibetans produce earthenware, often of fine quality, but porcelain has been regularly introduced from China, probably since the Ming period. For drinking their buttered tea and rolling moistened *tsam-pa* (roasted barley flour) into manageable balls most Tibetans use small wooden bowls, sometimes lined with silver, and since they are such inveterate travellers bowls of such a kind are clearly very practical for carrying on a journey.

The staple food of most Tibetans has always been *tsam-pa*, meat, butter, curds and barley-ale (*chang*). Tea was introduced very early from China, probably already in the eighth century, but the Tibetans very soon took to brewing it in their own manner, churning it with butter and salt so that it served as a light and stimulating broth. Just as in Britain, tea-drinking spread rapidly from being a foreign habit, cultivated by the upper classes, and became the national beverage for all Tibetans, high and low. To offer tea-ceremonies on a vast scale to a community of monks became a recognized act of merit, and in many monasteries it became the custom to expect such a tea-offering from a new member, and at various stages in a monk's academic career.

Cultural Limitations It might seem as though Tibet's chief cultural contacts were with India up to about 1200, and from then until the present day with China. But however attractive for its simplicity such a scheme might be, it would still be extremely misleading. Tibet's relations with India on the one hand and with China on the other were on an entirely different basis. We have already referred to the Tibetans' preoccupation with Buddhism in all their direct dealings with India (pp. 145–7), and we have described how they transported to Tibetan soil the whole active Indian Buddhist culture, developing it energetically until it permeated every sphere of Tibetan social life and became the psychological mainstay of every individual Tibetan. Compared with all this, Chinese cultural influences in Tibet have been superficial, limited for the most part to the cultured way of living of a wealthy minority. Apart from this, ordinary Tibetans and Chinese have nothing in common, and the Indian Buddhism which has penetrated so deep into the Tibetan soul makes a great gulf between the two peoples, which only its eradication might help to remove. Although Buddhism has flourished in China far longer than in Tibet, there has been no cultural contact worth mentioning between Tibetan and Chinese Buddhists. They speak a different tongue and their sacred texts are written in an entirely different language. Neither Chinese nor any other language for that matter, except Sanskrit, has even been taught in Tibetan schools and monasteries, and apart from their extraordinary enthusiasm for Indian Buddhism, the Tibetans have shown little interest in the literatures and cultures of their neighbours. Those who live in frontier areas and those who trade in any particular direction have picked up for colloquial use only as much of any local neighbouring language as may be useful in their affairs. Thus quite a number of Tibetans in Amdo speak some Chinese and not a few on their travels in *rGyal-rong* and beyond have stayed in Chinese Buddhist monasteries (this we know from present-day accounts) but nothing of great significance has permeated Tibetan cultural life from these slight personal contacts. Indian Buddhism apart, the Tibetans have shown right up to the present day an almost total lack of interest in their neighbours. From the thirteenth century onwards cultural contacts with the Mongols have been continuous, but the Tibetans are only interested in Mongols who have learned to speak Tibetan and have become Tibetan Buddhists in the full sense of the term. It is almost as though having procured for themselves 'the one pearl of great value', they care little about anything else. There is much that they might have learned from China of a technical and scientific nature throughout the centuries, but the only Chinese crafts adopted for general use seem to have been paper-making and especially printing from incised wooden blocks (xylographs). The Tibetan Buddhist Canon (*bKa'-'gyur*) was first printed in this way in Peking in 1411, and it is possible that this form of printing craft reached Tibet during the previous century or even earlier. To print in this way requires a school of highly trained wood-carvers, for every letter on the page has to be carved around with the utmost precision, so that it remains standing, with the rest of the wood cut away, ready to receive the ink. (page 194). A skilled carver might complete an average sized wood-block in seven to ten days. At the time of its introduction this form of printing was a great advance, and it was taken up eagerly by the Tibetans, for now they might make as many copies of their treasured Buddhist texts as they pleased. Although this early and laborious method has long since been surpassed in China, the Tibetans are so attached to it for traditional and sentimental reasons, that it was not until the mid-twentieth century that they began to take an interest in other more modern methods.

Tibetan Scholarship Before turning to *Tsong-kha-pa* (1357-1419), the next great figure to introduce still further complications into an already complex religious scene, we must summarize literary and religious developments from *Atīśa*'s arrival in Tibet (1042) until the end of the fourteenth century.

We have written so far chiefly of the *Sa-skya* and the various *bKa'-rgyud-pa* orders in so far as they have played an important part in political and social affairs from the early thirteenth century onwards, and now we need to emphasize the change that begins to take place in Tibetan scholarship about the same time. Up to 1200 India still had everything to offer in Buddhist studies, and so in Tibet it was the age of the Great Translators (*lo-tsa-ba*), such as *sKa-ba dPal-brtsegs*, *Cog-ro Klu'i rgyal-mtshan* and *Zhang Ye-shes-sde* in the eighth century, and after the eclipse of Buddhism *Rin-chen bZang-po* (see page 113) and *Ngog Legs-pa'i Shes-rab* in the tenth and eleventh centuries. The last named was a disciple of *'Brom-ston* (see page 131) and so is usually considered a *bKa'-gdams-pa* like his nephew *rNgog Blo-ldan Shes-rab*, also a translator, and the renowned scholar *Gro-lung-pa Blo-gros Byung-gnas*. These last two each wrote a general dissertation on Buddhist doctrine (*bsTan-rim*) which were important for later developments.

We have already referred to the importance of the translator *Mar-pa* (page 118) and *sGam-po-pa*, who was in a way the father of all the various *bKa'-rgyud-pa*

Village life   Herd of yaks transporting grain
in small sacks made of local
homespun

Ploughing in Dolpo with a single ox

Winnowing grain by shaking it
in the wind from a specially
scoop-shaped basket

Carrying in the barley harvest
for threshing

(*left*) Party of four women and
two men threshing rhythmically
with wooden flails

(*above*) Weaving homespun for local use on a domestic loom

(*right*) Interior of a small village house belonging to a painter of temple-banners. His 'canvas' is stretched cotton-cloth prepared with a coating of chalk and glue

Wooden effigy of a local
protecting divinity as sometimes
seen in *Kong-po* (see page 248)

Village doctor feeling the pulse
of a patient (see page 262). The
open bag in front of him
contains an assortment of
medicinal ingredients

Village youth playing a 'guitar' (*sgra-snyan*). An amulet hangs round his neck

(*left*) A village woman of *gTsang* tying up the watch-dog in front of her house

Ferry with a wooden horse
as its traditional figure-head

(*left*) Coracle made from willow-
boughs and yak-hides, used for
ferrying rivers

schools. He too wrote a general summary of the doctrine (*lam-rim*), and since another important but shorter work of his is available in English translation, the interested reader can easily gain an impression of this type of scholarly Tibetan literature.* With *sGam-po-pa* we pass from the age of the translator to that of the Tibetan Buddhist scholar who is now able to write dissertations on the doctrine on the basis of Tibetan translations which are available to him thanks to the quite extraordinary labours of others. Translators are still needed, but they are now subservient to master-scholars, who often know little or no Sanskrit.

With the *Sa-skya-pa* order we soon enter the world of master scholars with *Kun'-dga' snying-po* and the Great *Sa-skya* Pandit *Kun-dga' rgyal-mtshan*. The former systematized the teachings based on the tantric cults of *Hevajra* and *Samvara*, and as well as commenting on these same basic *tantras*, the latter wrote on philosophy, logic, grammar and poetics. He was also a renowned religious painter. *Grags-pa rGyal-mtshan* (died 1216) was the author of the earliest surviving history of early Buddhist developments in Tibet, and he was soon followed by another famous *Sa-skya* scholar and historian, *'Phags-pa* (died 1280), who also produced explanations of the *tantras* for his Mongol patrons, and invented the script for Mongolian which goes by his name.

As the period of translations came to an end, the main task of the new generation of Tibetan Buddhist scholars was the compilation of the Tibetan Canon, which must surely be the apotheosis of the Tibetan bent for selection, analysis and compilation. The destruction of the great Buddhist centres in India had left the Tibetans to work over the vast quantities of texts which they had translated and accumulated in the course of some five centuries of endeavour. It is now that the limitations of Tibetan genius begin to show. They knew extremely well what they had learned and they were able to put their new knowledge to practical use, where techniques of *yoga* and magical practices were involved. Amongst all peoples who had adopted Buddhism they seem to be quite unequalled in such matters. But with very few exceptions they show little power of imaginative invention, and the subsequent disputes between various orders, even when concerned with doctrine, do not arise from the doubts and questionings of the various parties, but come about mainly because they are arguing on the basis of the different Indian traditions that they have variously received. It is almost as though their thought and imagination were paralyzed by their implicit faith in the words of their masters. While this is doubtless also the main reason for the extraordinary potency of their religious practice, it results in their religious literature being for the most part extremely dull, for what they have been told, they simply retell again and again. At the same time they possess great ability in elaboration and exposition (dull as it may be) and in analysing and cataloguing. Thus when it came to ordering their accumulated Buddhist scriptures, they performed the complicated task with consummate skill. The great scholar and encyclopaedic writer *Bu-ston* (1290-1364) is primarily associated with this work, although much preliminary work had already been done on systematizing the texts that were finally included in the *bKa'-'gyur* (pronounced: Kanjur, literally 'Translation of the Buddha-Word'). *Bu-ston* seems to have been almost entirely responsible for arranging the second and larger section, entitled the *bsTan-'gyur* (pronounced: Tenjur, literally 'Translation of the Treatises') which includes all the available translations of commentaries, exegetical literature and discourses by Indian Buddhist scholars and yogins. Many lamas were interested in helping with funds and academic labour, and when the work was finished the lamas of *Rin-spungs* and the *Karma-pa* order had very fine manuscript copies prepared. The master manuscript copies were kept at *sNar-thang*, where very much later, in the eighteenth century, a printed edition was made in the traditional manner from carved wooden blocks (xylographs). *Bu-ston*'s work was really prodigious. He wrote on 'Perfection of Wisdom' literature and tantric texts generally with special reference to the *Kālacakra* (Wheel of Time) cycle of texts, and he also wrote a history of Buddhism in India and Tibet. Moreover he ensured that the Tibetan versions of all texts included in the newly compiled canon were carefully checked, and where necessary new translations made. This great compilation really marks the end of the labours of whole generations of Tibetan translators, and we cannot mention them for the last time without paying tribute once more to their patience and skill. It remains remarkable none the less that a people should devote such single-minded zeal in the matter of a particular kind of religious learning, and yet show not the slightest interest in any other form of foreign learning and literature.

rNying-ma-pa **Developments** All this scholarly endeavour was not without its effect on other groups, of whom little has been written so far in the present context, namely the *rNying-ma-pas* and the *Bon-pos*. The *rNying-ma-pa* (old) order is often listed with the *bKa'-gdams-pa*, *Sa-skya-pa*, *bKa'-rgyud-pa*, etc. as though it represented from the start a constituted religious order of much the same kind. In fact it represents an entirely different case, perhaps rather complicated to explain. Its followers claim as their Teacher and Buddha the yogin-sage *Padmasambhava* (Lotus-Born) who is said to have come to Tibet on a short visit in the eighth century during the reign of King *Khri-srong-lde-brtsan* (see page 78). Thus in theory their primary monastery should be *bSam-yas* and they should represent the type of Buddhism introduced in the time of the religious kings. In fact they represent in their real origins the remnants of early Buddhism, which continued to exist here and there throughout the land after the disappearance of all organized religion in the mid-ninth century. Buddhist teachers and yogins then lacked all centralized guidance and noble patronage, and those who were still interested in Buddhism just practised as best they could with such means as chanced to be available. As times changed for the better they returned to some of their old sites in Central Tibet and established small religious centres (monasteries would be scarcely a suitable term) at such places as *Yer-pa, La-mo, Thang-po-che, Ra-tshag*, and *rGyal*. Without any authoritative leadership their religious practice must have taken a great variety of forms, and it was because the kings of Western Tibet observed what a sorry pass the practice of Buddhism had reached, that they invited Indian scholars, trained translators, and generally began the process of reintroducing Buddhism all over again. Of that whole strange Buddhist 'underworld' we know practically nothing except for what may be deduced from later developments. We have already referred above to the rediscovered texts (*gter-ma*) which began to appear in the fourteenth century (page 154). A large number of such works were produced by religious practisers who claimed that they were now at last able to make available texts and traditions from the old royal period. Whereas the more recently established orders, the *bKa'-gdams-pa*, *Sa-skya-pa* and *bKa'-rgyud-pa* had their immediate roots in tenth and eleventh century India, the *rNying-ma-pa*, the 'Old Order' as it came to be called, claimed to be connected directly with earlier Indian transmissions to Tibet. Their 'rediscovered texts' reveal them for what they are, and although through lack of historical data little precise can be written about them, it would seem clear that their traditions are based primarily on the kind of officially unsponsored Buddhist practices which we have already referred to (page 105). They compiled, presumably in the fourteenth century, a 'Compendium of Old Tantras' (*rNying-ma'i rgyud 'bum*), which are not included in the Tibetan Canon, and which must have been introduced into Tibet as a result of the small-scale activities of Tibetan tantric enthusiasts working in co-operation with Indian yogins. The great importance they attach to *Padmasambhava*, who represents an Indian Buddhist yogin of a type quite well known, suggests that their contacts were primarily with his particular following. His deification and his close connection with the new popular divinity *Avalokiteśvara* remains unexplained, but there exists an interesting parallel in Nepalese Buddhism, where another Indian Buddhist yogin *Matsyendra* occupied a similar position. It remains possible that *Padmasambhava* is simply the ideal of yogin-magician and so represents any number of actual sages and is thus no one historical person at all. The details of the story of his visit to Tibet could quite conceivably be a later fabrication, intended to give authority to the teachings promulgated by his followers in complete analogy with the case of *gShen-rab*, the supposed founder of *Bon*. There is nothing in either 'biography' of which the historical validity is guaranteed.

Even in Tibetan Buddhism with its fantastic variety of theories and practices, *Padmasambhava* remains an unusual figure. He is the only main tantric divinity (and this is his chief function), who has the semblance of historical reality in a well-defined period. The other 'historical' buddha is *Śākyamuni* himself, but he remains the recipient of simple prayers, whereas *Padmasambhava* in his various divine manifestations is the centre of a number of tantric rituals. He appears as the 'Gentle Master' (*Gu-ru Zhi-ba*), as the 'Fierce Master' (*Gu-ru Drag-po*) when he is identical with the 'Tiger God' (*s Tag-lha*), which is a very early Tibetan divinity common to both Buddhists and *Bon-po*; he appears as the 'Union of the Precious Ones' (*dKon-mchog spyi-'dus*) where he is manifest as a whole complex of divinities based on the set of Five Buddhas in their fierce and tranquil forms;* he appears as the 'Perfector of Thought' (*Thugs-sgrub*) in either a red or a blue manifestation with his entourage of attendant divine forms. As a tantric divinity he serves as a 'god of knowledge', capable of consubstantiating his devotee in buddhahood, just like *Avalokiteśvara*, *Hevajra*, *Samvara*, and all the other great tutelary divinities. For these advanced processes of meditation and ritual he is as popular among the *Sa-skya-pa* and *bKa'-rgyud-pa* as the *rNying-ma-pa*, but the last named have an interest at the same time in his supposed historical existence, because they look back to him as the 'founder' of their 'order', just as the *Sa-skya-pa* look back to '*Brog-mi* and *Virūpa*, and the *bKa'-rgyud-pa* to *Mar-pa* and *Nāropa*. It is not unlikely therefore, that seeing how the newer orders were busy constituting themselves during the twelfth and thirteenth centuries, some genuine Tibetan followers of the older Indian Buddhist traditions that had been developing 'underground' since the eighth and ninth centuries should have set to work to make themselves into a recognizable and self-constituted order. They needed a founder, and having decided that this must be *Padmasambhava*, concerning whom a vast amount of legendary stories were already in existence, they set to work to produce his biography. The result was the 'Padma Scrolls' (*Padma thang-yig*), and it is likely that they used quite genuinely old fragments of legendary material. Ordinary Tibetans love fantastic stories, and great quantities of them were already available in the Indian Buddhist circles associated with the Eighty-Four Great Magicians (*mahāsiddha*). Many of these entered Tibet through the medium of generations of strange yogins and religious enthusiasts, of whom we can know almost nothing precise because they lived and operated free of any official interest or patronage. We know they must have existed because otherwise there could scarcely have been such quantities of legendary and ritual materials which go to make up all the *rNying-ma-pa* 'rediscovered texts'. No imaginative and roguish group of Tibetans sat down to invent all the stuff out of their heads.

***Bon-po* Developments** The *Bon-pos* are in a similar case so far as the collecting and promulgating of older legendary and ritual materials are concerned, but there is one very great difference. Whatever the more respectable Tibetan

Buddhists, those who were trained in philosophy and logic and the rules of monastic discipline, might think of the *rNying-ma-pas* and their free religious practice, they never suggested that the others were heretics. It was recognized that some of their lamas possessed the techniques by which buddhahood might be realized in a single life-time. As always, Tibetans are seldom perturbed by the most outrageous behaviour of men of religion, especially if they are thought to possess some kind of saving knowledge.

On the other hand the *Bon-pos* placed themselves beyond the pale by continuing to claim that they represented pre-Buddhist Tibetan religion, with the result that they became associated, often quite unfairly, with all the difficulties and opposition that the early Buddhists had faced in establishing the new religion in Tibet. As we now know from the earlier part of our story, such opposition as developed was either of a quite general and spontaneous nature, because no people likes to have to change its religion suddenly, or else political. Far from there being any real historical opposition between the two, the Buddhists adopted any local beliefs that people might be interested in, and the *Bon-pos* all they possibly could of Buddhist theory and practice. They had continued to develop their doctrines and practices through the early Buddhist centuries, working on Buddhist texts and adapting them to *Bon-po* terminology, performing their ancient rites for the welfare of their clients and the removal of harm of all kinds. Until the tenth and even the eleventh century they must have continued to exercise an enormous hold on popular interest, for their rites were needed by ordinary villagers and nomads in practical everyday matters. The battle for the hearts and minds of all Tibetans was a hard one for the Tibetan Buddhist clergy, and it was possible for them to replace the *Bon-pos* only by remaining to some extent *Bon-po* at heart and by acquiring greater proficiency in such non-Buddhist practices as the cult of local gods, oracles and divination, than the *Bon-pos* themselves. One of the results of this is the great number of indigenous Tibetan divinities who have made their way into the Tibetan Buddhist pantheon, and whose right to be there no self-respecting Tibetan, whatever his religious order, would question.

It is likely that already in the eighth and ninth centuries some *Bon-pos* possessed the beginnings of 'religious centres', even if these were only the houses or tents of particular practising 'priests'. Based upon these there gradually developed, in imitation of the Buddhists, a specialized literature and an organized religious life with temples and even monasteries. According to plausible *Bon-po* tradition the first real monastery was *gYas-ru dben-sa*, founded by *Bru-chen gYung-drung bla-ma* towards the end of the eleventh century in *gTsang* Province about thirty miles east of Shigatse. It was destroyed by a flood at the beginning of the fifteenth century and replaced by *sMan-ri*, which exists to this day. Again in imitation of Buddhist artists, painting and imagery were practised, and the forms given to the *Bon-po* divinities were simply skilful variations on Indian Buddhist themes. By the fourteenth century at the very latest the *Bon-pos* had organized their teachings as 'Nine Ways', which comprised in a consistent arrangement all the forms of religious practice, both pre-Buddhist and Buddhist, which were known in Tibet at that time.* Professing to be pure *Bon*, this work of synthesis in fact provides a convenient summary of all Tibetan religion as it was practised and understood in that period. Since they were concerned like everyone else to have an historical founder, they found one in *Mi-bo gShen-rab*, inventing a fantastic biography for him on the general model of that of *Śākyamuni*. As with *rNying-ma-pas* the whole process of development probably begins in the eighth century, or even earlier, as soon as intelligent *Bon-pos* made contact with Buddhist teachings. Borrowing and adaptation were probably quite spontaneous to begin with, but when later on they saw others equipping themselves with religious centres and approved teachings, they set to work deliberately in order to produce a recognized form of teaching for themselves, using their already existing traditional materials and taking whatever suited their argument and purpose from the now readily available Buddhist literature.

In the period when the various orders we have mentioned were constituting themselves (eleventh to fourteenth centuries) their relations must have been very close on a personal level. They were all competing for the interest and the support of the same villagers and nomads, and the layfolk were quite free to invite whom they pleased to perform their ceremonies. We read in the *Blue Annals* of a village ceremony where a celibate Buddhist teacher, a tantric yogin and a *Bon-po* were all invited together (*BA*, p. 112). In the early period Buddhist monks must quite normally have come from a *Bon-po* family background, and it was no matter for shame or surprise if a renowned lama was known to have started his life as a *Bon-po* (e.g. *BA*, pp. 466 and 743). Relations were sometimes quite friendly even between a practising Buddhist and a practising *Bon-po*, and the following incident is recounted about the *bKa'-rgyud-pa* lama *rGod-tshang-pa*:

> When he was returning to Tibet and had just reached the middle of the plain called *dPal-mo-dpal-thang*, his supplies ran out and his bodily strength became enfeebled. Then a *Bon-po* appeared and he asked him: 'O manifestation of *gShen-rab mi-bo*, is there anything to eat?'. He replied: 'This is just like you Buddhists, practising austerities at unsuitable times! Then he gave him a lump of moistened barley-flour and some offal, and munching this *rGod-tshang-pa* went on his way. Afterwards he used to tell this pleasing story, saying: 'That *Bon-po*'s present was better than the great offerings I receive nowadays.'†

But more often relations were not so friendly. For example the great *bKa'-rgyud-pa* Lama *bSod-nams rGyal-mtshan* (1386-1434) did not hesitate to remove a *Bon-po* accused of harming Tibetan hermits.

> As a yoke to crooked people, he was heavier even than a yoke of gold. Once when an agent of his was returning from Western Tibet, he was set upon by a lot of bandits led by *lHa-rtse-ba*, and simply by pronouncing an imprecation, he brought upon them a great sickness of voiding blood and sudden death, a punishment inflicted by the Defenders of Religion. In the same way a *Bon-po* named *dKar-gdung-pa* caused great harm to our (Buddhist) hermits in *sPu-hrangs*, and by pronouncing an imprecation in a general gathering of monks he caused the *Bon-po* with his whole family to leave the district.*

Like all national historians Tibetan writers of history see everything from a Tibetan point of view, and being fervent Buddhists as well, they inevitably see everything from a rather special Tibetan Buddhist point of view. Their view of the world around them is a simple one; in so far as it furthers the interests of their religion in general and their own religious order and monastery in particular, it is good; in so far as it works against their religion, their order and their monastery it is evil. Internally the *Bon-pos* tend to become the scapegoat for everything that had rendered the Buddhist conversion of Tibet at all difficult, while most Tibetan Buddhists themselves remain almost innocently unaware of the great variety of pre-Buddhist beliefs and practices that they have absorbed as an accepted part of their daily thoughts and actions.

It is during the centuries covered in this chapter, especially the eleventh to fourteenth centuries, that Tibetan civilization, life and thought take their characteristic form. It is the one great creative period of Tibetan civilization, creative as a result of the contact between Tibetan native religious genius and the fantastic philosophical and religious extravagances of late Indian Buddhism. Perhaps as a result of digesting so much in so short a time, the Tibetans realized unconsciously that they could absorb nothing else. In any event there were from now on very few contacts of a really creative kind.

However, during the fifteenth century, while *Byang-chub rGyal-mtshan*'s successors were still ruling, a new religious school came into being. Unlike the earlier schools it was not based upon fresh cultural contacts in India and Nepal, for this was no longer possible, but it represented a deliberate attempt to return to more faithful interpretations of reputable Indian Buddhist philosophical and moral teachings. It grew so rapidly and in such a way that within two centuries it was able to supplant the older orders of monks in both religious and political power. This was the *dGe-lugs-pa* order (the order of the 'Model of Virtue'), popularly known to Western readers as the 'Yellow Hats'. It grew from the teaching and following of the great religious genius *Blo-bzang Grags-pa*, known after his place of birth as *Tsong-kha-pa*, and by the honorific title of *rJe Rin-po-che* ('Precious Lord'). As the final victor in the struggles between the various religious factions, the 'Yellow Hats' might seem to bear the main responsibility for the developing tragedy. But this would scarcely be a just judgement, for as we have seen the stage was already set for future developments before the *dGe-lugs-pa* order even existed, and if we find that they show little mercy to the other monastic orders, we must remember that this is normal human experience, wherever religious authority has absolute political power.

PART THREE

The Yellow Hats

Chapter 7

Their Rise to Power

Life in Fourteenth- and Fifteenth-century Tibet By the end of the fourteenth century Buddhism of one form or another had permeated the whole of
Tibetan society. There can have been few Tibetans who did not acknowledge it
as the guiding principle of their lives, for even those who called themselves
Bon-po now shared identical religious beliefs and attitudes even if these sometimes went under other names. The demands of armed strife between the great
monasteries, each with its noble supporters, must have weighed heavily on
farmers and peasants, but warfare was mainly a seasonal occupation, pursued
after the harvest was gathered in, and if the assessment of taxes at one sixth of the
produce, as attributed to *Byang-chub rGyal-mtshan*, held good, there would have
been no great cause for complaint, at least in times of peace. There is, indeed,
no suggestion then or at any other time of peasant unrest in Tibet, and we may
presume that small people already had their stake in local monastic interests
through their family connections in the ever-growing communities of monks.

Religion was the sole motive force for all 'higher' cultural life, and all literature
was inspired by religious interests. But arts and crafts of a 'popular' kind continued to thrive, such as decorative motifs on tea-pots, sword-hilts, musical
instruments, on tinder-boxes and personal jewelry, even on churns for buttered
tea. Carpets and woollen cloth of bright and pleasing colours, derived from local
vegetable and mineral dyes, were woven, just as up to present times. Literature as
such may have been in the hands of the monks, but wandering bards sang the
glories of ancient mythical kings, identified with the great kings of the four
quarters, known conventionally as China, India, Persia, and the North, and
drawing upon a whole wealth of ancient myth and legend, now supplemented
with such popular religious traditions as the life-stories of *Padmasambhava* and
gShen-rab. Through the unusual strength of some local popular tradition and

probably the ingenuity of some anonymous monk chronicler in their entourage, the royal family of *Gling*, a small kingdom in north-east Tibet (fourteenth century onwards) became identified with the 'King of the North', also referred to as *Ge-sar* of *Khrom* (see page 49), and thus vast accumulations of legendary and popular religious material became associated with this epic hero, *Ge-sar* of *Gling* or of *Khrom*.*

These chants, often of enormous length, yet still allowing free scope for fresh elaborations, were spread by wandering bards throughout the length and breadth of Tibet. Then as now, popular songs, proverbs and lampoons were common in the mouths of the ordinary people, resembling when not actually identical with those which Tibetans, who are not encumbered with the dignity of monkhood, still sing today.

The established monastic orders continued to grow in size and influence, producing one generation after another of men of literature, skilled in their own religious traditions, as well as the more general subjects of logic, poetics, and philosophical exegesis. There was then, and there still is now, no real contact between this 'higher' form of literature and the popular oral traditions, which gradually began to receive written form. A Tibetan must be specially educated to read his own serious religious literature, just as a European normally requires specialized university training for the reading of Duns Scotus or Thomas Aquinas. Some of the great religious teachers, even the Great *Sa-skya* Pandit, wrote collections of moralizing verses, giving advice for ordinary worldly living, but in this they were simply following a well-established Indian tradition of moralistic verse-writing, and not manifesting some spontaneous Tibetan concern for their lay-supporters.

The religious writing of these monk-scholars was prodigious. The famous *Sa-skya* lama *Rong-ston sMra-ba'i Seng-ge* (1347-1449) wrote sixty-four manuals of instruction and forty-six works of exegesis. He came of a *Bon-po* family in *rGyal-rong* (to the far east of Tibet), but as a youth he went to Central Tibet and began studying at the feet of numerous teachers, becoming versed in all the types of doctrine available. He was renowned as a teacher as well as a writer, and he founded (1435) the monastery of *Nālandā* in *'Phan-yul*, named after the great Indian monastery of that name. He had two famous disciples, nicknamed as a pair *Go-Shā*. These are *Go-ram-pa bSod-nams Seng-ge*, who founded another famous monastery *Thub-bstan rNam-rgyal* (1478), and *Shā-kya mChog-ldan*, chiefly renowned for his work of exegesis on 'Perfection of Wisdom' literature.

Meanwhile another *Sa-skya* lama, *Kun-dga' bZang-po* (1382-1444), who was also a prodigious writer, founded the great monastery of *Ngor Evam Chos-ldan*, and from this foundation there developed a new *Sa-skya* 'sub-order' known as *Ngor-pa*. Yet another small order was started by the disciples of *Bu-ston* (see page 170) called *Zhva-lu-pa* after the monastery of *Zhva-lu*, where he had spent most of his life.

In addition to the six *bKa'-rgyud-pa* schools already mentioned (see pages 135–7) there came from out of this fold a seventh school which was really distinctive in its basic philosophical position. This was the *Jo-nang-pa* order, named after the monastery of *Jo-mo-nang*, rendered famous by *Shes-rab rGyal-mtshan* of Dolpo (1292-1361), the most renowned philosophical writer of this school. In its origins it can be traced back through *Shes-rab rGyal-mtshan's* teacher, *Kun-spangs Thugs-rje brTson-'grus*, who founded the monastery in *Jo-mo-nang*, through a series of seven teachers to *Yu-mo*, who was one of the many disciples of the Great Kashmir Pandit when he visited Tibet in the twelfth century, receiving from him the *Kālacakra* (Wheel of Time) Cycle. We have already referred to certain parallels in Buddhist and Hindu development during the last centuries of Indian Buddhism. These related mainly to the great increase in the Buddhist pantheon, and to the elaboration of new techniques of *yoga*. No Indian and later no Tibetan teacher seems to have thought of protesting against such developments, although they might occasionally try to remove any resulting abuses of these new practices. But in basic philosophical assumption there was no such laxity, for when monks were not engaged in physical battles with their opponents, they were engaged in philosophical dispute. Fundamental to the whole *Mahāyāna* development was the philosophical theory of 'absolute vacuity' (Sanskrit *śūnyatā*, Tibetan *stong-pa-nyid*), sometimes interpreted by Western scholars of Buddhism as 'absolute relativity'. It taught that every entity and every component element of that entity is absolutely void of any inherent self-nature. It is the original Buddhist doctrine of 'no self' (*anātmatā*) carried to its logical extreme. It was this doctrine which separated the Buddhists from orthodox Indian (viz. Brahmanical) schools, who held to the doctrine of a 'supreme self' despite their occasional use of a *via negativa*. If no one else, the tantric yogins, especially the 'Eighty-Four Great Magicians', who are named in both Buddhist and Shaivite tradition, were certainly affected by the more general Indian teachings of a 'self', and there is little difficulty in tracing them in some of the basic tantric texts included in the Tibetan Canon. But until such Brahmanical notions were formulated as a specific philosophical doctrine, no Buddhist academic seemed to have given them a moment's thought. It was left to *Shes-rab rGyal-mtshan* to formulate the 'heresy', and he did it in the most innocuous terms, namely by his theory of 'vacuity elsewhere' (*gzhan stong*), thus arguing that absolute vacuity was not just typical of every entity and every element, but was a kind of absolute quality, existing 'elsewhere', viz. apart from every entity while pertaining to everything. The parallel with orthodox Indian teachings of a 'supreme self' (*brahman*) manifest in individuals as an 'individual self' (*ātman*) might not seem so obvious to us, but it was enough to create what must have been the most bitter of philosophical battles between Tibetan religious orders, resulting eventually in the destruction of *Jo-nang-pa* monasteries and the burning of their books. We shall return to this below.

The material question in this religion-dominated world was which hierarch was to be politically as well as doctrinally dominant. Although *Sa-skya*, thanks to the support of the Mongol khans, had held in theory political power over all Tibet, the limit of their authority had really lain somewhere west of Lhasa. During their rule another antagonism became apparent, which has deeply affected Tibetan life, the rivalry between the provinces of *gTsang* and *dBus* with their capitals respectively at Shigatse and Lhasa. Only *Byang-chub rGyal-mtshan* had come near to gaining mastery over the whole of Tibet (see page 154). The *Rin-spungs* princes never succeeded completely in subduing all the remnants of the *Phag-mo-gru* domain, and although the kings of *gTsang* were for a short time rulers of nearly all Tibet, they were almost at once faced by a new challenge, which was partly the old struggle of *dBus* and *gTsang* and partly the old demand for religious instead of lay rule. This challenge came from the latest of Tibetan religious orders, the *dGe-lugs-pa*, whose 'founder' was the great *Tsong-kha-pa*.

Tsong-kha-pa In fact *Tsong-kha-pa* had no more intention of founding a new order than had most other great religious figures of Tibet. As always, it came about through the skill and determination of his more ambitious disciples. He was born in 1357 in the neighbourhood of the Kokonor, where his father was a local official. At an early age he was consecrated by the *Karma-pa* hierarch *Rol-pa'i rDo-rje*, and when he was seventeen he set out for Central Tibet where he visited all the most famous teachers of *mTshal*, *Sa-skya*, *Phag-mo-gru*, *Zhva-lu*, *Jo-nang* and elsewhere. His training exemplifies the close connections between all schools of teaching at that time and also the wide range of studies which an intelligent and devout young man could follow. These included studies in monastic discipline, 'Perfection of Wisdom' teachings, logical philosophy, rhetoric and debating, tantric cycles, medicine, religious chanting and dancing. The teachers who appear to have influenced him most were the *Sa-skya* lama *Red-mda'-pa* (a disciple of *Rong-ston* mentioned on page 178) and the *bKa'-gdams-pa* lama *dBu-ma-pa*, who first brought him into close contact with the revered traditions connected with *Atiśa*.

Tsong-kha-pa was trained in the usual mystic practices of concentrated meditation upon the great divinities, and the 'gods of knowledge' appeared to him in his meditation. After his full ordination at the age of twenty-five he began to become known as a teacher and writer, although he still continued to study under eminent lamas. His religious views seem to have taken their final form when at the age of forty he joined the great *bKa'-gdams-pa* monastery of *Rva-sgreng*, sanctified by both *Atiśa* and *'Brom-ston*, for there he had a vision of *Atiśa*. While at *Rva-sgreng* he wrote some of his most important works and began expounding his 'full account of the doctrine' (*Lam-rim*). He was also greatly affected by the ancient holiness of Lhasa, and in 1408 he established at the *Jo-khang* (Cathedral) the annual New Year ceremony of the 'Great Prayer' (*sMon-lam chen-mo*), which has continued until 1959. He intended it as a kind of yearly rededication of Tibet to the Buddhist faith. In 1409 he founded his own monastery of *Ri-bo dGa'-ldan* (The Joyous Mountain), where he meditated, taught and wrote, while supervising his community according to the proper rules of monastic discipline. Thus his followers were first known as *Ri-bo dGa'-ldan-pa* after the name of the monastery, and because of his insistence on proper monastic discipline, his teachings were sometimes called the new *bKa'-gdams-pa*. Only later did the name *dGe-lugs-pa* ('Model of Virtue') come to be used of his whole order. Westerners have borrowed from the Chinese the term 'Yellow Hat' for the *dGe-lugs-pa*, and have applied the term 'Red Hat' without any differentiation to all the earlier orders of Tibetan Buddhism, whereas it is applied by Tibetans just to one *Karma-pa* school, which is thereby distinguished from the 'Black Hat' (see page 137). Whatever little there may be to commend it, 'Yellow Hat' is at least unambiguous.

In and around Lhasa *Tsong-kha-pa* found ready support from the local nobility and people. This was a sort of border zone between the old religious rivals, *'Bri-khung* and *Sa-skya*, and had more recently come under the influence of the *Phag-mo-gru* and *gDan-sa-mthil* who gave a friendly welcome to the teachings of *Tsong-kha-pa* and his disciples. The example of a religious school which was as yet taking no part in the political rivalries of the day and insisted on the observance of strict monastic discipline, may well have appealed to many who were critical of the apparent worldliness of the older established orders. *Tsong-kha-pa* is sometimes presented in Western writings as a kind of self-appointed reformer of all the abuses of Tibetan religion, as a kind of 'Luther of Tibet'. This gives an entirely false impression both of *Tsong-kha-pa* himself and of the religious world in which he lived. He had no wish himself to interfere with the ways of others outside his monastery, and even if others were jealous of his successes, there is no sign of any open hostility between his community and others during his lifetime.

Tsong-kha-pa's reputation spread far, and Yung Lo, third Emperor of the Ming dynasty, who was intent on making contact with all influential lamas in Tibet, sent him an invitation in 1408 to visit China. *Tsong-kha-pa* refused the invitation himself, whether from personal dislike of such worldly activities or from unwillingness to appear in competition with other Tibetan lamas, and sent one of his chief disciples instead. The growth of his following in the Lhasa district led to the foundation by his disciples of two more monasteries very close to Lhasa, '*Bras-spungs* (Drepung – 1416) and *Se-ra* (1419). In 1419 the great master died, an event still commemorated in mid-winter every year, when lamps are lighted round every holy place and even every house. The tomb at *dGa'-ldan* (Ganden) containing his embalmed body is one of the treasures of his order and is guarded so scrupulously by the Abbot of *dGa'-ldan* that even the thirteenth Dalai Lama was not allowed to look inside it, although he sought an opportunity on the pretext of regilding the tomb.

The New Religious Order The first two successors of *Tsong-kha-pa* in the abbacy of *dGa'-ldan* were his close disciples *rGyal-tshab Dharma Rin-chen* and the more famous *mKhas-grub-rje*. The third was a younger follower, *dGe-'dun-grub* (1391-1475), who is said to have been *Tsong-kha-pa*'s nephew. It was his energy and ability which was mainly responsible for building up *Tsong-kha-pa*'s school into an active expansive order ready and anxious to compete with the others on an equal footing. Taking advantage of the complex pattern of loyalties among the nobility and the absence at that time of uncompromising opposition to the new order, he founded in 1445 another monastery, *bKra-shis-lhun-po* (Tashilhunpo) near Shigatse on the very edge of the territory dominated by the powerful princes of *Rin-spungs* who had the militant support of the *Karma-pa* Red Hat hierarch. Appreciating the prestige which older sects had gained through the system of reincarnating lamas, *dGe-'dun-grub* may well have arranged before his death that the same means of succession should be adopted by the *dGe-lugs-pa*. At all events in due course a successor was found whose birth came sufficiently close to his death. Named *dGe-'dun rGya-mtsho* this successor was treated subsequently as a reincarnation and regarded retrospectively as the second of the Dalai Lamas. Despite the mystique with which some Westerners like to regard the whole practice of reincarnating lamas, the custom was clearly adopted and maintained primarily for reasons of statecraft. We should emphasize too that the *dGe-lugs-pa* Order did not initiate the practice, as has sometimes been quite wrongly supposed.

During the lifetime of this 'second Dalai Lama' the growing prestige and authority of his order aroused the increasing hostility of the powerful *Karma-pa* prelates and their lay patrons, so that most of his life he was unable to live in the great monasteries established by his predecessors around Lhasa. But he continued the work of *dGe-'dun-grub* by travelling and teaching widely throughout the rest of the country, thus winning a great missionary reputation and increasing support. *dGe-lugs-pa* lamas were even asked on occasions to mediate in disputes between other rivals, and all the time the numbers of their monastic foundations and of the inmates were on the increase. By the time of *dGe-'dun rGya-mtsho*'s death there were at least 1,500 monks in *'Bras-spungs* (Drepung), which from now on became the principal seat of the 'Dalai Lamas' and the largest monastery in the whole of Tibet.

As Abbot of *'Bras-spungs* he was succeeded by another child, *bSod-nams rGya-mtsho* (1543-88), who was recognized as his reincarnation. It was from this time that the monastery of *bKra-shis-lhun-po* (Tashilhunpo) was entrusted to a series of adult lamas (*viz.* not yet reincarnating) who came to be regarded later as the spiritual predecessors of the *Pan-chen* Lamas (see pp. 219-20). *bSod-nams rGya-mtsho* had the advantage of coming from a distinguished family, connected with *Sa-skya* and the *Phag-mo-gru*, and as well as extending still further the missionary efforts of his predecessors, he even colonized some monasteries of the older orders, especially those of *'Bri-khung* and *Phag-mo-gru* which had been abandoned during the periods of interminable civil and religious strife. The *dGe-lugs-pa* Order, despite its successes, was still untarnished by temporal power, and with its appeal of monastic simplicity, religious devotion and calm austerity, it must have made a great contrast with the others, which always seemed to be involved, despite the sanctity and learning of some of their lamas, in selfish and worldly activities. No one can fairly begrudge the *dGe-lugs-pas* their final success, if only because the first rounds of the contest were clearly won by the excellence of their religious practice.

The Mongol Interest Then *bSod-nams rGya-mtsho* took a step which was to produce the same situation as had existed under *Sa-skya* rule and was to transform his order from a purely religious to a political religious force of exactly the same kind as the others. He accepted an invitation to visit Altan Khan, chief of the Tumed branch of the Mongols, and in 1578 Lama and Khan met near the Kokonor.

It was over two hundred years since the emperors of the Yüan dynasty, the descendants of Genghiz Khan, had been driven out of China back to the steppes where they belonged. Continual dissension and rivalry between the various tribes had spared China another Genghiz or Kublai, but there were periods when a forceful leader, such as Esen in particular, succeeded in uniting a majority of the Mongol factions, causing alarm and humiliation to the Ming emperors. Although there was now (1578) no overall leader, Altan Khan was the most powerful chief among the tribes nearest China's borders.

dGe-lugs-pa historians like to represent this historical meeting between this Khan and their Grand Lama as the renewal of contact between Tibet and Mongolia broken since the fall of the Yüan dynasty, but there is evidence that a tenuous link had been maintained all the time by the *Karma-pa* and others.

While the Ming dynasty had been anxious to cultivate a connection with Tibet by means of monastic missions which enjoyed lavish commercial concessions, they viewed with suspicion, at first, and sought to discourage, any initiative by the Mongols to increase their own religious intercourse with Tibet. Later, with the realization that Mongol militancy might well be softened by Buddhist influences, Chinese policy changed, and Tibetan lamas who had contacts in China were encouraged to make visits to the Mongol chiefs.

Yet the lamas of the older orders do not seem to have displayed much zeal in instructing the Mongols. So although *bSod-nams rGya-mtsho* was breaking no new ground, he was certainly entering a mission field which was ready to receive him.

The two great figures met in an atmosphere of intense reverence and devotion. They exchanged honorific titles, the Grand Lama receiving that of *Ta-le* (written as 'Dalai' by Westerners), which means simply 'Ocean' (as does Tibetan *rGya-mtsho*) presumably with the implication of 'Ocean of Wisdom'. The Khan received the title of *Chos-kyi rGyal-po lHa'i Tshang-pa* 'King of Religion, Majestic Purity'. This third Dalai Lama (the title is used retrospectively of his predecessors) and this Khan of the Tumed Mongols may well have felt they were re-enacting the bond which once existed between *'Phags-pa*, Grand Lama of *Sa-skya*, and the great Kublai Khan, but there was still one great difference. The Khan might be willing to be 'patron', but he was in no position to bestow upon his 'priest' authority over any part of Tibet. For the time being he contented himself by sending rich presents to the *dGe-lugs-pa* monasteries and to the lay nobles who supported their Grand Lama. Later he arranged an invitation from the Chinese Emperor to *bSod-nams rGya-mtsho*, who would have gone to Peking but for his death in 1588. He had been continually urged by his followers to return to Tibet, but he was unwilling to do so, for in Mongolia he had a promising mission field, and his success was really remarkable. At his insistence the Khan issued a proclamation forbidding blood-sacrifices and the worship of ancestral images. *bSod-nams rGya-mtsho* also travelled throughout Eastern Tibet, which had long been the sphere of influence of the *Karma-pa*, and he won from them the support of their great patron, the king of *'Jang-sa-tham* (Likiang). At *Tsong-kha-pa*'s birthplace in the Kokonor region a great new monastery, named *sKu-'bum* (A Thousand Images) was founded during his time. He travelled not only through those parts of Mongolia which were under the authority of the Genghizide khans, but also within the Oirat confederacy, establishing a new 'religious empire' outside Tibet of such size and potential importance that it is not surprising that the Chinese Emperor should be anxious to invite him to Peking and grant him a diploma.

On his death in 1588 (he was only forty-five years old), his reincarnation was discovered in a great-grandson of Altan Khan. By this piece of diplomacy the

Cultural objects: 1

A 'magic dart' (*phur-pa*) used especially for the ritual slaying of the human effigy (*liṅga*) who represents the particular foe under attack, whether a supposed enemy of the doctrine, human or divine, or in more philosophical terms the 'demon of the self'

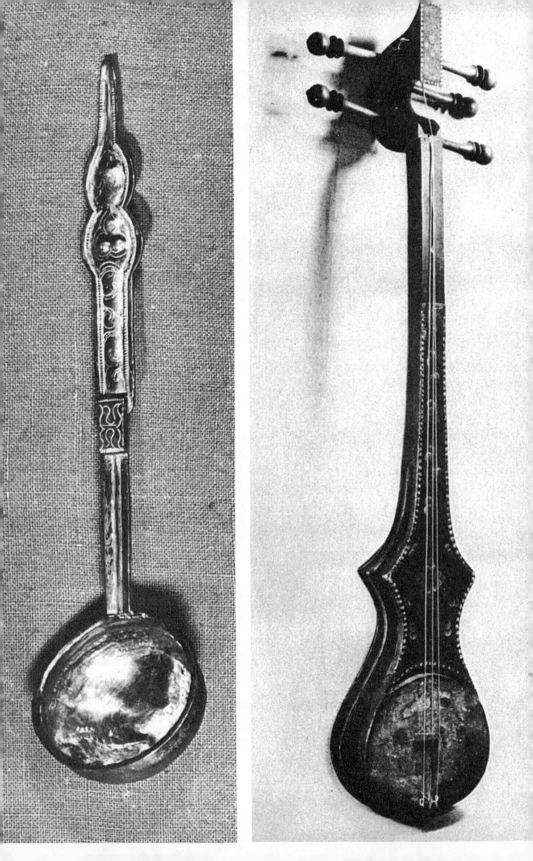

(*opposite, left*) A domestic brass ladle as used in a well-to-do Tibetan family

(*opposite, right*) A Tibetan 'guitar' (*sgra-snyan*)

(*above*) A conch-shell, most commonly blown in order to summon monks to a ceremony

(*right*) A conch-shell used as above, but adorned with a plaque of worked silver showing *Mahāmāya*, the mother of *Śākyamuni* Buddha, at the moment of his birth. He was born from her right side while she supported herself on a tree

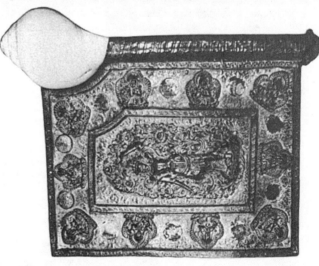

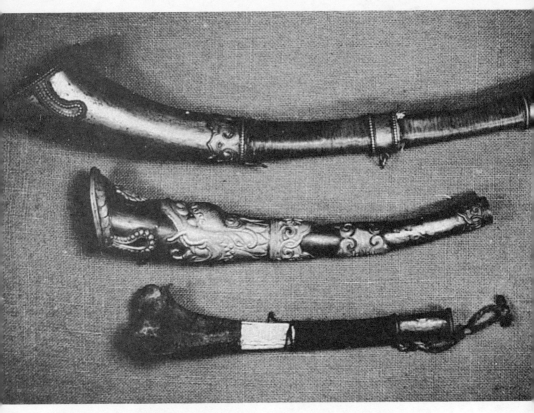

Three designs of the Tibetan 'horn' (*rkang-gling*). The top two are made of copper embossed with silver, and the lower one is made of a human leg-bone. The last one is used by Buddhist and Bon yogins (*rnal-'byor-pa*)

(*below*) A Tibetan temple drum

A teapot made of copper decorated with brass, used only on ceremonial
occasions, as the flavour of the tea tends to spoil

Mask and dress of brocade silk as used in monastic dances ('*cham*) (see page 246)

(*opposite*) A conch for blowing adorned with a worked silver plaque. The design is of two dragons holding a jewel (*nor-bu*)

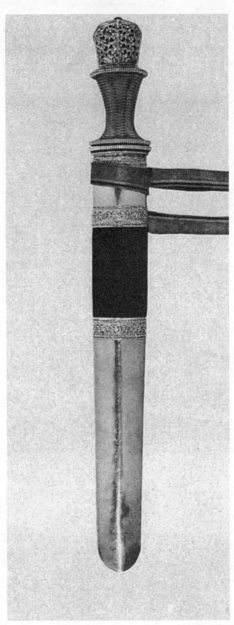

(*left*) A metal pen-case

(*centre*) A long Tibetan dagger

(*right*) Set of eating instruments, chopsticks,
knife and spoon, in a case

dGe-lugs-pa Order gained conclusively the interested support of the Mongol ruling family, and so took the second step, which was bound to involve foreign influence in Tibetan affairs sooner or later. In 1601 some of the principal lamas of the order together with supporting nobles and officials, including a representative of the *Phag-mo-gru*, travelled to Mongolia to receive the child, who had been vouched for as a true reincarnation of *dGe-'dun-grub* and his successors by the Abbot of *dGa'-ldan*. A great retinue including many Mongols escorted him all the way to Central Tibet. He was taken to *dGa'-ldan* (Ganden), to the *Jo-khang* (Cathedral), and wherever he went there were receptions and celebrations of the most lordly kind. There was no sign of immediate opposition, but this evidence of *dGe-lugs-pa* strength and pretentions, not to mention the presence of armed Mongol supporters, soon provoked reactions from the *Karma-pa* Order. The Black Hat hierarch was still a minor, but the Red Hat, whose branch was usually the more militant, sent messages to the new Dalai Lama in a patronizing vein and with allusions which the *dGe-lugs-pas* regarded as insulting. They replied in similar terms, and thus relations became embittered at once, and this led to further rounds of insults and acts of petty violence. The *dGe-lugs-pas*, despite their fine beginnings, were now operating on the same worldly terms as the older religious orders.

Trouble began on a serious scale in 1610 when the *Phag-mo-gru*, whose fortunes had lately revived thanks to their connections with *dGe-lugs-pa* successes, carried out a raid in the Lhasa Valley. The *gTsang* ruler, still the chief political power in Tibet, retaliated and secured for the first time complete control of *dBus* Province, so that from this time his line can justifiably be called 'kings of Tibet'. The King of *gTsang* seems to have acted with considerable restraint, even handing over to the *dGe-lugs-pas* authority to act as his representative in Lhasa. He also asked for certain religious consecrations (*dbang*), but these were refused, and in the present dangerous context such a refusal was both rude and provocative. Incensed by the monks' behaviour, the King attacked *'Bras-spungs* (Drepung) and *Se-ra* with such violence that the Dalai Lama took flight. The monks tried to secure the mediation of *sTag-lung*, which seems to have managed to keep apart from recent disputes, but they also took the third disastrous step, now almost inevitable, of calling upon the help of their Mongol supporters. Although there was no immediate fighting, foreign intervention in Tibetan affairs was now once more a reality after two and a half centuries of freedom from this menace. The Dalai Lama died in 1616 at the age of twenty-five, probably poisoned. There must have been many who were concerned at the course events were taking, and even within the *dGe-lugs-pa* Order itself counsels must have been divided.

The Triumph of the Yellow Hats A successor was soon found in Central

Tibet. This was *Ngag-dbang Blo-bzang rGya-mTsho* who was born in 1617 at *'Phyong-rgyas*, where the old kings of Tibet lie buried. His family was *rNying-ma-pa* (one more sign of the good possibilities of religious accord) and had connections with *bSam-yas* and with the *Phag-mo-gru*. Presumably because of its influence, the *Karma-pas* had already sought to claim the same child as one of their reincarnations. After his recognition, many Mongol leaders with their armed escorts came to do him honour and, by their presence, made it possible for him to be formally installed at Lhasa. One may wonder how they were thinking. National memories are long and the days of Kublai Khan and his Tibetan connections can hardly have been forgotten. To the King of *gTsang* they appeared as a threat of that foreign domination which had been shaken off by *Byang-chub rGyal-mtshan* and which he too was determined to resist. He had a good claim to be regarded as the rightful king of Tibet. His main allies were the *Karma-pa* but it is likely that he would have been willing to accept all the Tibetan religious orders on equal terms. This was, perhaps, the last chance which Tibet had of establishing a lay administration, devoted to religion certainly, as was the case in other Buddhist countries, but keeping affairs of state out of too interested religious control. As we have seen, religious rule in Tibet had meant control by one religious order at the expense of the others and to the inevitable detriment of national unity and strength. But by now the die was cast.

Repeated Mongol intervention in Tibet roused the King of *gTsang* to firmer measures against the *dGe-lugs-pas* on whose behalf they came. In 1621 a large Mongol army entered Tibet to protect the *dGe-lugs-pas*. A battle seemed imminent; but the *Pan-chen* Lama of *bKra-shis-lhun-po* and other Lamas came forward as mediators and arranged a truce. It seems, therefore, that there were many *dGe-lugs-pas* willing to come to terms with *gTsang* rather than risk too close a connection with the Mongols. They might be useful at times, but since the death of Altan Khan they were no longer under the leadership of a single and reliable person. The bands of Mongols now visiting Tibet consisted of a haphazard mixture of Genghizide and Oirat tribes; and it seems that, whether invited or not, support for the Dalai Lama had become an excuse, at least in some cases, for merely adventurous excursions into Tibet. Since there was no unity in Tibet, there was no way of stopping this uneasy course of events, which took on a fresh and concentrated impetus when a new power, the Qośot branch of the Oirats, took advantage of the dissension among the Genghizide tribes to establish a strong and orderly government in the Kokonor region on the borders of Tibet. They were an offshoot from the homeland, around Chuguchak, of the Western Oirats who are from now on usually referred to as the Dzungars. Unlike the Genghizides they could claim no historic connection with Tibet, but their leader *Gu-shri* Khan had been on a secret pilgrimage to Lhasa in 1638 and had been deeply impressed by the person of the Dalai Lama. He therefore required very little encouragement from those *dGe-lugs-pas* whose minds were set on political domination to offer his armies as champions of their cause against the King of *gTsang*. By 1640 he and his *dGe-lugs-pa* friends emerged victorious. There was bitter fighting, but resistance was made difficult for the King of *gTsang* by the weakness and dissension of his main religious supporters just at that time. On the one hand the tenth Black Hat hierarch was no asset at all in the political field, for he was of a gentle disposition, loving wild animals, painting religious pictures, delighting in austerities such as carrying stones and water for the building of temples, and altogether disapproving of the militancy of the King of *gTsang*, however justified it might be. On the other hand there happened to be a vacancy in the succession of the Red Hat Lama, whose party was usually more competent in political and military affairs. Also at the same time the King of Ladakh embarked upon a totally unprovoked invasion of Central Tibet, and this was the final undoing of *gTsang*. The King was but a young man, only recently come to the throne. After the defeat of his army by *Gu-shri* he was captured, and although his life was spared for a time, he was later put to death, apparently at the instigation of the monks of *bKra-shis-lhun-po* (Tashilhunpo). The officials (*sGar-pa*) of the Red Hats hierarch refused to accept defeat, and more fierce fighting was necessary at their *Kong-po* stronghold before *Gu-shri* and the fifth Dalai Lama were finally masters of Tibet. The Black Hat hierarch escaped the fighting and lived for many years sometimes disguised as a simple monk and always accepting hardship of every kind, but before he died he was reconciled to the Dalai Lama. He was a remarkable character, typical of the best of Tibetan lamas, but to his tragedy he was caught up in political events totally at variance with his quite proper religious way of life.

The Fifth Dalai Lama *Gu-shri* and the Dalai Lama were now able to enact the parts of patron and priest to their full satisfaction. The original intention was that the Dalai Lama himself should be the religious ruler, as his nature was supposed to be eminently spiritual, and that he should have a regent to conduct the administration with the Khan himself as overall protector, ready to step in whenever there was need. The Dalai Lama, however, had far greater power than *'Phags-pa* had ever had, for he was present on the spot, whereas *'Phags-pa* had been a kind of hostage-viceroy at the Mongol court. Moreover in establishing his authority he had the great advantage of the unstinting and devoted support of the powerful Khan. The pacification of the whole of Tibet took quite a long time, but by *Gu-shri*'s death in 1656 the Dalai Lama's régime stretched from Mount Kailas to *Khams*. He even attempted to assert his authority in Bhutan, but here he was less successful, and to this day, the *bKa'-rgyud-pas* of the *'Brug-pa* branch hold their own there. Together with *Gu-shri* he visited monasteries of every order throughout the country, making a survey of monks and of monastic property. Where he saw fit, he transformed monasteries of the older orders into *dGe-lugs-pa* establishments and replaced local landlord-governors with his own supporters. If one takes into account the decades of dispute and bitterness which preceded his triumph and the inevitable cruelty and excesses of the actual fighting, one is bound to acknowledge his tolerance and even generosity, now that the battle was won. He kept in his service some of the most able ministers of *gTsang*; and once he had brought the *Karma-pa* monasteries to heel and stripped them of most of their property, he allowed many of them to re-establish themselves. Towards other branches of the *bKa'-rgyud-pa* who had not opposed him with the bitterness shown by the *Karma-pa*, he was even more generous; and his treatment of the *rNying-ma-pa* was responsible for later critical gossip (which reflected on his birth), that he was in fact a crypto-*rNying-ma-pa*. It was during his rule that the chief *rNying-ma-pa* monastery in Central Tibet, namely *sMin-grol-gling*, which probably existed previously simply as a small religious centre, was established as an important monastic teaching centre (1676). *rNying-ma-pa* establishments had always been small, consisting for the most part of a lama, often married, who was revered for his special powers of meditation and the consecrations which he was able to give, so that he would always be surrounded by a small group of religious practisers. Thus up to 1676 *sMin-grol-gling* seems to have belonged to the lama-descendants of a famous 'discoverer of hidden texts', *gTer-bdag gling-pa* who lived in the fourteenth century, and this line continued as abbots of the new monastery. The fifth Dalai Lama certainly practised *rNying-ma-pa* forms of meditation, and it is by no means impossible that his personal interest was responsible for the sudden flourishing of *sMin-grol-gling*. Be this as it may, the existence of well ordered *dGe-lugs-pa* monasteries certainly seems to have encouraged the *rNying-ma-pas* to follow suit, and they gradually founded several monasteries in eastern Tibet, well away from the main centres of *dGe-lugs-pa* power.

Having no political pretensions, the *rNying-ma-pas* and the *Bon-pos* had least to fear from *dGe-lugs-pa* domination, and since their centres of religious practice were generally small, there was little to destroy and little worth taking, even if enemies did threaten them. It is noteworthy, however, that the main *Bon-po* centres developed in the far east of Tibet, Amdo and *rGyal-rong*, where they continued to operate as local monasteries and small teaching centres until the 1950s. Neither they nor the *rNying-ma-pas* seem to have suffered much at the hands of the *dGe-lugs-pas*. For the most part they were simply ignored.

The chief sufferers were the *Jo-nang-pas* (see page 179). Their last great representative was *Tāranātha* (1575–1634),* a famous writer and historian, and after his death the fifth Dalai Lama closed all the *Jo-nang-pa* monasteries, and transformed them into *dGe-lugs-pa* centres. The chief monastery of *Jo-nang*, where *Shes-rab rGyal-mtshan* had lived and worked, was renamed as *dGa'-ldan Phun-tshogs gling*, and as such it existed until 1959.

As for the *Sa-skya-pa* monasteries, they continued to flourish, at least so far as their teaching and religious life were concerned, and despite certain doctrinal differences with the *dGe-lugs-pas*. Although Lama *Red-mda'-ba* (see page 180) had been one of *Tsong-kha-pa*'s revered teachers, other *Sa-skya* lamas, especially the pair referred to as *Go-Shā*, had been his vigorous opponents. Yet we can see from the biography of a Dolpo lama, *bSod-nams-dBang-phyug* (1660-1731), who was a student at the great monastery of *Thub-bstan rNam-rgyal* from 1682 onwards, visiting other *Sa-skya-pa* and *Ngor-pa* establishments as well as doing the round of all the holy places in Central Tibet (in 1687), that by his time conditions of life were quite normal once more.* The older orders may preserve some bitter memories of the fifth Dalai Lama, for no one likes a diminution of wealth and power, but there is no doubt that without his moderating and controlling hand, their lot might have been very much worse. It must also be said that at that time, despite their new political interests and responsibilities, the *dGe-lugs-pas* remained the freshest and most zealous of the Tibetan religious orders. The centuries of disputes between the older groups had resulted in general religious disorder and lack of sense of direction, and thus in their well-ordered monastic life and in their return to sound Buddhist doctrine, based on the treatises of the great Indian Mahāyāna scholars, such as *Nāgārjuna*, *Asaṅga*, *Diṅnāga*, the *dGe-lugs pas* were providing a great deal for the revitalizing of Tibetan religious life. The standards they set clearly had their effect on scholars and religious practisers in other orders. Even the *Bon-pos* began to develop schools of logical philosophy, based entirely on Buddhist materials, and eventually they introduced the *dGe-lugs-pa* system of academic degrees.

The fifth Dalai Lama led in a great age for Tibet, and during his lifetime it seemed that the use of a foreign power to establish his régime had been a risk well worth taking. China had shown no interest in recent events in Tibet, for she had troubles enough of her own at the time. A new power, the Manchus, had appeared on her north-western borders, and having won over or subdued the Mongol tribes around them, they laid claim to China itself. By 1633 they were claiming the title of Emperor for themselves, and in 1664 by a combination of force and diplomatic skill they ousted the Ming dynasty from Peking. Thus was established the Ch'ing dynasty of the Manchus, which survived until 1911. The *dGe-lugs-pas* and the Manchus became respectively rulers of Tibet and China at just about the same time, and it is important to note that relations between the two countries developed mainly in the form of diplomatic contacts between the *dGe-lugs-pa* hierarchs and the Manchu court.

Communications had been tentatively opened with the Manchus in 1640 when all the parties involved in the Tibetan struggle for power, *Gu-shri*, the fifth Dalai Lama, the King of *gTsang* and the *Karma-pa* hierarchs, sent envoys to the Manchu court, trying to secure the support and favour of what was clearly the rising power in Asia. The Manchus were not then emperors of China, nor had *Gu-shri* submitted to them. At the time the Manchus sent diffident and temporizing answers, which influenced in no way the course of events in Tibet. Some eighty years later, when the Manchus, who were then the Ch'ing emperors of China, were looking for some pretext to intervene in Tibet, they cast back to this distant, inconclusive exchange of missives, interpreting them in a vague way as an act of submission by Tibet. But this observation anticipates events.

Once the Manchus were firmly established as rulers of China, *Gu-shri* persuaded the Dalai Lama to make a state visit to Peking. Whatever interpretation was placed upon this afterwards by the Chinese, it was clearly a meeting between equals. The Emperor himself, in the hope of winning over those Mongols who were still hostile but whose devotion to Tibetan Buddhism seemed to be undiminished, was prepared to disregard the protocol of his new empire and go to the borders of his country to meet the Dalai Lama, while his Chinese advisers even tried to prevent the meeting taking place at all, lest China's authority might be compromised by showing excessive respect for a foreign ruler. It must be remembered always that Chinese political theory excluded entirely the possibility of equal diplomatic relations with any other country whatsoever.

As for the Mongols who had helped the *dGe-lugs-pas* to power, their suzerainty became entirely nominal, a development which helped *dGe-lugs-pa* historians to gloss over the fact that their authority in Tibet had been established by a foreign conqueror called in by their Dalai Lama. After *Gu-shri*'s death (1654) his two sons succeeded him jointly, but later divided the kingdom, so that *bKra-shis B'a-tur* took the Kokonor territories and Tibet fell to the lot of Dayan, who appointed a regent while he himself lived mainly in the upland hunting grounds some eighty miles north of Lhasa, which he visited only occasionally. All real power in Tibet, including even that of appointing the regent, gradually fell into the hands of the fifth Dalai Lama. Gradually the Mongol connection was played down, and new ceremonies were devised to recall the old days and enhance the prestige of the new ruler. Like *Byang-chub rGyal-tshan* two centuries before, the fifth Dalai Lama called to mind the glories of the remote past, seeing himself as the successor of the great Religious Kings. Visits from neighbouring rulers were encouraged, and Shah Shuja, the Muslim ruler of Bengal, and the Malla Kings of Nepal sent envoys. The Kings of Lo (Mustangbhot) and Jumla, between whom the whole of modern western Nepal was then divided, came in person. Bhutan proved less amenable, which is hardly surprising after the attempts made to dominate it. Ladakh also was guarded at first, but later after a Tibetan expedition had driven the Ladakhis out of the parts of Western Tibet which they had occupied since the times of King *Seng-ge rNam-rgyal* (died 1642), a state of qualified subordination to Lhasa was generally acknowledged. One may note that the wars in Western Tibet and the final collapse of what remained of the old royal dynasties resulted in the neglect and consequent dilapidation of the temples and monasteries there, which we referred to in a previous chapter (page 114). Many of them were transformed into small *dGe-lugs-pa* establishments, but they never regained anything of their past glory.

Tibet's meeting ground with the new Manchu dynasty still lay in Mongolia, and more than once the Dalai Lama was asked by the Emperor to use his great influence amongst the Mongols in order to prevent danger to China from that quarter. The cultural connection between Tibetans and Mongols was now real and enduring. Just as the Indian masters of Buddhist doctrine and practice had once had everything to give (or to sell) to Tibetans who were so anxious to learn, so now the Mongols continued to learn from their Tibetan masters in religion all they could of Buddhist doctrine. Mongol students came to Tibetan monasteries, especially *'Bras-spungs* with its direct association with the person of the Dalai Lama, just as Tibetans had once visited the great monastic universities of northern India. Some Mongols rapidly became recognized religious masters themselves, and right up to 1959 the most renowned teachers in *'Bras-spungs* were often Mongols.

The fifth Dalai Lama built up the stature of Tibet in many ways. During his reign new monasteries were founded, mainly in Central Tibet, but a very important one, *bKra-shis-sgo-mang* of *Bla-brang* (Labrang) was founded in *Khams* (eastern Tibet). From now on a more assertive and grandiose style begins to appear, typical of the new sense of *dGe-lugs-pa* grandeur and triumph. Instead of sheltering in the folds of mountains or on the lee of a protecting hill, some of the new monasteries were built on hill-tops, proudly dominating the surrounding country. The culmination of this new spirit in architecture was the Dalai Lama's own majestic palace, the *Potala*, dominating Lhasa itself (pages 37 and 45). There had been buildings on that commanding hill for many centuries, whether fortress, palace or monastery, going back at least to the time of *Srong-brtsan-sgam-po*. But now from about 1645 there was continuous effort in building, so that the whole long high ridge was crowned by a connected series of massive buildings, which seem to grow out of the rock at different heights and different levels, and for all their solid weight, to be straining and leading upwards to the sky. Indeed the two turrets, one at each end, are called the wings of the *Potala*, and it is said that when a great flood comes which has been prophesied, they will lift the whole palace above the waters. Even now it seems to float. The contrasts of colour are breathtaking: the dark red central mass hung with a black curtain; the long expanses of whitened stone with windows, outlined in black and tapering upwards, very small on the lower expanses and larger in the upper stories. The wide steep stone stairways enhance the effect of the sheer rock on which the palace is built, and the dazzling accents of the small gold canopies relieve the militant squareness of the flat roof-tops. If only this survived of all Tibetan achievements, they would have staked an incontrovertible claim to the unique genius of their own national culture.

This palace is named after the holy mountain *Potala* in southern India, which is sacred to Shiva as 'Lord of the World' (*Lokeśvara*). For the Tibetans the name never had a geographical significance, for *Potala* had already become the accepted name of *Lokeśvara*'s divine palace in his Buddhist manifestation of *Avalokiteśvara*, the 'Lord who looks down in compassion' (see page 117). The Dalai Lamas now came to be consciously identified as manifestations of this most popular of Tibetan Buddhist divinities. A similar idea of divine kingship, but in an entirely non-Buddhist context, had been attributed to the early kings of Tibet, and other parallels might be quoted from many oriental countries. The closest are to be found in the Indian-inspired civilizations of South-East Asia, where kings also once liked to regard themselves as royal *bodhisattvas* or divine monarchs, and the great monuments of Angkor Vat and Borobuḍur remain to bear witness to this ideal. Thus although they have since become mingled, the two ideas, that of a lama conceived of as a reincarnation of his predecessor, and that of a lama or a ruler conceived of as a manifestation of a particular divinity, are really quite distinct. According to popular Buddhist notions, all living creatures are reborn as other creatures, higher or lower in the scale according to their past actions, so we are all supposedly reincarnations of one kind or another. On the other hand kings and great lamas could be regarded as particular manifestations of 'would-be buddhas' (usually reserved for kings and rulers like the Dalai Lama) or *buddhas* (reserved for great lamas) without there necessarily being present any idea of an identifiable reincarnation of a previous human being. The three 'Religious Kings' (see page 73) were regarded in this way; so too were the *Sa-skya* lamas and many others.

The fifth Dalai Lama was the first Tibetan ruler who effectively united in his person both the spiritual and the temporal power, for it was clear to all Tibetans that here was a true religious king enthroned in his mountain palace in their midst. He was served by able ministers, worldly politicians despite their religious exterior. *bSods-nams Chos-'phel* who was Regent from 1642 to 1658 seems to have been a capable, though arrogant and self-seeking man, and he is said to have urged the Dalai Lama to assert himself over the *Pan-chen* Lama, his own teacher, an old and greatly revered figure. The next great Regent was *Sans-rgyas rGya-mtsho*, the adviser of the Dalai Lama's advancing years. He even concealed the death of his master (1682), retaining absolute power for himself, while he brought up the child who had been discovered as the new incarnation, and completed in the name of the Dalai Lama the building work of the *Potala*.* The *dGe-lugs-pa* Order continued to revere above all others the name of their founder *Tsong-kha-pa*, who was regarded as a manifestation of the divine 'would-be buddha' (*bodhisattva*) *Mañjuśri*, but one may reflect on what *Tsong-kha-pa* might think of his royal successors. *Tsong-kha-pa* was altogether a man of religion, an abbot responsible for his own devoted community and with his own chosen disciples as his personal entourage. This new head of his order lived and moved in the centre of a royal court with hard-headed politicians and pragmatic advisers for company. It could not be otherwise, for this is a necessary concomitant of secular power. Yet this shows the character of the fifth Dalai Lama to even greater advantage, for he demanded and received the loyalty of his ministers and he maintained his reputation for tolerance in times when tolerance might well have been strained. Moreover he found time to exercise his literary ability, not only inspiring others to write but also composing several works himself, a commentary on the *Abhidharmakośa* ('Treasury of Philosophical Notions'), works on rhetoric and astrology, a treatise on monastic discipline, a guide to the *Jo-khang*, a history of Tibet, which is filled with theories attempting to reconcile discrepancies, sometimes wrong-headed, but always showing independence of thought and freedom from blind acceptance of tradition. His style is difficult and allusive, reaching the point with some labour, and his manner of writing sometimes impatient and arbitrary. He encouraged others to study Sanskrit, a subject all too often neglected by the later Buddhist scholars of Tibet, and he renewed scholarly contacts with India by inviting qualified Indian teachers. He was responsible too for encouraging all the religious arts and crafts, and the large gifts received from his Mongol supporters facilitated the building and adornment of temples and monasteries.

Foreign Contacts It would be of little use to look for new artistic trends, for Tibetan painting and wood-carving, metal work and architectural decoration had all assumed their characteristic forms. The main influences continued to be China in the east and Nepal in Central Tibet, but neither country had anything essentially new which the Tibetans had not already received from the same sources. Relations with Nepal were very ancient indeed, but it was not until about 1590 that there is any mention of a formal treaty between the two countries. This secured some kind of extra-territorial rights for Nepalese traders and craftsmen resident in Lhasa, which gave a still further impetus to their crafts of image-casting, metal-work, especially in silver and gold, wood-carving and jewelry. Nepal (then little more than the Nepal Valley) was ruled by the three Malla kings of Pātan, Kathmandu and Bhatgaon, and the important cultural and trading connection with Tibet was mainly in the hands of the predominantly Buddhist city of Pātan, some of whose citizens married freely with Tibetans of Lhasa and adopted the religious beliefs and practices of the Tibetans, which were in any case very close indeed to their own. This Tibetan-speaking sympathetically disposed Nepalese (Newar) community, small as it was, represented for centuries an important Tibetan link with the outside world. Yet the Tibetans never attempted to make use of the contact for wider cultural purposes. It survived the Gorkha conquest of the Nepal Valley in 1768-9 and in the nineteenth and early twentieth centuries a few Tibetan lamas came on missionary visits to Newar communities, quite apart from the regular stream of ordinary Tibetan pilgrims making the winter rounds of the holy Buddhist places in the Nepal Valley. It has been a strange but somehow typically Tibetan relationship. They were interested in the Newars, just as they were interested in the Mongols, for the services they rendered to 'holy religion', incorporating them, as only the Tibetans know how, in the Tibetan 'spiritual empire'. Except for a little acquired for trading purposes, Tibetans hardly ever learned Mongol or Newāri, any more than they learned Chinese. The onus of maintaining the contact always lay with the others, while the Tibetans continued to show general indifference to social, cultural, and political developments in surrounding countries unless they touched upon Tibetan Buddhist religion. By the seventeenth century the Tibetans regarded themselves as the one people who practised true Buddhism, and they do not appear to have been willing to go out of their way to learn about other religions and philosophies, although they were quite happy to allow them to exist in their midst, at least until there was any sign of conflict with the established Tibetan way of life. For the present, however, the only foreign community in Lhasa seems to have been the Newars and since those who came belonged normally to Nepalese Buddhist castes and rapidly adopted Tibetan Buddhist religion, there was no occasion for conflict on this score. Their interest in gold and silver work, reserved in Nepal to the Buddhist religious caste of *ba-re*,* resulted in their securing for the kings of Nepal the monopolization of the right to strike coinage for Tibet.

By the beginning of the eighteenth century Armenians were established in Lhasa, and in 1707 the first Christian missionaries arrived, the Capuchin Fathers François de Tours and Giuseppe d'Ascoli, followed in 1709 by Father Domenico da Fano. But this anticipates a little. The first missionary to enter Tibetan territory was the Jesuit, Father Antonio d'Andrade, who reached Tsaparang, capital of the Western Tibetan kingdom of *Gu-ge* in 1624, having made his way there from Ladakh. He laid the foundations of a small mission which continued with varying fortunes until war between Ladakh and *Gu-ge* brought it to an end in 1640. The earlier success in *Gu-ge* encouraged another Jesuit mission, and in 1630 Fathers Cacella and Cabral travelled through Bhutan to Shigatse, where they received a warm welcome. In their ignorance of Tibetan language and literature, they were at first not quite sure whether or not they had found their way into an ancient Christian community of debased practices. The images of Tārā (Tibetan *sGrol-ma*, 'the Saviouress') might well have appeared to those who did not know her as an oriental version of the 'Mother of God', and the by now stylized set of three images of *Tsong-kha-pa* and his two chief disciples might have been some curious representation of the Trinity. Traders who had reached Ladakh previously had already spread the rumour that the people there worshipped 'Our Lord' and 'Our Lady'. However, the death of Cacella prevented the founding of a proper mission at Shigatse, and nothing came of this early contact. Yet another group of Jesuit missionaries travelled through Lhasa in 1661 on the long journey from China to India. The missionaries were poor and unassuming in their behaviour, but there could be no real contact with the Tibetans, simply because at this time they could not speak their language. Presumably the Tibetans they met simply treated them with kindly curiosity, regarding them as just one more kind of harmless religious practiser.

Ladakhi Muslims were already well known in Western Tibet, and after the fifth Dalai Lama had brought Ladakh within his sphere of religious influence, a small community of these Muslims began to grow in Lhasa, most of them traders, but also some butchers.

Chapter 8

Manchu Overlordship

Problems of Succession The death of the fifth Dalai Lama produced an unprecedented problem for those responsible for Tibetan state affairs. The first ruler who effectively combined in his person both the religious and the secular power, his authority had remained unquestioned and he had succeeded in holding the country together by his immense personal prestige. In accordance with the now accepted method of succession, a child successor would have to be discovered and it would be eighteen years before he came of age and resumed personal control of the country's affairs. The system of reincarnating lamas had been adopted in the first place for heads of some religious orders and monastic establishments. Now as a result of a combination of historical circumstances, it was being applied for the first time in the case of an effective head of state. Even with normal hereditary succession there is no guarantee that a son will be capable of continuing his father's work, but it may be easier to replace him than a young lama who occupies his position by unquestioned divine right. Succession by rein-carnation also involves the additional risk of eighteen years interregnum between the effective rule of one Dalai Lama and his successor.

Sangs-rgyas rGya-mtsho (Sang-gye Gyamtso), Regent of the fifth Dalai Lama's last years, tried to solve the last mentioned problem by concealing the death of his master, which occurred in 1682, and maintaining the fiction that the Dalai Lama had entered upon a long bout of strict meditation, he continued to rule in his stead. He was much criticized for this afterwards and was even accused of treacherous duplicity by the Chinese, but since Tibet was not beholden to China in any way at this time, the charge of treachery at least is irrelevant. Whatever his personal motives may have been, he probably acted in the wisest way possible so far as Tibet's best interests were concerned, and if his choice of a child successor had been more fortunate, Tibet might have survived intact as an independent power, at least until the same problem of an interregnum occurred again. As it was, he managed to hold his own almost unchallenged until 1695, when his secret leaked out and he hastily enthroned his protégé as the sixth Dalai Lama *Tshangs-dbyangs rGya-mtsho* (Tshang-yang Gyamtso). Unhappily for him, the new supreme ruler proved a most unsuitable choice.

It will be remembered that all this time Tibet was still nominally committed to the descendants of *Gu-shri*, Khan of the Qośot Mongols, who still retained the title of 'King of Tibet', although the fifth Dalai Lama's extraordinary ability and the lack of interest of *Gu-shri*'s successors had reduced the relationship to mere formality. Then in 1697 *lHa-bzang* became 'King'. Like the Regent *Sangs-rgyas rGya-mtsho*, he was determined to make his impact on the world. He had established his claim to be Khan by the murder of his elder brother, and it soon became clear that he did not intend to remain a mere cipher in Tibetan affairs, as his immediate predecessors had been. This brought him into conflict with the Regent, who had exercised absolute control of Tibetan affairs and was now under criticism from the Emperor for governing so long under false pretences. The principal cause for contention was the behaviour of the young Dalai Lama, which seemed totally unsuitable for a head of state, and especially for a Grand Lama of a great religious order, whose primary claim to distinction had been the excellence of its strict monastic discipline. It was certain that events had developed in a most extraordinary way since the first preaching of *Tsong-kha-pa* two centuries earlier, and it is not surprising that *lHa-bzang*, supported by some Tibetan lay nobility, should object.

It may appear ironic that at so critical a time it should have been possible for the peace and stability of Tibet to be fatally affected by the personality and character of the young Lama. If he had proved an able, conscientious leader like his predecessor, or even if he had been dull but discreet, the worst results of Tibet's internal dissension and external entanglements might have been avoided. But on the very first occasion that the successor of a supreme ruler was chosen by the principle of reincarnation the dangers of the system became tragically obvious. *Tshangs-dbyangs rGya-mtsho*, a gay libertine, the writer of charming lyrics celebrating his romantic nature and love of women, could have lived without much comment, even as a lesser lama, in the tolerant society of Lhasa. But although he was by nature unfit to be a religious leader and showed no interest in administrative matters, he was, whether he liked it or not, caught up in a high place from which there was no escape.

Many Tibetans can still recall the traditional account of his appearance – in the blue silk robe of a lay nobleman, wearing his hair in long black locks, bedecked with rings and jewelry, and carrying a bow and quiver. His lyrics have retained a universal popularity throughout the country; and as a poet of a most unusual kind for Tibet, *Tshangs-dbyangs rGya-mtsho* (his name means 'Ocean of Pure Melody') deserves an important place in any cultural history. His talent can scarcely have been unique, but no one would have troubled to record poetry of such a kind from the mouth of anyone less than a Dalai Lama, since only that which is religious and didactic in context is deemed to have value. But since he was a Dalai Lama, some of his devotees have tried to give hidden meanings to his quite spontaneous songs.

> The young shoots of last year's planting
>   have become this year's trusses of straw.
> A young man grows old and his body
>   is stiffer than our southern bamboo.

> O that the one who has entered my heart
>   might be my lifelong companion!
> It would be like gaining a precious gem
>   from the very depths of the ocean.

> The lass with the sweet perfumed body
>   was my friend by the way as I travelled.
> T'was as though I had found a white turquoise
>   and cast it aside straight away.

> When I recall the fine complexion
>   of that great official's daughter,
> It seems like the ripe dropping fruit
>   at the top of a tall peach tree.

> My thoughts are so set on the matter
>   that sleep eludes me at night.
> By day my hopes go unrealized.
>   How weary, so weary, my mind!

.   .   .   .

> I went to seek instruction
>   at the feet of my worthy lama.
> But my thoughts could not be kept there.
>   They escaped to my beloved.

Though called to mind, my lama's face
  does not rise in my thoughts.
Not called to mind, my loved one's face
  gently pervades my thoughts.*

Tshangs-dbyangs rGya-mtsho readily renounced his monastic vows but the idea of
a reincarnating religious ruler had already fastened itself so strongly on Tibetan
minds that he had the unquestioning devotion of the mass of ordinary monks and
laymen and even the highest religious dignitaries and lay nobles, after using the
most earnest persuasion, were unable to influence him. Caught this way, as they
were later to be caught again, in the trap unwittingly laid for themselves by adher-
ence to an ostensibly irrational system, the Tibetans were incapable of resolving
their internal dissensions or of finding a way out of their entanglement. Thus they
were caught up in a complex external situation where the feuds of the Mongols
involved them in a threat to China.

The fifth Dalai Lama had exercised considerable influence in Mongolian
affairs, and an important connection existed between him and one particular
group of Mongols, the Dzungar Oirats of Chuguchak, who had now come right
to the fore. Their previous leader B'atur had been a close associate of *Gu-shri*,
and B'atur's son Ganden, Khan since 1676, had once been a monk in Lhasa, and
continued to maintain close relations with the Regent *Sans-rgyas rGya-mtsho*.
These same Dzungars were the greatest thorn in the Chinese side at this time,
and although they suffered a severe defeat in 1695 and Ganden himself died two
years later, his nephew and successor *Tshe-dbang Rab-brtan* still remained, ready
to cause further trouble.

The direction of Chinese affairs was now in the hands of the great K'ang Hsi,
second Manchu Emperor of China (since 1662) and the saviour of his dynasty.
He had had serious revolts to deal with in southern China, and he could not
afford to tolerate uncertainties on his northern frontiers. Tibetan involvement
with the Dzungars who were causing him so much trouble, and various other
incidents, such as their self-interested dealing with the Chinese rebel Wu Shih-
pan who was found to be trying to win Mongol support against the Manchu
dynasty, were more than sufficient to cause him anxiety. Furthermore the manner
in which *Sangs-rgyas rGya-mtsho* had deliberately concealed from him the death
of the fifth Dalai Lama was in itself an unfriendly act, even allowing for Tibet's
independence of China at the time. Such mistaken acts of policy arise from the
Tibetans' endemic lack of interest in foreign countries to which we have referred
above; they seem only to be able to recognize and grasp the immediate advantage.
They knew the Mongols as good Tibetan Buddhists and as generous benefactors,

and so they overlooked altogether the dangerous instability of the Mongol régimes as opposed to the solidly based power of imperial China. Rather belatedly, in 1693, *Sangs-rgyas rGya-mtsho* seems to have tried to establish some understanding with the Emperor, and he received recognition of his position by a special seal. Thus once again if his choice of the sixth Dalai Lama had proved a success, Tibet might well have emerged unaffected by his several diplomatic errors.

Meanwhile the Dalai Lama continued to live unrepentantly the life he pleased and tension grew between the Regent *Sangs-rgyas rGya-mtsho* and *lHa-bzang Khan*, the 'King of Tibet', supported by some members of the lay nobility, who were restive under the Regent and his ecclesiastical régime. The Regent was still on friendly terms with the Dzungars, who were not only the enemies of China but also enemies of the Qośot khans. Thus in 1706 *lHa-bzang* with the full moral support of Emperor K'ang Hsi, gathered a small and efficient army, marched on Lhasa where he captured the Regent and put him to death. The Emperor then sent an envoy bestowing formal recognition upon *lHa-bzang* as Governor, and in return for an offer of tribute, Tibet became in effect the formal vassal of China. *lHa-bzang* next tried to remove the young man who was such an unsuitable Dalai Lama. Recognizing that in spite of his way of life and his public disavowal of spiritual powers, he was none the less still regarded with reverence by Tibetans and Mongols, *lHa-bzang* tried to persuade the leading lamas of Lhasa to disown him as a true reincarnation. Since none dared take this responsibility, *lHa-bzang* himself took the young man into custody, and, with the Emperor's concurrence, set out with him to China and exile.

Tshangs-dbyangs rGya-mtsho was twenty-four or twenty-five at the time, and with a self-abnegation which makes his fate all the sadder, he refused to take advantage of the strong popular feeling in his favour, and voluntarily went with his captor. On the way to China he died, and even if the inevitable suggestion of murder cannot be substantiated, K'ang Hsi showed the more petty side of his nature by ordering that his body should be dishonoured. In his place *lHa-bzang* installed one of his protégés, a monk of whom little is known and who had been born soon after the death of the fifth Dalai Lama, declaring that this one was the true incarnation and that *Tshangs-dbyangs* had been chosen by mistake. *lHa-bzang*'s nominee was ignored by the people of Tibet, who were soon affected by reports that *Tshangs-dbyangs* had reincarnated as the seventh Dalai Lama far away in eastern Tibet, as foretold in one of his poems, which was now quoted to this effect.

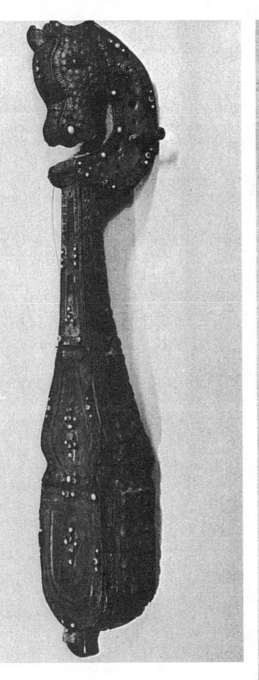

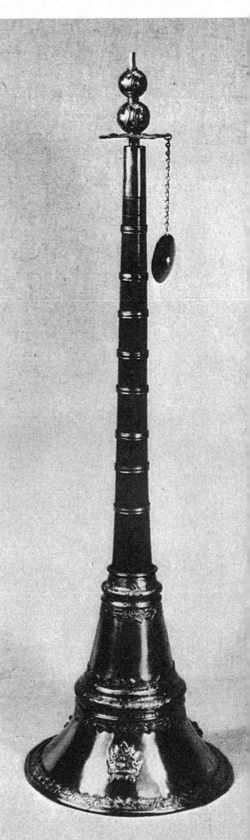

Cultural objects: 2

(*above*) A Tibetan 'guitar' (*sgra-snyan*) as used by wandering minstrels

(*right*) A Tibetan 'shawm' (*rgya-gling*) as used in all kinds of religious ceremonies. It is made of wood and copper, bound with silver

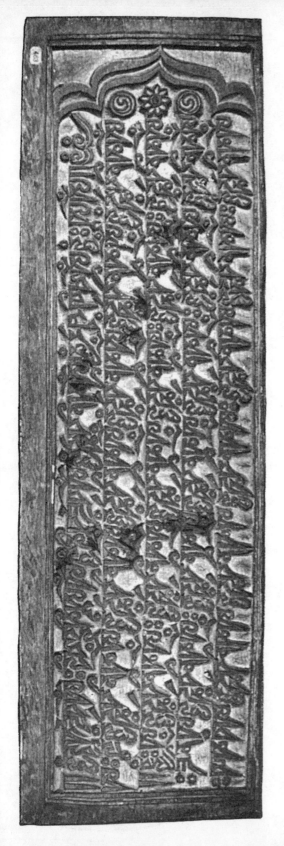

(*above*) Decorative dragon-head of a 'guitar' (*sgra-snyan*)

(*left*) A wooden printing-block. The wood is cut away by a master wood-carver so as to leave the letters upstanding in reverse. They are then inked and paper pressed upon them (see page 160)

(*opposite*) A painted scroll illustrating the Great Religious King *Srong-brtsan-sgam-po* and events in his life. His two queens are just below him

Detail of lotus-flower pattern from table below

(*left*) A Tibetan side-table, carved and painted, for ordinary domestic use. It is decorated with a lotus-flower pattern

Group of men from an aristocratic estate dressed up in old military costume for taking part in the New Year ceremonies (see also page 122)

(*left*) Ceremonial dress as supposed to have been worn by the early kings. Certain officials are appointed to wear it for the New Year ceremonies

(*top*) A copper teapot decorated with designs in silver and gold

(*above*) An ornamental belt made of leather and silver, as worn by nomad women

(*left*) A steel and tinder pouch

An inkpot, made of copper, decorated with silver, and fitted with a wooden lid

(*left*) A quiver-shaped bamboo container for sticks of incense

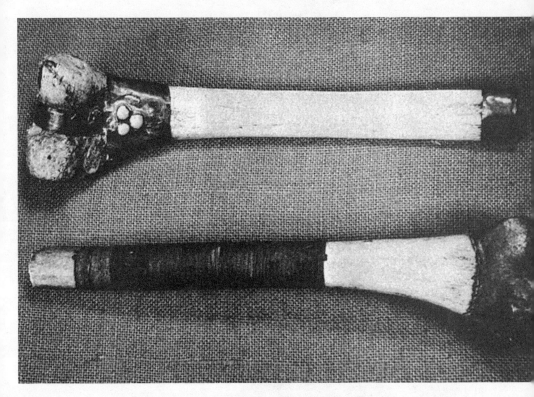

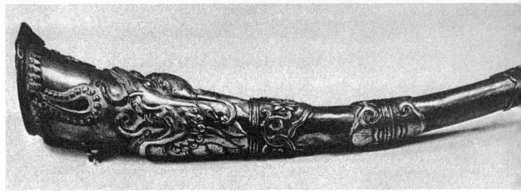

(*top*) Two 'horns' (*rkang-gling*) as used by yogins and made of human leg-bones, bound with leather and thread (yak-hair)

(*above*) A 'horn' (*rkang-gling*) made of copper decorated with silver, as in normal monastic use

Bird! white crane!
Lend me your wings!
I shall not go far,
Just to *Li-thang* and back again.*

Manchu Interests Established   *lHa-bzang*'s position, difficult for a while, came
to be generally accepted. He had the support of an envoy sent by the Emperor,
and he could rely on the help of two able Tibetan noblemen, *Kang-chen* and a
young man *Pho-lha*. It is interesting to have from now on the occasional observations of independent Western witnesses in Tibetan as already in Mongolian
affairs. The first Christian missionaries entered Lhasa in 1707 and 1709 (see
page 202), and the reports of these pioneers show *lHa-bzang* in a bad light as the
slayer of the Regent and the destroyer of the Grand Lama. His unpopularity is
mentioned, especially with reference to his status as a tributary of the Emperor.
Later on when he had established his position and other missionaries came to
Lhasa, he is depicted very favourably. Both he and his minister *Kang-chen* were
friendly to the new missionaries, especially to the famous Jesuit Ippolito Desideri,
the first Western scholar of Tibetan. He remained in power until 1717, when the
great monasteries of Lhasa, which had not forgiven him for removing the sixth
Dalai Lama and eclipsing ecclesiastical power, achieved his downfall by com-
bining with a foreign ally of theirs, the same Dzungars who had been in association with the former Regent. They planned to destroy *lHa-bzang* and bring to
Lhasa the child who had been discovered in *Li-thang*, and who by the political
foresight of the Emperor was living under loose supervision in the monastery of
sKu-'bum. The Dzungars despatched one force from Khotan across the wastes
of north-western Tibet to march on Lhasa, and another to the Kokonor region
to get the boy from *sKu-'bum*. The latter force failed in its task, but the former,
by using the cruel deception of pretending to bring help to *lHa-bzang* in a
campaign against Bhutan, reached their objective unopposed. *lHa-bzang* was
deceived into trusting these Dzungars, because they had recently concluded
a matrimonial alliance with him through his son. He was taken by surprise and
defeated in spite of skilful fighting by the young *Pho-lha*; then, helped by
treachery, the Dzungars stormed Lhasa and killed him.

The monks and people of Lhasa welcomed the Dzungar army as deliverers,
but they soon received a rude shock. Apart from not bringing the Dalai Lama,
they also behaved as savage and rapacious masters, looting all and sundry and
even ransacking the tomb of the fifth Dalai Lama. The minister *Kang-chen* was
captured and tortured, but managed to escape. *rNying-ma-pa* monasteries were

especially victimized, but even *dGe-lugs-pa* foundations and lamas were persecuted and robbed on the pretext that they had allowed their discipline to become
lax. Nor were the humble Capuchin fathers spared. The Dzungars appointed an
elderly nobleman, *sTag-rtse-pa*, to act as Regent, who mitigated as far as he
could their reign of terror.,

K'ang Hsi could not risk the danger which might result if the Dzungars won a
position from which they could manipulate to their advantage the influence of
the *dGe-lugs-pa* 'church' in Mongolia. He was well informed of the course of
events, and as well as forestalling the Dzungar raid on *sKu-'bum*, he immediately
prepared an army to send to Lhasa. The first force of 7,000 which he sent was
totally wiped out. Meanwhile *Pho-lha* and his Tibetan following were attacking
the Dzungars wherever they could, and even before the second Chinese force
approached Lhasa, the Dzungars, more interested in raids and booty than in
peaceful administration, were already pulling out of Central Tibet. In the event
Dzungars and Chinese did not meet. The main trump in Chinese hands was the
new Dalai Lama, whose reception, in the words of Desideri, was rapturous. Thus
the Chinese arrived as friends and deliverers from the hated Dzungars, and the
Emperor appeared as the true protector of the boy *bsKal-bzang rGya-mtsho*, who
was duly installed (1720) as Dalai Lama.

K'ang Hsi now resolved to establish representatives at Lhasa to guard against
future dangers to China from such vagaries of Tibetan policy. This represented
an entirely new relationship between Tibet and China, but it was justified by a
lengthy decree (1721) which assumed quite wrongly that Tibet had been in the
position of tributary vassal for eighty years already. In this respect K'ang Hsi
referred to those messages sent to his ancestors by the contending parties at the
time of *Gu-shri*'s conquest of Tibet and before the Manchus were emperors of
China (see page 198). From this time onwards the Manchu emperor was technically the overlord of Tibet; the relationship was based on no treaty or written
document, and the Tibetans have persisted in envisaging it in terms of the
traditional concept of 'patron and priest'.

The effects of this new connection between Tibet and China have been far-
reaching, despite the lightness and often the total non-existence of Chinese control of Tibetan affairs. After a decade of readjustment the new Chinese interest
provided conditions in which the social unity of the country was able to develop
under a stable central government in Lhasa. Chinese advice had some effect on
the form of the administration, but little on its manner. The organization of a
Tibetan army was perhaps the most effective innovation inspired by Chinese
models. In other functions of government, although the number of officials was

varied from time to time by imperial decree, Tibetan customs, good and bad, continued almost unchanged.

K'ang Hsi's proclamation of 1721 did not at once initiate a new era of unity and peace. Having reorganized the Tibetan government and staged a gruesome public execution, his representatives stood apart from the actual administration. However, two thousand Chinese troops were left as a garrison, and almost at once there appeared a constantly recurring source of friction in Sino-Tibetan relations. The presence of these troops at Lhasa caused an immediate shortage of supplies, a consequent rise in prices and the growing unpopularity of the protecting power. When K'ang Hsi died in 1722, his son Yung Cheng was influenced by this Tibetan discontent and withdrew the powerful Chinese presence from Lhasa. The immediate effect of its removal was the upsurge of old rivalries amongst the ruling nobles, resulting in the murder of *Kang-chen* and a bitter civil war, from which *Pho-lha*, fortunately for the Tibetans, eventually emerged as victor. In the meantime there was anxiety lest civil war in Tibet should again attract the marauding Dzungars. Once again the Emperor sent an army, but this arrived after the trouble had been decided. As before, there was no fighting between Tibetans and Chinese, the government was reorganized, a public execution staged, and imperial representatives with a strong body of supporting troops settled down in Lhasa. The new reorganization resulted in twenty years rule by *Pho-lha bSod-nams sTobs-rgyas*, a golden age of good government in Tibet under a truly great Tibetan.

In the general pattern of Tibetan history this régime exemplifies the ascendancy of lay over clerical elements, and, to a lesser extent, the ascendancy of *gTsang* over *dBus*. It is a mark of *Pho-lha*'s greatness that although his supremacy involved the subordination and at times the exile of the seventh Dalai Lama, he was able by his conciliatory and just behaviour to keep monastic resentment to a low level. In his relations with China he shrewdly saw that as long as Tibetan policy did not endanger the wider interests of China in Central Asia, Chinese overlordship in Tibet could be reduced to a mere formality so far as internal affairs and even Tibetan relations with her Himalayan neighbours were concerned. Thus the substance of Tibetan independence was preserved thanks to Chinese protection but without fear of Chinese interference. His success was complete; he won the full confidence of the Emperor by his competence and reliability, and in Lhasa his dealings with the Ambans, as the Chinese representatives were called, were firm but friendly, so that they remained little more than observers and diplomatic agents of their Emperor.

The Pan-chen Lamas In one matter, however, the Emperor did interfere in the internal affairs of Tibet in a way which had lasting importance. The *Pan-chen* lamas have been mentioned before (page 183), but without explanation. Leaving aside later hagiography, we note that the title *Pan-chen* (an abbreviation of *Paṇḍita Chen-po*, 'Great Scholar') was given to the abbots of *bKra-shis-lhun-po* (Tashilhunpo) Monastery, for at first they were learned men, like the present *Khri Rin-po-che* of *dGa'-ldan* (Ganden), who were appointed at a mature age. The principle of reincarnation was applied to their selection, when the fifth Dalai Lama pronounced that the *Pan-chen* Lama of his time, the learned and venerable *Chos-kyi rGyal-mtshan* (1570-1662), who was his tutor and a much respected figure in Tibet, would reappear after his death in a recognizable child-successor. Thus it was that the first reincarnation, technically the second *Pan-chen* Lama *Blo-bzang Ye-shes*, was discovered in 1662 and duly installed. In the civil war of 1727-8 the seventh Dalai Lama and his family were suspected, not without reason, of fomenting trouble. They had backed the losing side, which had been flirting with the dangerous Dzungars, and so the Dalai Lama himself was sent into virtual banishment. Then in order to have some counter-balancing force within the *dGe-lugs-pa* hierarchy, the Emperor arranged that the *Pan-chen* Lama should be built up into a temporal and administrative power. Thus in 1728, before *Pho-lha*'s authority had been established and without any formal Tibetan concurrence, the Emperor made the *Pan-chen* Lama sovereign of *gTsang* and of Western Tibet. The Lama prudently accepted only a part of the donation, and the Dalai Lama and his successors never regarded it as conveying anything more than the subordinate position similar to that of a local hereditary ruler. During *Pho-lha*'s rule this division of authority had no great political significance, but when the *dGe-lugs-pas* came into power again, it was a frequent source of embarrassment and internal weakness, manifesting its fatal effects right down to 1959.

Christian Missionaries *Pho-lha*'s régime, among other events, saw the end of the Christian missions in Lhasa. Since these missions and the causes of their ending throw so much light on Tibetan character and Tibetan civilization at the time, they merit some detailed consideration. Here was a connection which, based on common cultural and religious interests, might have brought Tibet into closer contact with the outside world, and perhaps hastened its adjustment to foreign ideas. The responsibility for failure lies to some extent on the Western side, for Tibetan religious authorities seem to have been far more receptive then to strange philosophical and religious ideas than they are now (after almost two centuries of self-enclosure), while the Christian religious authorities, in ignorance of the nature of Tibetan civilization, sent missionaries who with one notable exception, the great Jesuit Father Ippolito Desideri, were incapable of understanding the depths of Tibetan feelings and convictions.

The Jesuit interest in Tibet, which had been established by Father Andrade in Western Tibet and by Fathers Cabral and Cacella in Shigatse (see pp. 202–3), was renewed in 1716 by Desideri's mission to Lhasa. It happened, perhaps due to the prevailing geographical uncertainty about Tibet, that the Holy See had already sanctioned a mission to Lhasa by the Capuchins, who had established themselves there from 1707 to 1711, when this mission of theirs was closed through lack of funds. Thus it came about that soon after Desideri's arrival a fresh Capuchin mission came to Lhasa under Father Orazio della Penna. There was immediate, though outwardly restrained rivalry between the two groups about the right to conduct the Lhasa mission. The case went to Rome and was decided after some years in favour of the Capuchins. So in 1721 Desideri sadly left the place where he had studied and taught and recorded Tibetan life and religion as no foreigner has done before or since. Meanwhile the Capuchins were not always able to secure adequate or regular financial support, and in 1733 their mission was again abandoned while they went to Rome to raise funds. It was reoccupied in 1741 and abandoned finally in 1745.

From the start the approach of the Capuchins had been tentative. This was an age when Catholic missionaries travelling about India sometimes felt compelled to disguise themselves as naked Hindu ascetics in order to avoid trouble with Moghul officialdom, especially the toll and *octroi* gatherers. So in Tibet the Capuchins did not at first wear their religious habit or declare their faith. They wore dark blue Tibetan cloth and made their impression on the Tibetans mainly by their practice of medicine, for which they always found a ready welcome. On their arrival in Lhasa they had the help of the Armenian merchants, already established there, without whose charity they would scarcely have survived. There was no hostility on the part of the Tibetans, rather a kindly social tolerance, and thanks to their Armenian connections they obtained entrance to the houses of some of the nobility. But during their first mission from 1707 to 1711 they do not seem to have disclosed their faith, except very discreetly. However, when they returned in 1716 they found to their surprise the Jesuit Father Desideri, who had been there only a few months, not only wearing his habit, but openly established as a priest and celebrating the mass without concealment. Moreover he already knew quite a lot of Tibetan, was discussing religious questions with the nobles, and was even received in a kindly and respectful manner by the king, *lHa-bzang* Khan. He had been fortunate in falling in with a Qošot princess on the arduous journey from Ladakh to Lhasa, and by her motherly kindness to this foreign holy man his hardships on the journey were reduced and he secured useful introductions on his arrival in Lhasa. He was received by *lHa-bzang* and his minister *Kang-chen,* and he formally asked permission to practise and preach his faith. He found remarkable 'affection, honour and friendship' in high places, and soon he was greatly in demand for discussions in religious circles. This is surely evidence not only of his transparent piety, sincerity and strength of character, but also of a genuine tolerance, natural kindness and even intellectual curiosity amongst Tibetans. The Capuchins, encouraged by his example, now also took up the profession of their faith and shared in the social advantages won by Desideri. But the contrast is seen unmistakably in the eloquent records recently edited by Professor Luciano Petech.* Desideri was an educated man of penetrating intellectual powers, able within a short space of time to master sufficient Tibetan to write an account of the essentials of Christianity, and a little later to master the content and meaning of Tibetan Buddhism, as expounded to him by *dGe-lugs-pa* teachers, and to write in Tibetan his refutation of their doctrines. In his *Account of Tibet*,† although he necessarily condemns those doctrines of Buddhism which conflict with his faith and philosophical conceptions, he never indulges in abuse, and although he criticizes what he sees as the weak points of Tibetan character, he is full of praise for the greater good which he sees in it.

The Capuchins, on the other hand, happened to be men of far less education, trained rather for the emphatic preaching of slogans than for the intellectual discussion and analysis of their own and other people's religious beliefs. All but one of them, Orazio della Penna, who lived for twenty years in Tibet, found it impossible to learn Tibetan sufficiently well to discuss religious matters. Their proselytizing efforts consisted in the translation of a few simple catechisms containing for the most part moral views and injunctions with which Tibetans would in any case be in complete agreement. Ignorant of Tibetan religion, they regarded the acceptance of these points as signs that the faith of the Tibetans, even of the Dalai Lama himself who expressed kind agreement, was wavering and that a mass conversion of Tibet was imminent. They even wrote with satisfaction how they had proved to several reincarnating lamas that such a kind of rebirth was impossible, and that the lamas expressed 'great interest'. Meanwhile they did not trouble to try to understand the theory and practice of Tibetan religion, but simply condemned it with extravagant abuse. Serious tension was bound to develop between such simple but pretentious men and the truly religious intellectual Desideri, with the result that they did not hold back from the most unChristian accusations and complaints against him in their letters to superiors. But with the finer characters of the Capuchin mission he established friendly relations, and in company with Father Orazio della Penna he was allowed to live in the *Ra-mo-che* Temple, and later on in the great monastery of *Se-ra* itself, in order to study the Tibetan language and religious literature. It is another and remarkable evidence of Tibetan tolerance that the mass was allowed to be regularly and openly celebrated in these *dGe-lugs-pa* strongholds. (But we must remember that the consecration of the sacred species has interesting parallels in Tibetan religious practice, and having once received these priests as men of religion, Tibetans would expect them to perform ceremonies of consecration.) They further treated them with special generosity in · the matter of living accommodation, and even gave them concessions to help them build a chapel.

Why, one may well ask, in the midst of such kindness and consideration, was the mission eventually closed. The answer is a very simple one: until 1741 no Tibetan converts to Christianity were made. A few Newars and Chinese were converted, and many Tibetan children were baptised *in articulo mortis*. At such a stage any rite might be worth trying, and it could scarcely do harm. But after the reoccupation of their mission in 1741, they made special efforts at conversion, possibly in accordance with instructions from Rome, where some results might be expected from a mission field which had been worked for thirty years. Including their servants with their families and a butcher with his family, the Capuchins made twenty-six Tibetan converts in all. But within eleven days of their baptism one of them, Tomaso, formerly Tenzin, seems to have gone out of his way to seek martyrdom. He was sent in the course of his duties to carry presents to the Dalai Lama at a public audience, where he refused rather ostentatiously to prostrate himself. An inquiry was ordered and for some days the city magistrates of Lhasa, showing surprising patience, argued with Tomaso and his fellow Christians, not without threats to be sure. The fathers, who made great efforts to protect them, were told that they might no longer teach their religion. Particular offence had been caused by their teachings that the Dalai Lama was not a reincarnation, and that *Śākyamuni*, the historical Buddha, was not a true saint. Eventually the magistrates, even then with reluctance it seems, ordered that if they would not recant, five of the Christians should be given twenty strokes. (This punishment is extremely light by Tibetan standards; a Tibetan monk of our acquaintance received twenty-five strokes for hitting a fellow monk on the head with a key.) The five Christians bore their punishment with admirable staunchness and courage, which greatly moved the Capuchin fathers. But now their days in Tibet were numbered. They were shunned and ignored by the nobles and lamas who had been their friends for so long, and after several months of ostracism they were summoned to the presence of *Pho-lha*. He received them with the usual courtesy, but upbraided them sternly at what could only appear to the Tibetans as an abuse of their kindness and hospitality. *Pho-lha* himself had already protected them from attack some time before, when the building of their chapel had been followed by a severe flood, and the monks insisted that there must be a connection between these two events. Why, after all the friendship and concessions they had received, should they now suddenly offend against the person of the Dalai Lama and against Tibetan religious beliefs? Let them instruct Newars, Chinese and Ladakhis, if they wish, but Tibetans must be left alone in future and not taught to insult their ruler. Thereafter the mission dragged sadly on for a while, but it was short of funds and Orazio della Penna was old and ill. In 1745 they finally left, and almost before they were out of sight of Lhasa their chapel was razed to the ground. Orazio, struck down with grief at such an end to his twenty years' mission and by his severe illness, died soon after reaching Kathmandu. Later attempts to reopen the mission came to nothing and the last heard of the converts was a message from Lhasa in 1769 asking for a priest to be sent to them. One would like to think that the staunch Tomaso and his wife Agata were among the senders. One trusts that the hardships and loneliness of this little band of foreign missionaries was lightened by the friendliness of so many Tibetans, while this lasted, by the beauty of Lhasa itself, by the climate and mountain scenery of *Kong-po* where a small branch-mission did nothing but make wine, and by the interest of studying and recording Tibetan ways, thought and history. One relic remains of their mission: a fine bell hanging in the main approach of the Cathedral (*Jo-khang*), the most holy of Tibetan temples, and inscribed with the words TE DEUM LAUDAMUS.

The great intellectual contribution of the mission is the information on the history of the period and on Tibetan life and religion, which is contained principally in Desideri's *Account of Tibet*, but also in the writings of Domenico da Fano, Orazio della Penna and Cassiano de Macerata, all illuminated further by the letters included in Petech's remarkable work. It is evidence, if proof were needed, that Tibet was not then a closed country. Not only could the fathers come and go as freely as the difficulties of terrain, weather and transport allowed, but there is also mention of other foreign visitors, including a French merchant and an adventurous Dutchman. As well as the Armenians already mentioned, there were some Russian traders, and the Capuchins describe Lhasa as a busy market-city of some 80,000 inhabitants, depending on trade for its existence. The Dzungar looting of Lhasa put an end to the Armenian and Russian trading communities, but Newars, Ladakhis and Chinese continued to take advantage of *Pho-lha*'s peaceful administration.

Rule by Regents This golden age of lay administration came to an end with *Pho-lha*'s death in 1747. The son who succeeded him proved irresponsible, arrogant and cruel, and when he began to intrigue with the Dzungars, the Chinese representatives, receiving no reply to their urgent reports to the Emperor, took matters into their own hands and murdered him. A furious Tibetan mob, who would not even listen to the Dalai Lama's remonstrances, killed the two Ambans. Within twenty-four hours, however, the Dalai Lama had restored order, thus forestalling the despatch of an army which the Emperor had ordered. In the event a small expedition arrived, not to chastise the Tibetans, but to inquire into the causes of the trouble. Once again there was no question of fighting between Tibetans and Chinese, a spectacular execution was staged, the Tibetan administration was reorganized, and the Chinese troops in Lhasa sent up the cost of living and brought themselves into early unpopularity.

A great change in the administration of Tibet resulted from the Emperor's decision that never again should one Tibetan be in such a position of power as that achieved by *Pho-lha* and misused by his son. The Dalai Lama was restored to power with a council of four ministers, of whom one would be a monk, and thus the period of lay supremacy ended for ever.*

Thus from 1757 onwards there came a period of 130 years during which the head of the administration was a *dGe-lugs-pa* lama regent, assisted by monk officials of his order and lay officials of the *dGe-lugs-pa* nobility. The eighth Dalai Lama lived to the age of forty-seven, but he was disinclined to worldly activities. After him four Dalai Lamas all died young, at the ages of ten, twenty-one, seventeen and twenty. There is good reason to believe that the tenth Dalai Lama was assassinated, with the connivance of the then regent. Western writers have also expressed suspicions about the early deaths of the others, which resulted in power remaining in the hands of some dignitary of the *dGe-lugs-pa* 'church', but this is not supported by anything in Tibetan or Chinese records or by Tibetan oral tradition. Whatever the truth may be, this rule of regents produced a considerable variety of character. Some were revered and peaceful, while others were harsh and unscrupulous. In the main the country remained peaceful and the regents remarkably free of Chinese control. The emperors often complained of the poor quality of their representatives in Tibet, and the men chosen to fill the post of Amban tended to regard the appointment as a punishment, for life in Tibet at eight months distance and more from their homeland seemed little better than exile. Thus it came about that after a burst of brisk activity following some crisis, Chinese interest in Tibet would languish until the next crisis.

In the eyes of the Tibetans the regents lacked altogether the aura of a Dalai Lama, and it was therefore possible for an outstanding *Pan-chen* Lama to acquire considerable influence as a person worthy of respect and devotion. Such a person was the third *Pan-chen* Lama, *Blo-bzang dPal-ldan Ye-shes* (1737–80). We have an unusually intimate picture of him, as he befriended George Bogle, the first British visitor to Tibet, sent there by Warren Hastings in 1775 to investigate ways of increasing trade between India and Tibet. His account of his visit, as well as containing valuable commercial and political information, depicts the warm hospitality, intelligence, good humour and gaiety of Tibetan society. He observed that rivalry existed between the *Pan-chen* Lama's following and the administration at Lhasa, headed by the Regent, and that the overlordship of

China, confined in practice to Lhasa itself, was disliked and rather reluctantly admitted. He also had the distinction of marrying a Tibetan lady, a relation of the *Pan-chen* Lama, and of introducing, at Warren Hastings' suggestion, the potato into Tibet*. Both he and his friend the *Pan-chen* Lama died prematurely, the latter in Peking where he had been invited by the Emperor. In 1782 Samuel Turner, sent on a mission by Warren Hastings, set out to visit Shigatse, thus strengthening the friendly relationship, which was further encouraged on the British side by the grant of a site in Calcutta for the establishment of a small monastic community. Unhappily nothing came of this, due to the next crisis in Sino-Tibetan affairs.

Relations with Nepal In 1768-9 the ruler of Gorkha, a small principality some thirty miles west of the Nepal Valley, which comprised in those days the three small kingdoms of Pātan, Kathmandu and Bhatgaon, to which the name 'Nepal' then applied, seized by means of intrigue and treachery the whole of the Nepal Valley and proceeded to make himself master of the much larger kingdom, which now goes by the name of Nepal on modern maps. In the west he appropriated the ancient kingdoms of Jumla and Mustang, and together with Mustang the old Western Tibetan region of Dolpo fell into his hands. No authority in Western Tibet or in Lhasa seems to have thought of protesting at these depredations, and despite some recent suggestions to the contrary, China had no idea at that time of holding a frontier along the Himalayas, where boundaries were vague in a way which seems incomprehensible to many modern political theorists. Then in 1792 as a result of an incident which was largely due to the incompetence of the Chinese Ambans and the Tibetan government in Lhasa, Gorkha troops invaded Tibet and looted the *Pan-chen* Lama's own monastery of *bKra-shis-lhun-po* (Tashilhunpo). Thus the Emperor Ch'ien Lung had to send a costly expedition across Tibet in order to drive the aggressive Gorkhas from the country. This was done with great efficiency, and the expedition was followed as usual by a further reorganization of the Tibetan administration, which theoretically conferred upon the Ambans greater responsibility for directing Tibetan affairs. The changes existed mainly on paper, since this was, as it happens, the last occasion on which the Chinese were able to undertake their responsibilities of overlord and protector of the Tibetans, for after the death of the last great Emperor Ch'ien Lung, China entered upon one of the most ruinous centuries of her whole history. Meanwhile, through the Gorkha conquest of Nepal, the Tibetans lost their friendly contacts with the small Newar kingdoms of the Nepal Valley. The Newar kings, even the king of the Buddhist city of Pātan, ruled over societies which were organized according to locally devised caste-systems, allowing for both Buddhists and Brahmans and for all who belonged to the two main religious groupings. The whole valley was filled (and still is filled) with Buddhist and Brahmanical temples existing side by side, and this extraordinary civilization, the direct heritage of pre-Muslim India, existed as the result of some fourteen centuries of continuous creative activity by the original inhabitants, the Newars. Now as a result of the Gorkha conquest, their chief citizens were slaughtered, cruelly maimed and totally impoverished. For reasons of prestige the new Gorkha régime was concerned to establish a claim to pure Hindu orthodoxy, and thus the Buddhist cities of Pātan and its off-shoot Kīrtipur suffered most destruction to begin with and thereafter most neglect. Despite many handicaps Buddhist Newars maintained their position as traders and craftsmen in Lhasa, and so an important cultural and trading connection was not lost to the Tibetans. Having stabilized their kingdom, the new rulers of Nepal were by no means indifferent to trading advantages, but the Tibetans had lost within a few years a whole complex of friendly relationships, based upon common religious beliefs, along the major part of their southern frontier. All this was but part of the almost total cultural isolation to which they would soon be condemned.

A Closed Land After the death of the Emperor Ch'ien Lung in 1799 rebellions began to break out all over China. Although the Manchu dynasty hung on feebly and desperately until 1911, it was in no condition to come to the aid of its neighbours. Ever menaced with troubles within and fearful of disruptive influences from without, the Manchus adopted the deliberate policy of excluding foreigners. The Tibetans were directly affected by this xenophobia, for the Chinese inspired them with the belief, probably quite sincerely felt, that the country would be endangered if they allowed any foreigners, particularly anyone who might be British or Russian, into Tibet. The nineteenth century is the only period when Tibet might justly be described as a 'forbidden land'. The Tibetans were led to believe that British machinations were responsible for the recent Gorkha invasion, and this unhappy policy of a closed frontier led to mutual ignorance and misunderstandings between British India and Tibet. There were one or two small breaches of this Tibetan seclusion, interesting in themselves, such as the private visit of Thomas Manning in 1811 and the remarkable journey of two Lazarist missionaries, Fathers Huc and Gabet, from Peking through Mongolia to Lhasa in 1846. From the well-written and informative account of their travels, *Souvenirs d'un voyage dans la Tartarie et le Thibet** one gains a vivid impression of the distance between Peking and Lhasa, of the inevitable sense of isolation, so close to exile, felt by the Chinese who were stationed in Lhasa, contrasting so strongly with the warm friendliness of the Tibetans, who were genuinely pleased to receive foreign visitors and ask them about their religion and their homeland. Nevertheless they were treated with the greatest suspicion, and were thoroughly searched, especially for maps, which might so easily imply plans for foreign invasion. Despite the kindness received at the hands of the Regent himself, they were made well aware of the general Tibetan fear of foreign agents, and after some two months in the capital they were expelled under pressure from the Chinese and forced to make the fearful eight months' journey back the way they had come, instead of the so much easier one months' journey south to the Indian frontier, which was then regarded as closed.

The Administration This long period of guarded seclusion enabled the *dGe-lugs-pa* hierarchy to establish itself firmly in the Tibetan saddle. Chinese 'overlordship', by its mere guarantee of general stability, permitted the development of a new form of Tibetan government, entirely composed, it would seem, from the already existing Tibetan elements. The main force in Tibet was religion, as represented since the mid-seventeenth century by the *dGe-lugs-pa* order with its politically minded prelates, and secondly the ancient nobility and local hereditary rulers, who still held considerable power in their estates and domains. As a unifying force, religion, even of a single dominant religious order, was of primary importance, for it had its powerful representatives throughout the length and breadth of the country, who were united in many common interests, despite their occasional domestic disputes. With an external power ready to prevent armed discord, the *dGe-lugs-pa* order no longer needed to fight to preserve its primacy; the mere maintenance of the *status quo* was enough to ensure the continuance of the power and prestige which it had already acquired. This primacy was first achieved in the person of the fifth Dalai Lama during the seventeenth century, but it was not until the end of the seventh Dalai Lama's reign (1757) that the *dGe-lugs-pa* order, assisted by the *dGe-lugs-pa* nobility, became the established unifying power in the land.

Apart from the unfortunate period of the Gorkha invasion, no Dalai Lama since the 'Great Fifth' had exercised personal rule for more than a few months, and thus the incumbent became simply a symbol of power, by whose authority the regents and their ministers governed. To oppose the government in any way was to oppose the sanctity of his divine person, as represented by some great prelate of the *dGe-lugs-pa* 'church'. In practice the office of regent became almost the special preserve of the Incarnate Lamas of *Rva-sgreng* (Reting), *bsTan-rgyas-gling* (Ten-gye-ling) and *Tsho-mo-gling* (Tsho-mo-ling). The *dGe-lugs-pa* order with its tradition of learning and strict discipline had the makings of an effective bureaucracy, and with the increase in governmental responsibilities, this administrative potentiality was soon put to good use. There developed a whole class of monk officials, corresponding to the lay officials of noble family, who were employed in government service. In theory lay and monk officials had equal responsibilities in the administration of the country, but since the régime represented primarily the *dGe-lugs-pa* order, and all lay officials recognized the Dalai Lama and his Regent as their religious head, the 'church' in fact predominated.

The officials of the lay nobility who were beholden to the state in the person of the Dalai Lama, held their private estates in return for services rendered to the government. They provided a 'civil service' much as we understand the term, specially trained for their duties, not tied to any one function, and rising in position in accordance with seniority. This represents a very great change from the older nobility, where a chief held a territory by hereditary right, and he might normally expect the particular high office of state that he performed to become the inherited responsibility of his son. This older nobility continued to exist, especially in districts far from Lhasa, and they usually retained the local title of 'king' (*rgyal-po*). Very similar to them were the heads of the great monasteries, many non-*dGe-lugs-pa*, such as *Sa-skya*, where the grand lama would govern his estate with the same amount of local independence as the local 'kings'. They would acknowledge the Dalai Lama, represented by the Lhasa government, as overlord, and the amount of interference they might suffer would depend upon their relative strengths at any particular time. The greater part of inhabited Tibet, however, came to be administered by local governors, always appointed in pairs, usually one lay official and one monk official, directly responsible to the Lhasa government. They were properly part of the 'civil service' referred to above. How much the development of this system owed to the proddings of the Chinese, who were frequently at pains to reorganize the Tibetan administration and how much to the genius of *Pho-lha*, it is difficult to know. But in any event the whole structure suited the existing conditions so well that its elaboration must have been Tibetan. The support for the whole framework was provided, as always, by the peasants and the nomad-herdsmen, the fruits of whose labours maintained their superiors and the whole system of administration. It is important to realize, however, that no noble family held an estate without administrative responsibility, whether it provided hereditary local chiefs, or lay officials for the Lhasa administration. The *dGe-lugs-pa* monasteries also provided a small but steady flow of monk-officials, and these monk-officials themselves might hold private estates. Moreover a considerable administrative staff was required to maintain the great monasteries, and the manner of their operating can be roughly compared with that of a British university, composed of several well-endowed colleges. Quite clearly the monks were a large privileged body in Tibet, but they had their own particular responsibilities, duly acknowledged by the other members of Tibetan society.

It would be easy to point to abuses and injustices in the Tibetan system of government and administration, but as we well know, every system has these.

Perhaps they appear more obvious when authority remains decade after decade within the same limited circle, but at least in the Tibetan system it was clear for all to see who actually wielded the power and so to demand or engineer the removal of any official who acted with continuing injustice. (We have the recent case of a monk-official at *sKyid-grong*, appointed as usual for three years, but whose behaviour was so outrageous that within twelve months the people had protested to Lhasa and secured his replacement.) One would hardly expect to find in this Asian society the modern Western idea of service to one's fellow men as a kind of social duty. But one can find enlightened self-interest, and this is often the more practical ideal. An estate where the peasants are reasonably contented is likely to be a better paying concern than one where they are continually overtaxed and brutally treated, and the more permanent and personal the link between master and dependent, the more likely is the relationship to be a happy one. Thus an administrative change which involved increased responsibility by a central government and the appointing of local governor-officials on a short-term basis, probably was not a change for the better so far as the peasants were concerned.

Perhaps the worst effect of two centuries of *dGe-lugs-pa* administration, especially when combined with the complete closure of the country against any foreign ideas and influences, was the sense of power and self-sufficiency which developed in the large monk-bodies, especially in the monasteries of *dGa'-ldan* (Ganden), *Se-ra* and *'Bras-spungs* (Drepung). These came to dominate the whole administration of government, thus forming a kind of special *dGe-lugs-pa* power within a wider *dGe-lugs-pa* order. There is a marked change between the beginning of the eighteenth century, when Desideri could be freely received in their midst, and the first half of the twentieth century, when they would oppose any innovation which seemed to threaten their particular religious interests with the passionate conviction that they were doing right. We later see this powerful monk-body resisting changes desired by the Dalai Lama himself, and holding fiercely to all the special privileges that they have gained for themselves during the long period of *dGe-lugs-pa* rule.

Cultural Life A certain sterility is now apparent in Tibetan crafts, art-forms, literature, imagery and all the rest. But as the various things produced continue to be true to traditional form and always beautiful in themselves, one hesitates to make adverse comment on this score. But the question arises: what now becomes of Tibetan civilization? Does it continue to flourish, always in the same stereotyped forms, contrary to all we observe elsewhere in the history of civilizations? It is almost a general rule that when any culture becomes cut off from outside influences and ceases to develop new forms, it is already moribund. Is it possible that Tibetan Buddhist civilization was an exception? Although by the seventeenth century we already know almost its whole content, there seems no inherent reason why, left to itself, it should not have continued to live on as it lived until the mid-twentieth century. Good religious paintings in the accepted styles continued to be produced; books were still printed by the laborious but extremely skilful craft of carving wooden printing blocks; learned commentaries, mainly on philosophy and logic, were still written by masters for their pupils; texts and schools of teaching were analysed; catalogues of deities, teachers, images and temples were drawn up; sacred places were described as pilgrims' itineraries; new monasteries and temples were founded. Since works such as these continued right up to present times, it would be best to make this point by quoting examples in the following chapter (see page 245ff.).

Chinese influences upon Tibet during the eighteenth and nineteenth centuries were not profound or creative. It is true that they continued to affect the style of Tibetan religious painting and modes of interior decoration, especially in the homes of the wealthy, but all this was nothing new, and as we have observed above, these influences had already been absorbed creatively into styles which remained distinctively Tibetan (see page 157). The effects of closer Chinese contacts were apparent in such obvious matters as dress, insignia and decorations, in the increased use of Chinese porcelain, in the use of chop-sticks in upper circles, in the profusion of vases, incense-burners, jardinières, lion-figures, even lacquer bowls and screens, that appeared in the monasteries and in aristocratic homes. But all this remains entirely superficial to Tibetan culture as a living force, as superficial as the perfumes and make-up, the fountain-pens and Swiss watches, which thanks to the British contact began to adorn the members of higher Tibetan society during the twentieth century. Chinese cuisine began to be appreciated by the upper classes, and noodles (known in Tibetan as *rgya-thug*, 'Chinese soup') and small dumplings stuffed with spiced minced meat, known as *mo-mo* (the name is borrowed direct from Chinese) became the most popular of Tibetan party dishes. A whole range of new spices and delicacies were gradually introduced by those who could afford them, and the great houses would employ Chinese cooks, much as French chefs have been employed in Britain. But unlike tea-drinking, these foreign styles of eating remained luxuries for the most part, enjoyed by the not so wealthy only on special occasions, and by the great number of peasants and nomads scarcely at all.

Unfriendly Neighbours During the nineteenth century Tibet was involved in two foreign wars from which she emerged with varying fortunes. In a series of small but bitter campaigns the Dogras, an Indian tribe from Jammu, attacked and annexed Ladakh, which since 1647 had been in a loose tributary-trading relationship with Lhasa. This interrupted the regular and lucrative trade between Tibet and Ladakh. Then in 1841–2 the Dogras made two campaigns into Western Tibet. They were defeated and lost their great general Zorowar on the first attempt, but later they successfully counter-attacked, when the Tibetans ventured too far into Ladakh. As a result the trade between Lhasa and Leh (the capital of Ladakh) was restored, the Dogras taking the place of beneficiaries, which formerly belonged to the kings of Ladakh. Then in 1856 the Gorkhas invaded Tibet for a second time, and were only persuaded to leave in return for a long-term indemnity. Both these wars tended to emphasize the friendlessness of the Tibetans on their southern and now their western frontier, to which we have already referred above.

The last great event of the nineteenth century, which looks forward to the present one, was the accession of the thirteenth Dalai Lama, born in 1876 and receiving full power in 1895. He survived an attempt at assassination, for which his regent was condemned, and lived to be the only great Dalai Lama since the fifth who ordered the destiny of his country throughout the whole of his long life.

Chapter 9

The Twentieth Century

The British Intrusion During the nineteenth century the Tibetans had become deeply suspicious of any foreigners who wished to enter their land, and even a lama who had unwittingly helped a secret agent from India was put to death by drowning. They were particularly fearful of British encroachments, and while on the one side they were taking advantage of increasing Chinese weakness to make the imperial connection ever more of a fiction, they continued to hide behind it whenever it suited them. Thus they argued that they could have no direct dealings with the British, for this would be displeasing to their Chinese overlord. Over against this obscurantism the British in India were inspired by a typically Western respect for exact frontiers and precisely determined international relations, and by the quite understandable feeling that it was desirable to have friendly relations and regular trading arrangements with neighbours along so many hundreds of miles of effective frontier. Lacking reliable information and unable to communicate with those who were responsible for the government of Tibet, they sought to make agreements about Tibet with China, only to find that they were repudiated by the Tibetans. This impasse, rendered more acute by fears that while British overtures were being rejected, the Tibetans were accepting those of Russia, led eventually to the Younghusband expedition of 1904 and the signing of a treaty in Lhasa directly with the Tibetans. The British force, to the great surprise of the Tibetans, having obtained their treaty on trade-marts and fixed an indemnity (which they later reduced unilaterally to a third of their original demand), simply withdrew, expecting the provisions of the new agreement to be put into effect. But although some leading Tibetans had come to realize that their southern neighbours were not as ruthless as they had previously imagined, the development of closer understanding was interrupted for a time by the resurgence of Chinese activity in Tibet. This was made possible by the withdrawal of British influence and by a subsequent treaty between Britain and China.

The Dalai Lama had fled to Mongolia as the British advanced, and the Chinese agreed that he should be temporarily deprived of his powers; later, after he had visited Peking and received instructions, he was allowed to return to Lhasa, but in their eyes as a kind of vassal of China. Meanwhile a Chinese general, Chao Erh-fêng, having forcibly seized the eastern parts of Tibet, was planning to advance to Lhasa in order to establish the actual physical supremacy of China over the whole of Tibet. In 1910 his forces reached Lhasa, only to find that the Dalai Lama had fled, this time to India, together with his leading ministers.

Although the British had precipitated the trouble, they continued to look the other way, until the Chinese Revolution in 1911 enabled the Tibetans to shake off once and for all their now unwanted connection with the Manchus. We may note that the period between 1907 and the fall of the Manchu dynasty was the only time during which the Chinese tried to impose their authority on the Tibetans by force, and their attempt was bitterly resented. The new Chinese Republic still claimed to be overlord, but the Tibetans persistently and effectively rejected this claim. The British government was willing to take advantage of this situation in the interests of India's frontiers, and in 1914 they once again made an agreement with Tibet as equal partners. But in other respects they studiously refrained from committing themselves definitely to the principle of Tibetan independence.

From 1910 onwards when the Dalai Lama was an honoured guest in India, and especially after 1912 when he returned to Lhasa, relations between British and Tibetans, both on an official and unofficial level, became ever more friendly. The British refrained from establishing a representative in Lhasa, so long as the Chinese did not have one there as well, but the Trade Agency at Gyantse and all the other practical provisions of the 1904 agreement were now able to operate effectively.

All this initiated for us the slow process of understanding the workings of the Tibetan mind and the peculiarities of Tibetan civilization. Even before 1904 L. A. Waddell had been studying the nature of Tibetan religion, making good use of local informants in Darjeeling, and patiently accumulating a vast amount of information about rituals and charms, oracles and prayer-flags, serious religious beliefs and popular superstitions. His work, *The Buddhism of Tibet or Lamaism*, published in London in 1895, remains one of the 'classics' on Tibetan religious beliefs. Like the first Capuchins (see page 203), he noticed many similarities with Catholic practices even before he ever entered Tibet, and with a loathing for priestcraft, typical of many of his fellow-countrymen, he seems to have been as much appalled as fascinated by Tibetan religion. Unlike Desideri, it was very hard for him to see any good in an ecclesiastical order, which reminded him so vividly of the papacy. During 1904 he was able to travel in Central Tibet, and wrote good descriptive accounts of what he saw, but he never changed his opinion of Tibetan religion. From this time on there appeared several books, mainly by British officials, providing a good deal of first-hand information about Tibetan customs, attitudes and social behaviour. Just before the Younghusband expedition a remarkable Japanese monk, Ekai Kawaguchi, had succeeded in entering Tibet secretly, and he is the first to give a description of life in Lhasa at the turn of the twentieth century.* But soon several books, filled with useful information collected by British officials during their residence in Tibet, made their appearance, and Tibet ceased to be a strange unknown land. There is the account of the whole British expedition and everything connected with it by Younghusband himself (*India and Tibet*, London 1910), descriptions of Lhasa and parts of central Tibet by Waddell (*Lhasa and its Mysteries*, London 1905) and by Landon (*Lhasa*, also London 1905), but most important of all for first-hand reporting of the Tibetan scene and the Tibetan people were the later works of Sir Charles Bell, who had long personal contacts with many Tibetans including the thirteenth Dalai Lama in particular, and since he also mastered one important Tibetan historical work, the *Blue Annals*, he may be said to have written the first cultural history of Tibet.†

But the main function of the new relationship between Tibet and India was not academic research. The Tibetans, like the British, were primarily interested in trade. This had the rapid effect of producing a prosperous Tibetan middle class of traders, and Indian border towns, such as Kalimpong in particular, became a second home for them. The railway from Calcutta to Siliguri, and the roads from there to Darjeeling, Kalimpong and Gangtok, provided a far more effective trade-route than the ancient one that passed through Pātan and Kathmandu with no railway available until one reached the Nepal-Indian frontier. The great bulk of Tibetan trade southwards was very soon drawn to the new route. The chief Tibetan export was, as always, wool, and in return a whole variety of desirable things entered Tibet – cotton cloth, kerosene, hardware, sugar, soap and matches; British broadcloth was greatly prized, and British hats, especially the trilby. So important was the new trade-route with India that even the Chinese trade with Tibet began to be partly diverted to sea-routes, far preferable to the months of hard and hazardous travel with pack-animals across the wilds of north-west China and eastern Tibet. Thus Kalimpong became a market not only for Indian and Tibetan goods, but for brick-tea from China specially packed for the Tibetan traders, and for Chinese brocades and porcelain. Attempts were made to win the Tibetans over to India tea, though without success, but harsh aniline dyes began unhappily to replace the indigenous vegetable and mineral dyes which hitherto had been used invariably in Tibetan weaving and carpet making, while Tibetan ladies, always addicted to cosmetics, took in due course to the products of Coty and Dior.

We referred above to the generally rather superficial character of Chinese cultural influences. A few material things, such as tea, and to a lesser extent silk and porcelain, have penetrated into normal Tibetan life, but almost everything else has simply served for the adornment of a few monasteries and noble houses. The one important craft learned from China had been that of block-printing, but this and Chinese landscape motifs in Tibetan religious painting have already been mentioned. There has been no Tibetan interest in Chinese religion, philosophy and literature, or even in Chinese painting for its own sake; their interest in Chinese medicine seems to have been limited to the practical application of certain remedies and drugs, without their making any effort to absorb and reinterpret the theories upon which the practices were based. There is an extraordinary pragmatism in their approach to new things (if they decide to approach them at all), which might seem to be completely at variance with the mystical and philosophical preoccupations of their religious life. With the British, too, they showed the same pragmatic attitudes, adopting a few practices in a superficial manner, without really absorbing them into their own culture. When the British agreed to supply them with a limited quantity of modern armaments in the early nineteen-twenties, they were anxious to possess the new weapons, but without being greatly interested in the theory of their use. There remains always this remarkable difference between the Tibetans' approach to the Indians and to the Nepalese, when they were interested in Buddhist religion, and their approach to any other people and culture with which they have since come into contact. As we have already illustrated in the previous chapters, where Buddhist theories and practices were concerned, no effort or cost seemed too much. Judging alone by the way in which they created a whole new vocabulary, one might assume that Tibetans are expert linguists, and so they were for this one purpose. Judging by their skill in mastering complicated techniques of *yoga* and their profound knowledge of the workings of the human mind, one might assume that Tibetans are good psychologists, and so they are, for the one purpose of practising Buddhist religion. But in their practical dealings with both Chinese and British they failed consistently to understand the other's thought, and what is more, they seemed unaware of any need to try to understand. The great miracle of Tibetan civilization was the zeal and competence which they showed for Indian Buddhism in all its varied forms. It has remained throughout their history the one pearl of great price for which they seem to have sacrificed everything else, even their independence as a nation.

The Monks Since the mid-eighteenth century the *dGe-lugs-pa* Order was in control of the government and the administration of the whole of Tibet, but except for a very few years no Dalai Lama exercised any personal authority. As we have observed already, the ninth, tenth, eleventh and twelfth Dalai Lamas all died very young. Thus the country was ruled by a regent (acting for the Dalai Lama) through a monastic bureaucracy, whose main concern (like bureaucracies elsewhere in the world) was the maintenance of its own power and prestige. The centre of its power was Lhasa, where it was overshadowed by the three monasteries of *dGa'-ldan* (Ganden), *Se-ra* and *'Bras-spungs* (Drepung). *'Bras-spungs* was already in the time of the fifth Dalai Lama the largest monastery in Tibet, with its 1,500 monks. In the twentieth century it was still the largest, but with at least 8,000, and together these three great monasteries housed more than 20,000 monks. They were therefore incontrovertible by sheer weight of numbers. This situation was special to Lhasa, and one has to bear in mind that in many ways these three monastic establishments, whose power, owing to difficulty of communications, was in practice limited to the Lhasa area, were not typical of the religious life of the country. Nevertheless since political decisions were made in Lhasa, the Tibetan government could not dare to risk their displeasure in domestic and foreign affairs. At the same time it would be a mistake to think that the great prelates were primarily concerned with political matters, manipulating them with Machiavellian subtlety. So far as the outside world was concerned, it would be fairer to regard them as ignorant and rather naïve. As for their internal affairs, they conducted these for the most part with efficiency and decorum, maintaining high standards of scholarship by traditional Tibetan standards, which were still those of the great Buddhist monastic universities of India of a thousand years ago. The main subject of their studies was 'logical philosophy' (*mtshan-nyid*) as applied to the five main branches of non-tantric canonical literature, namely logic (*tshad-ma*), the doctrine of 'universal emptiness' known as the 'Perfection of Wisdom' (*phar-phyin*), the doctrine of the 'Middle Way' (*dBu-ma*) as taught by *Nāgārjuna* and his successors, the 'Treasury of Philosophical Notions' (*mngon-chos-mdzod*=Sanskrit *Abhidharmakośa*) and 'Monastic Discipline' (*'dul-ba*). One's competence in these five branches of literature was tested by means of formal debating, and thus as a course of study they are all comprised under the general subject of 'logical philosophy', which provided the method for arguing one's points. The *dGe-lugs-pas* had been responsible for two reforms of the monastic life, a return to stricter discipline and the reinstating of the scholastic tradition, but with all the extraordinary developments which had taken place since the time of *Tsong-kha-pa*, it was no longer practicable for most monks to be scholars, even if they had been so inclined, and with such a vast increase in numbers as well as material wealth, it was impossible that all should be well disciplined. Monks came from every rank of society and they represented every kind of disposition and propensity. A monastery of 5,000 to 8,000 monks required as much administration as a small town, and there were almost as many varieties of occupation. Apart from occasional help with the harvest, monks did not work the land or herd cattle, but some of their number were responsible for supervising the peasants and nomads, who belonged to their estates, while others were responsible for business and trade. The provision of tea, butter, *tsam-pa* and other items of general consumption demanded continual labour on the part of some bodies of monks, while the temples required regular attention and material needs had to be catered for. It was impossible that such an establishment should be enclosed like Western monasteries in the twentieth century. The monks were not cut off from the life of the land; rather they tended to influence it in all its various departments. While the great prelates controlled the government, insignificant monks might be running a prosperous restaurant. Unless you were a serious monk with a good teacher to watch over you, you might come and go much as you pleased, for permission for outside excursions was easily obtained.

To explain how the great monasteries were ordered and administered would be as complicated as explaining the differencies between the Universities of Oxford and Cambridge in all their various activities, but a brief general description may help to remove the false impression that a 'monk' is necessarily a man of religion any more than the inmates of European universities such as Oxford, Cambridge and Paris were all necessarily serious scholars three or four hundred years ago. The great monasteries were each divided into colleges (*grva-tshang*) of unequal strengths. Thus *'Bras-spungs* (Drepung) had four colleges, one with about 5,000 monks, one with 3,000 and two with about 300 each. *Se-ra* had three colleges, and *dGa'-ldan* (Ganden) just two. Each college consisted of a number of 'houses' (*kham-tshan*); for instance the largest college of *'Bras-spungs* had twenty-three houses. These houses were of varying size, some with as many as 700 monks, some with only 150, but whatever its size, the house was the basic unit. If one wanted to become a monk, one had to apply to the chief teacher of the house of one's choice, much as one might apply to an Oxford or Cambridge college. A novice was put in charge of an older monk, who might have as many as seven novices at a time, especially just before the New Year ceremonies, when with the prospect of offerings and gifts on a vast scale, large numbers of 'would-be' monks used to present themselves. The ease with which a new monk was taken on, even in these *dGe-lugs-pa* establishments with their supposedly strict discipline, is noteworthy. Having become a monk, often at the age of five or younger, one's life and future, depended entirely upon one's own aspirations and the company one kept. In every college there would be those who were 'scholars' (*dpe-cha-ba*) and those who were ordinary monks, but again the numbers were variable. The 'scholars' were usually well disciplined and correspond more or less to what our readers would expect a monk to be. Also many of the 'lay-brethren' would be sufficiently well behaved, but since their duties often took them into the town and sometimes far away on trading ventures, their way of life could scarcely be described as monastic. All *dGe-lugs-pa* monasteries and most monasteries of the older orders may be said to show this primary distinction between 'scholars' and ordinary monks, because both groups are necessary to the life of a religious community, and here (with many reservations) one might quote as a parallel the distinction between choir-monks and lay-brethren in Christian monasteries.

In most monasteries, whether large or small, about half the monks were 'scholars', but this term has a very different meaning from that which we give to it nowadays in the West. The subjects of study were the five branches of non-canonical literature as listed above (page 237), followed sometimes by special tantric studies. In the major *dGe-lugs-pa* establishments, especially the Three Great Monasteries around Lhasa and also in *bKra-shis-lhun-po* (Tashilhunpo), the main emphasis was on learning by rote to such an extent that writing and note-taking were discouraged when not actually forbidden. Learning to write and compose good Tibetan was regarded as the work of clerks and officials, and so positively harmful to the acquisition of true religious knowledge. Serious studies in the colleges of the great Lhasa monasteries might begin for a young scholar of the age of fifteen or sixteen and continue for a minimum period of thirteen years, for there were thirteen classes through which he passed upwards year by year. There might be delay in taking one's final examinations, for the numbers who could present themselves each year at *Norbu Lingka*, where the examinations were held, were limited to few more than twenty. Examinations were entirely oral, taking the form of conventionalized debates, and successful candidates would have to display an extraordinary knowledge both of doctrines and of the relevant texts, from which they would quote with precision and great verbal accuracy. In the course of their years of training they would have learned by heart considerable quantities of sacred literature, so that they became, as it were, repositories of the doctrine, able to produce from their store any text or quotation which served the immediate argument. It is noteworthy that despite the existence of a well-established written language, such a tradition of oral scholarship, clearly based on ancient Indian styles, should have continued right into the mid-twentieth century. But at the end of their long training some of these highly expert 'scholars' might be unable even to write their own name properly, however well they might read. It was as though all their concentrated effort went into absorbing texts for oral reproduction only.

However, other monasteries apart from the major *dGe-lugs-pa* establishments maintained a better balance between reading and learning by rote on the one hand and written reproduction of texts and even composition on the other. In these monasteries the highest degree of 'geshey' (*dGe-bshes*) might be gained in five or six years, and the course represented a far more general kind of literary education (always within the limits of the five branches of study listed above) than the highly specialized skills of philosophical debating for which the great Lhasa monasteries were famous. Thus many scholars, having completed their studies in their own local monasteries, would go on to Lhasa to follow the courses there. They might come already well equipped academically and it would often be the best of such as these who became famous teachers and writers, of the kind we have often referred to above. Having completed their training and received the Lhasa degree of 'geshey', to which the special title of *lha-ram-pa* was given, they might return as teachers to their own monasteries, receive one of the many appointments in the great Lhasa monasteries, or take up special tantric studies at the two Lhasa colleges specially concerned with these, known as the *rGyud-stog-pa* and the *rGyud-smad-pa*. Here they would concentrate on studies of ritual, including both liturgy and the arrangement of symbolic offerings, especially as relevant to the 'mystic circles' (*maṇḍala*) of the great tantric divinities. Thereafter the same kind of openings would exist as before, but with greater possibilities, or in some cases a scholar might retire for several years for quiet meditation and reading, or for writing, if he was one of the few equipped to produce literary compositions. Education of this kind inevitably remained an entirely monastic pursuit, in which the layfolk could have no possible share. Even the reading of Tibetan historical and biographical literature lay outside the monastic curriculum, and it has become in effect the special preserve of well-educated aristocrats and officials. Thus one can imagine how difficult it is for the Tibetans in exile suddenly to produce qualified teachers capable of teaching in a twentieth-century context, now that they have suddenly been forced willy-nilly into coping with modern ways.

The great monasteries around Lhasa possessed, as an extraordinary exception, a special category of monks, drawn from the ranks of the 'lay-brethren'. These were nicknamed 'dop-dop' (*ldab-ldob*), a term which possibly means 'the swanks'. With rather more knowledge than we possess of conditions in old European universities, perhaps German ones in particular, one might find parallels to these 'dop-dop' groups in some of our more aggressive student fraternities. The 'dop-dop' existed as self-constituted groups within the colleges (*grva-tshang*), choosing their own leaders and co-opting their new members. Any tough and good-looking novice, who joined the college, would be likely to be recruited by them, especially if he were not academically gifted and lacked a tutor who was concerned for his welfare. They performed their regular monastic duties like any other 'lay-brethren', but they operated strictly as an enclosed fraternity. An insult to one of them from an outsider, whether an individual or a member of a 'dop-dop' group of another college, might lead to serious retaliation from the group as a whole. It was easy therefore for traditional feuds to develop between different groups of 'dop-dop', resulting in small organized skirmishes and sometimes in duels between individuals. Any 'dop-dop' apprehended by the monastic authorities for such lawless conduct would be liable, at least in theory, to serious punishment, but since many of the senior administrative posts in a college might be occupied by older 'dop-dop', it was often possible to avoid all penalty. Thus in '*Bras-spungs* for example, each college had two chief 'disciplinarians' (*dge-skos*) rather like the proctors of our ancient universities; they were appointed for six months at a time, and regularly chosen from amongst the 'scholars' for the six summer months, and from the 'lay-brethren' for the six winter months. Due to pressures that they could bring to bear as a group, the lay-brother disciplinarians would often be 'dop-dop', and during their period of office the group-members would enjoy far greater licence. Even a 'dop-dop' known to be guilty of having killed a fellow-monk in a duel would escape punishment, for the duel was secret and none of his brethren would bear witness against him. If the crime occurred during the office of the 'scholar-disciplinarians', it would be wise for the killer to keep away from the monastery until the next change in the rota, and thereafter he might rejoin his community just as before. Like other fraternities the 'dop-dop' had their own code of honour and their own particular virtues. On the better side they were characterized not only by generosity within their own group, but often by light-hearted, almost reckless, charity to those in great material need, the beggars and the poor. Moreover as their blood cooled with age, and Tibetans age very young, or at least think they do, many of them would settle down to the single-minded practice of religion, not necessarily the book-religion of the scholars, for which, at least in their youth, they would express contempt, but the true religion of the heart, best known to us in Christianity perhaps from the practice of simple unlearned Russian monks. The extraordinary thing about the 'dop-dop' is how with their own special *esprit de corps*, their own distinctive hair-style and personal ornamentation, and their often quite outrageous conduct, they nevertheless had their recognized place within the general body-politic of the great Lhasa monasteries. Their uses and their virtues were clearly recognized by those in authority, even by the 'scholars', and so their strange misdemeanours might wherever possible be overlooked. Out of a total monk population of over 20,000 in the Lhasa district, the 'dop-dop' must have numbered several thousands, and this is some force to be reckoned with by any government which possesses no regular military or police force of its own. But most of the time they would go peaceably about their duties, blowing the shawms and long trumpets, carrying processional banners and awnings, or serving tea during the long monastic ceremonies, while outside the monasteries they would earn money by helping with the harvesting, or with the plastering of houses, or even by acting as private guards in noble families who had need of special protection. They were also in demand for their sports displays, high jumping, long jumping and stone-throwing, and at the request of nobles or wealthier monks they would put on a show in return for generous entertaining. Thus these 'dop-dop', of whom it would be so easy to write nothing but ill, played a significant part in religious and lay affairs, and if they looked fierce and hostile when the British appeared in strength in 1904, they were merely giving frank expression to the feelings of the monks generally and probably most layfolk as well.

It seems almost impossible that Tibetans and Westerners, represented primarily by the British, should have understood one another. The negotiation of the 1904 treaty was the first occasion when these two parties, whose basic ways of thinking were so different, confronted one another with the need to work out practical solutions acceptable to both sides. It is to the lasting credit of the *Khri Rin-po-che* (the Enthroned of Ganden), who had been left in charge by the Dalai Lama when he left for Mongolia, and of Younghusband, that on the basis of so much mutual miscomprehension, inevitable in the circumstances, they should have established such close relations of mutual trust and respect.

The treaty of 1904 between British India and Tibet represented the first Tibetan lesson in the Western concept of international law, and they must be pardoned if this lesson was not easy to understand; within a few years of their signing the treaty it was changed in the interests of a third party, without their even being consulted, let alone giving their consent. Meanwhile obstructions on the Indian-Tibet frontier continued just as before, but this time it was the Chinese and not the Tibetans who were responsible. All that came out of the Younghusband Expedition was the opportunity for establishing friendly relations between the individual British and Tibetan officials who had dealings with one another. When a few years later the Tibetans found themselves at serious enmity with China, it was to the British that they turned for sympathy and support. Thus the Dalai Lama spent two years of exile in India, until revolution in China made it easy for his people to drive the unwanted Chinese from Tibet.

The Dalai Lama returned to Tibet in 1912 with several problems to solve. Desultory war continued with China on the eastern frontier, and the British seemed equivocal in their dealings with his country. He was also the first Dalai Lama for about 150 years to assume personal control of the government, and he had to come to terms with a well-established bureaucracy, and with the twenty thousand monks who lived in the vicinity of his capital. His position was very different from that of the great fifth Dalai Lama, who was really a power unto himself. Given similar freedom of policy and action the thirteenth Dalai Lama might have led his country into closer relations with the British and thus towards general recognition by other countries of Tibet's effective independent status. In the early 1920s, thanks to the exertions of Sir Charles Bell, closer relations were established between the British and Tibetan governments, but by then the initiative had already been lost and new problems faced Tibet. Relations with the Nepal of the Gorkhas continued to be hostile, and in 1922 there very nearly occurred a third war between Tibet and this belligerent neighbour. Internally there were constant misunderstandings and recriminations between the Dalai Lama's government and the administration of the *Pan-chen* Lama at *bKra-shis-lhun-po* (see page 220), and these finally led to the *Pan-chen* Lama's flight to China in 1923, whence he never returned. The Dalai Lama could not show that friendship with the British had brought great practical advantages to Tibet, and above all there had been no settlement with the Chinese.

The monks, and most other Tibetans for that matter, can have had little comprehension of the great changes which were taking place in China. They remembered the generous benefactions of the Manchus to their monasteries, which were still adorned with all the signs of Chinese munificence. It was not only a matter of bronze incense burners, silk hangings and gilded canopies, although things of this kind were impressive enough; whole monasteries at Lhasa, such as *Kun-bde-gling*, *bsTan-rgyas-gling* and *Tsho-mo-gling*, had been built up into wealthy and resplendent establishments. Lay officials too had shared in the judiciously applied bounty of the emperor, for the occasion of an annual parade had been used for the distribution of large presents of silver and silk. Even the servants of officials could be dressed in silk on ceremonial occasions. Chinese distinctions of rank had been imported in the form of different ornaments, patterns of brocade, buttons of office and peacock-feathers. Grant of rewards had even been extended to the sacred images in the temples: a peacock's feather and button of the first rank had been awarded to the image of *Padmasambhava* at *rGya-mda'*, when the emperor heard that a famine had been averted through his power, while over the entrances of many monasteries there hung large ornate painted panels with inscriptions in gilded Chinese characters. It is true that since the death of Ch'ien Lung, their chief benefactor, there had been considerable diminution of such gifts, and since 1911 there was not even an emperor. But despite the recent fighting, which after all was taking place a long way from Lhasa, the Chinese in the person of the emperor were still remembered as benefactors of Tibet's holy religion.

On the other hand, it might well have appeared to Tibetans that, although the British had given shelter and help to the Dalai Lama in exile, their support since his return was less than had been hoped; in particular they had failed to bring about a political settlement with China. Moreover the danger to established customs and monastic authority which might result from contact with a foreign power became apparent in the innovations which followed the visit of Sir Charles Bell to Lhasa in 1921. The formation of a modern army and police force had in fact been used by the Dalai Lama as a direct threat to monkish independence. Education at the new English school in Gyantse, which was opened in 1924, might also in time subvert established religious authority. Further warning of the dangers of change and new ideas may have been seen in recent events in Mongolia, where in 1924 a republic had been declared on the death of the Grand Lama of Urga, who reincarnated no more. There was no knowing whether British methods might not lead to the same sort of result. So monastic opinion began to exert itself more strongly on the Dalai Lama. He too was by now disappointed at the failure to reach agreement with China, for on this rested his hopes for the stable independence of Tibet. He had never broken off all contact with China, which was still visited from time to time by high monk dignitaries, and while always stubbornly resisting Chinese attempts to impinge upon his independence, he may have been susceptible to suggestions that perhaps the British were acquiring too dominant a position over him. At all events he yielded to criticism of his modernizing tendency, closed the school at Gyantse which had already achieved remarkable results in the space of two years, allowed the army and police force to deteriorate, and introduced an aloof note into his correspondence with the Political Officer in Sikkim, who was responsible under the British Indian government for Tibetan affairs.

This attitude changed appreciably in 1932 when after twenty years of military success in eastern Tibet, things went for a time against the Tibetans. The Dalai Lama sought a *rapprochement* with his Indian neighbours, but although he was anxious to receive fresh supplies of arms and ammunition and even sent a few non-commissioned officers for training at Gyantse, he never again showed any zeal for Western innovations; nor did those lay nobles who would have been glad to send their sons to India for education, venture to do so during his lifetime.

The Dalai Lama's interest in modernization had been aimed principally at bringing Tibet into a condition where it could hold its own against others. When he found that monastic opinion was against even the limited measures he introduced, he was content to adopt a policy, which he expounded in his 'last testament', of seeking to maintain a state of balance between his two powerful neighbours. He can hardly be blamed for assuming that it would be possible to continue Tibet's foreign relations in this way for an indefinite period, or for failing to foresee that within a generation China would prove a far more ruthless innovator than ever the British could have been, even if they had aspired to govern

Tibet. Even if he had possessed such vision, it would have taken more than a gift of prophecy to shake monastic conservatism, and so the opportunity which was open after 1914 of bringing Tibet into closer contact with the outside world was lost. This may seem to us to have been the last hope for Tibet to establish her national identity and to find fresh sources of inspiration for her culture. But in the complex of historical and cultural circumstances reviewed in this book, it was not possible for the Dalai Lama and his advisers to see things in this way. Thus the door which had begun to open was once again pushed to; and time was running out.

Meanwhile life in the monasteries continued just as before. Since the time of the fifth Dalai Lama *dGe-lugs-pa* scholars continued to write whole successions of commentaries, mainly on their favourite subject, logical philosophy (*mtshan-nyid*). After the writings of the Great Fifth and his Regent *Sangs-rgyas rGya-mtsho*, they showed little interest in history, but an exception was *Sum-pa mKhan-po* (1704-86) who produced not only a large-scale historical work, but also a short account of his homeland in the 'Annals of the Kokonor'. All the *Pan-chen* Lamas were prolific writers, and there are many other famous names, such as *Klong-rdol* Lama, '*Jam-dbyangs-bshad-pa* and many others.

The last named was the founder of the great monastery of *Bla-brang* (see page 199), where his writings were used as prescribed texts right up to 1950. Among his successors there were many notable scholars, all producing their commentaries in the same rather stereotyped style. A contemporary writer of this school is *lHa-mo Tshul-khrim*, whose works were well known even in the great Lhasa monasteries. In Lhasa each college would have its own traditionally prescribed texts, such as those of *bSod-nams Grags-pa*, who was abbot of one of the '*Bras-spungs* (Drepung) colleges at the beginning of the seventeenth century. His works were studied not only in his own college, but also in *Se-ra* and *dGa'-ldan*.

It may be healthy to mention some literary rebels and innovators, if only to indicate that a few exist. *rDo-yul Shes-rab*, a favourite of the thirteenth Dalai Lama, was later banished, and he went to China where he recently became president of the Chinese Buddhist Association. He is said to have translated *Tsong-kha-pa*'s *Lam-rim* ('Survey of the Doctrine') into Chinese. A pupil of his, *dGe-'dun Chos-'phel*, who came to '*Bras-spungs* from *Bla-brang*, even wrote a treatise against the *dGe-lugs-pa* philosophical position, entitled 'The Ornament of *Nāgārjuna*'s Thought' (*Klu-sgrub-dgongs-rgyan*). He also wrote a history of the kings of Tibet, *Deb-ther dKar-po*, and while in India he translated the *Kāma-sūtra* into Tibetan. Later he was involved in political as well as literary disputes with the *dGe-lugs-pa* hierarchy, and he died in Lhasa about 1950.

All the other religious orders have produced their own scholars and writers, and we cannot pretend to knowledge of them all. Among *rNying-ma-pa* lamas, who claim to represent the oldest Buddhist traditions in Tibet, we might mention *sDe-dge Mi-pham*, who wrote a large number of commentaries, including one on a work well known to European scholars, the *Bodhicāryāvatāra* ('Entry of the Course towards Enlightenment'), and also *O-rgyan 'Jigs-med chos kyi dbang-po* who wrote the *Kun-bzang Bla-ma'i Zhal-lung* with its pleasing stories and anecdotes, the sort of writing in which Tibetans really excel, when they can escape from their more usual dry scholasticism. Both these lamas lived in the nineteenth century. The present *bDud-'joms Rin-po-che*, now an exile in India, has just written and published 'A History of the *rNying-ma* Order' in Kalimpong. It is important to realize perhaps that Tibetan literary activities have not been stopped entirely by the recent Communist occupation of the country, and they are still actively engaged in printing their 'established' works.

Among *Bon-pos* we should mention *Zla-ba rGyal-mtshan*, an Abbot of *sMan-ri* (see page 173), who founded the neighbouring monastery of *gYung-drung-gling* in the mid-nineteenth century. Then there was *bKra-shis rGyal-mtshan* of *Khams*, who produced fifteen volumes of works, including a history of *Bon*. He lived the life of a hermit, and when he died some forty years ago, he is supposed to have disappeared leaving no mortal remains behind. Such lamas are known as 'rainbow-bodies' (*'ja'-lus-pa*). Only the *Bon-pos* and the older orders make such claims, for the *dGe-lugs-pas* are more prosaic in their religious practice.

A feature of Tibetan religious life, often mentioned by travellers and usually miscalled a 'devil dance', is the ritual mystery drama known as *'Cham*. Unlike the *a-che lha-mo* (see page 258), which combines an element of entertainment with religious instruction conveyed by a moral tale, *'Cham* is a solemn performance by trained monk dancers, acting the role of various divinities, as constructively imagined in meditation upon their conventional forms. Most, but not all, of the manifestations are helped by the wearing of awesome masks, usually of the 'oath-bound' protectors of the doctrine (see page 109), and the fierce forms of their entourage. Each movement and gesture of the dance, which is accompanied by the music of long trumpets, shawms, drums and cymbals, follows a strictly ordained symbolism. Tibetans believe that this form of religious dance originated in India, and this is confirmed by religious dances of a similar kind which may still be performed within some of the old temple-precincts of Nepal. However, the Tibetan styles, which are far more complex and widespread, have been developed according to local needs and interests.

The primary function of *'Cham* seems to be the physical manifestation of the great protecting divinities, who have already been invoked and propitiated during preceding ceremonies which may have lasted two or three days. The choice of divinities invoked will depend, as always, upon the particular religious order and the particular monastery, for everyone normally adheres to his own tutelary divinities. The action of the manifested divinities in this ritual dance is directed towards the overpowering and expulsion of evil, usually represented by a small sacrificial model of a human body, known as the *linga* or 'sign'. Having imbued its 'life-force', the dancing performers ritually slay and dismember the human effigy, thus performing a kind of general exorcism of evil for the whole community which sponsors the rite.* Most monasteries have a yearly performance of this rite of 'renewal', while it was regularly performed on a national level for the great New Year festival in Lhasa, known as the 'Great Prayer' (see page 181).

A whole variety of subsidiary dances, some didactic and some pure entertainment, have been added gradually as a kind of supporting programme. There is a dance recorded which represents the slaying of *Glang-dar-ma*, the apostate persecutor of Buddhism, another acting a well-known story of *Mi-la Ras-pa* and the huntsman; there is a skeleton-dance of the 'Lord of the Cemetery', and another of 'Indian Teachers' (Sanskrit *ācarya* corrupted into *a-tsa-ra* in Tibetan) who seem to appear rather in the role of clowns, an interesting commentary perhaps on the way these former masters of Buddhist doctrine were regarded by most Tibetans, for such a view of them is completely at variance with the accounts given of them in the *Blue Annals* and other religious histories. Although a performance of '*Cham* is always essentially a serious ritual for those who know its meaning, for the villagers and visiting herdsmen who throng the temples and surrounding courtyards it serves mainly perhaps as an impressive and colourful spectacle, which helps to brighten their lives. Holy days are also holidays, and while monks and religious-minded laymen take part in the ceremonies inside the temples, layfolk may be happily performing their own non-religious dances just outside the temple precincts. At least this seems to be the usual pattern of events at the many small monasteries in country districts.

Apart from a number of very large monasteries, such as the 'Big Three' around Lhasa, the *Pan-chen* Lama's monastery of *bKra-shis-lhun-po* (Tashilhunpo), *sKu-'bum* and *Bla-brang* in Khams, the famous *Sa-skya-pa* monastery of *sDe-dge*, the main *Sa-skya* estate, and some medium-sized monasteries with five hundred monks or so, other Tibetan monasteries were comparatively small with fifty to two hundred monks, and often far less. These small communities possessed little or no land and depended for their existence mainly on the families whose members were actually monks. Thus most monasteries developed in close relationship with nearby villages, providing for the religious, educational and in large part the cultural needs of the community. Monks and layfolk lived in such close association, joining in so many activities together, that it completely falsifies the real nature of Tibetan society if one sets monks in opposition to layfolk, as Communist apologists have tried to do (pages 126 and 127).

The Laymen Just as in the monasteries, so in the villages, the passing of the years was scarcely noticed. The land was still worked by wooden ploughs drawn by a pair of dzo (crossbreed of a bull and a *'bri*, female of the yak), or in some places by a line of men with long-handled, long-bladed spades. The crops were cut with a short reaping hook and taken to the threshing-ground on the backs of donkeys; threshing was done with wooden flails or by driving cattle round and round over the sheaves; and the grain was winnowed by the wind as it dropped from basket-work scoops (pages 162–3). There were no wheeled vehicles in the country until early in the 20th century, and no revolving mechanism except for water-mills (used for turning prayer-wheels as well as for grinding) and pedal-worked lathes.*

Some signs of the expanding trade with India might be seen: an aluminium cooking pot, coloured Chinese prints of seductive girls, often on bicycles, a cheap clock from India perhaps or some gaudy Japanese brocade over the seat of honour, and very rarely even a kerosene lantern; nowhere would there be glass in the windows. Every house had its prayer-flags, wafting skywards their spells of good fortune, and its cluster of long sticks next to the incense burners on the roof. Over the doors of some houses might be seen realistic phallic symbols to ward off ill luck. These survivals of pre-Buddhist superstitions existed even at Lhasa on the wall surrounding the summer palace of the Dalai Lama and under a small canopy on the roof of the Cathedral (*Jo-khang*) itself. In a few remote villages there still stood grotesque wooden images, known as 'tom-be', and serving as local protectors, but seemingly receiving little attention (page 166).

The tempo of life was easy, but the young Tibetan began to learn his work at an early age. Young boys were sent off in charge of sheep or yak, and might live with them on the high grazing grounds for days at a time with only a sling and a dog to protect themselves and their flocks and herds from wolves and leopards. Even the girls might go with the animals, when they were considered old enough, but it is more likely they would go and help in the fields, if there was work to be done there. Father might go off with his donkeys on a job of porterage, while mother would milk the three or four family cows, or settle down to her weaving. Amusements were few and simple: visits to the local temple added some colour and awe to life, and there would be happy and spontaneous singing and dancing wherever there were local festivals and ceremonies. In the middle of the fields there would be a white stone dedicated to the local water-sprites (*klu*), and the crops might be blessed by a *Bon-po* priest as well as by a Buddhist monk. There

Temple-banners and artefacts

Carved Tibetan wooden book-covers

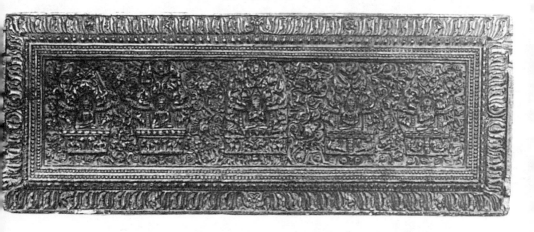

Temple-banner illustrating *Padmasambhava* in his paradise known as the 'Glorious Copper-coloured Mountain' (*zangs-mdog dpal-ri*) (*opposite*) Temple-banner illustrating *Śākyamuni* before he abandoned his princely life. An eighteenth-century painting perhaps, and showing distinct Chinese influence (see page 157)

Temple-banner of the 'Lord of Death' (*gShin-rje* skr. *Yama*) with his female partner and attendant demons

Temple-banner illustrating the Dolpo lama *bSod-nams dbang-phyug* and events from his life (see page 197). It was painted in Dolpo in 1961

Temple-banner illustrating a pilgrimage to an unidentified *stūpa* and surrounding holy places. It seems to be a site sacred to *Mi-la Ras-pa* near the Nepalese border

'Lords of the Cemetery' (*Dur-khrod bdag-po*) performing a macabre dance over a human corpse

Image of the great tantric divinity, the 'Destroyer of Death' ('*Chi-bdag 'joms-pa* skr. *Yamāntaka*) clasping his female partner (*below*) The 'Lion-headed Goddess' (*gSeng-ge gDong-ma*) who plays a leading part in rituals

The gentle goddess known as the 'Saviouress' (*sGrol-ma* skr. *Tārā*), the most popular of feminine divinities (*below*) The 'oath-bound' (*dam-can*) protector of the doctrine *rDo-rje Legs-pa*

Section of Tibetan carpet: dragon and bird designs

A silver bowl, presumably of Central Asian origin, which was brought out of Tibet about 1950. The Greco-Bactrian figures, the Indian tree-motif, and on the base the Chinese fish design represent three distinct spheres of ancient culture around Tibet's borders

would be a yearly procession round the village, carrying sacred texts, in order to ensure a good harvest, but few villagers would be able to read them. Most houses would have a few religious books kept respectfully, sometimes in special racks around the images in the best room, which was arranged for use as a little chapel. Reading the sacred texts and reciting prayers would be a task for a mendicant monk or for one invited specially from the local monastery (page 123). In any case there would not be much light for reading from the mustard-oil lamp when the day's work was done. Keeping the accounts of the villagers' dues and payments was the responsibility of the village-headman, and this he would be quite capable of doing.

Sometimes villagers and nomads would find the occasion for making long pilgrimages to holy places (pages 124-5). Then they would offer butter-lamps and burn incense before the temple images and make repeated circumambulations of the sacred buildings. Both monks and laymen might make large numbers of prostrations before certain images or in the process of their circumambulations, counting religiously on their beads the full complement they had vowed to perform. Anyone so inclined might make special offerings to a whole community of monks in payment for the performance of a particular ceremony. This might involve simply the reading of sacred texts, for example some of the 'Perfection of Wisdom' literature, or the complex performance of an 'after-death' ceremony for the benefit of a deceased relative or friend.* The most common kind of general offering to a community of monks was the *mang-ja*, the 'general tea ceremony', when the benefactor would offer tea and possibly other refreshments to a whole community and often also a separate gift of money to each monk in return for a general recitation of texts and prayers on behalf of his family. The main intention of all such religious activities is the building up of merit, which will counteract the effects of evil deeds committed and eventually ensure a happier rebirth for those to whose account the merit is credited. Such innocent mercenary considerations infuse the practice of much Tibetan religion, and laymen seem to have been usually content that they received fair returns for their money.

Within the household the typical Tibetan gaiety would be expressed by singing or dancing, by playing the flute or guitar (pages 167 and 186), or by competitions in repartee using four-line verses. The same kind of four-line verses also serve as a vehicle for comment on topical affairs. They were pointed and witty, but seldom crude, for the use of skilful allusion and concealed implications was so highly developed and so much liked by Tibetans that openly indecent songs were rare. In Lhasa verses of this kind were an anonymous and effective way of giving expression to public opinion, and they were usually sung by the women who went to the river to fetch water every morning. It was very rare that official action was taken to suppress a lampoon of this kind.

In some places traditional rivalries existed between neighbouring villages, and these would find expression in competitions in riding and shooting with arrows and matchlocks from horseback, or again by contests at repartee in verses, when a large number of villagers would meet at their common boundary, advance in line and sing their verses, to which the other side had to find an apt reply.

For other entertainment, not of their own making, there were the occasional travelling bards, men of nomadic origin (*hor-pa*) who chanted sections of the great *Ge-sar* epic, and sometimes there were singers and dancers. Then with a didactic bias there were itinerant monks who told religious stories (*ma-ṇi-pa*), illustrating them from a religious scroll which they carried with them. On rare occasions there would be a performance of the immensely popular *a-che lha-mo* at some great monastery or wealthy noble's house, and villagers would travel miles to see it. The *a-che lha-mo* are sung performances of religious drama which tell the stories of figures of the past famed for their piety and miraculous achievements. The custom is attributed to a fifteenth-century innovator, *Thang-ston rgyal-po*. A number of the most highly trained troupes from all over Tibet had to come to Lhasa in the autumn and offer their performances as a sort of tax to the Dalai Lama after which they were free to perform for profit at the great monasteries and in private houses. There were many other lesser companies which performed in a less ambitious way for their own and neighbouring villages. The repertoire of such dramas was not very large but each troupe cultivated its individual style in their presentation, although the general framework of the performance was the same. The tale was unfolded in operatic recitative and chorus, relieved by interludes of circular dancing to the accompaniment of a drum and cymbals; there were also comic scenes and mime often acted with great brilliance. The more important companies might number up to forty and in them the parts were all played by men and boys; but in the smaller troupes, which might be no more than eight persons, women often took the less important parts.

The keynote of Tibetan life before 1950 was its ready acceptance of the traditional order of things. Conditions might often be hard by modern Western standards, but scarcely comparable with the degrading soul-destroying poverty which existed in nineteenth-century England. Moreover the hardness of life affected all more or less, and it was relieved by compensating factors which we have perhaps lost, especially a deep sense of social unity and spontaneous friendliness to all and sundry, expressed best perhaps in the simple observations: 'we are all but men'. There was thus a very large tolerance of the behaviour of others, unless it offended against society and accepted traditions, when the punishment would usually be swift and effective. A thief caught red-handed one night in a villager's house would be flogged publicly the next day to the satisfaction of the whole village, and the culprit was clearly made to feel that he had offended against society generally and not against one household in particular. There must have been a direct relationship between this social solidarity and the low level of crime in ordered Tibetan society. Westerners often comment on the wonderful behaviour of Tibetan children, and let it be added that Tibetans who have visited Britain and the USA in recent years have been astounded at the way-wardness and rudeness of our children. Tibetan children behave well, simply because all members of society with whom they come in contact insist on it, seldom with compulsion because this is unnecessary where no one questions the traditional order of things. We may prefer our theories about the need for self-expression, and so must be ready to accept the logical consequences. Tibetans have preferred to keep to older ways, and who would dare declare them wrong?

Although the government at all levels was based on a strictly authoritarian principle, in practice the country was lightly administered. Of a body of 350 officials, half monk and half lay nobles, about half were to be found in Lhasa, while the others were mostly in charge of the various districts into which the country was divided. These officials depended entirely upon the traditional acceptance of their authority by the people, for there was no police force and the official had only a small group of servants at his personal command. Each was sent to his post with a strict letter of instructions in the name of the Dalai Lama, laying down how he should act, and the various dues and privileges of his office were known to all concerned. For all their outward air of polite submissiveness, the village-headmen were strong upholders of their customary rights. No district official or local landlord, even in a remote area, could afford to exceed the cus-tomary limits of strictness or exaction, for the ultimate sanction of his authority was popular consent guided by traditional usage. Certainly some of them might try to do so and even succeed in their practice of injustice for a while, but those under them soon rose in quiet protest, and the least that might happen to the offending official would be removal from his post. With their strong sense of self-reliance and firm conviction of what is traditionally right, the Tibetans are a people whom it is extremely hard to oppress, unless one subjects them with armed force, and this their own rulers and administrators never did.

After the death of the thirteenth Dalai Lama in 1933 Tibet returned to the usual interregnum of rule by regents. The Chinese, officially excluded from Lhasa since 1913, sent a small delegation to commiserate on the Dalai Lama's departure from life and this stayed on as the unofficial representation in Tibet of the Chinese Republic. In 1936 a small British mission went to Lhasa in order to try to mediate between the Tibetan government and the *Pan-chen* Lama who had been in China ever since his flight there in 1923. Attempts at mediation failed, but the mission stayed on with the acquiescence of the Tibetan government, which was glad to have another power represented so as to counterbalance the Chinese presence.

There had been a Nepalese representative in Lhasa for a long time (since the sixteenth century), but he was primarily concerned with looking after the business interests and special rights of the Nepalese community. The Chinese were intent on trying to establish the position, or at least the appearance, of being an office with supervisory authority over Tibetan affairs. They did not want the Tibetans to have official dealings with any other power except through the Chinese government, but although senior Tibetan officials from the regent downwards were happy to accept large presents (which might after all be construed as a continuation of the bounty once enjoyed under the Manchus), they conceded nothing to the Chinese overtures. Traders and aristocratic circles in Lhasa were by now well aware of the great value of the British connection, and they were not likely to cast it lightly away. Moreover the great monasteries, whatever reservations they might have in the sphere of foreign cultural ideas, had not been slow to realize that they too could share in the profits of the Indian trade.

In spite of occasional fluctuations this trade had shown a steady increase since 1913, but with the outbreak of the Second World War in 1939 profits rose to undreamt-of heights. To begin with the Indian government found it necessary to place quota restrictions on the export of such goods as cotton cloth, kerosene, sugar and metals, and this had the immediate effect of placing a high premium on them in Tibet. At the same time Britain and China had become war-allies, and discussions were initiated on the subject of opening a supply-route right through from India to China. The Tibetans, who had resolved to remain neutral during the war, showed the greatest determination in resisting pressure; despite threats from the British government as well as troop movements against their eastern frontier by the Chinese authorities, on no account would they allow a route for motor vehicles to be constructed across their country. The issue was largely political, for in fact no such route could very well have been made at that time. Eventually the Tibetans agreed to allow the passage by normal means of everything except war materials. But in fact the traffic was already operating in the hands of private merchants, who were making vast profits on whatever could be transported across Tibet from India. All animals, mules, donkeys, yaks and bullocks, were drawn into this trade, and every available man, woman and child besides. The value of the Tibetan quota of restricted imports from India soared to fantastic heights and Tibetans began to travel all over India in search of any kind of goods to sell to the Chinese. In spite of high initial prices, the ever-increasing cost of transport, and the exactions of border-officials, great profits were made at the other end by the Chinese who succeeded in getting the consignments into their own country.

At this time Tibetan principles regarding material profits were under considerable strain and perhaps lasting damage was done to the primitive Tibetan virtues. Looting of caravans by bands of robbers became common, even on the Gyantse trade-route, where formerly one could leave one's baggage unattended anywhere. But it was still not unusual for an official or trader, who had made great profits, to spend large sums on some grand religious gesture, payments towards the Great Prayer Festival at the New Year, having a fine new image made, or gilding lavishly existing images or tombs of lamas. Some landlords made so much from their wool and their trade that they no longer worried about profits from their lands, to the great benefit of their tenants. For good and ill it was a feverish and unrealistic period.

New experiences in India led some Tibetan nobles to introduce innovations in their own houses. Glazed windows, still rare in 1936, were accepted as quite normal by 1944. Steel girders were used for the first time in building, and wide concrete staircases began to replace the old steep wooden ladders. High society was even influenced by British cuisine; cooks from the noble houses came round to the British Mission to learn how to bake bread and cakes, while lamb-chops came to be regarded as a fashionable way of serving good Tibetan sheep. Even knives and forks began to appear, but their advantage over chop-sticks or fingers was doubtful. Great prestige attached to such things as watches and pens, so that only the most famous and expensive makes were likely to be acceptable, and as for materials, only the best broadcloth or brocade was esteemed. But a serious breach was being made in the traditional order, marked by a rapid decline in appreciation of colours and designs. Perhaps a welcome influence of the British Mission in domestic matters was seen in the far greater variety of vegetables, flowers and fruit-trees, which were spread by roots and seeds and cuttings all over Lhasa and beyond.

As for medicine, the British hospital was always busy. Monks and lamas, as well as layfolk, made use of its services, and patients travelled from long distances seeking treatment. British, Sikkimese and Indian doctors were welcomed on the most friendly terms in the houses of the nobles and in the apartments of high-ranking lamas. Western medicine, especially 'injections', became a matter of prestige, and traders would bring back from India hypodermic needles and almost any kind of serum, entrusting them to the Mission Hospital, but perhaps more often to some totally unqualified friend or lama for administration. Several books have appeared recently on the subject of Tibetan medicine, suggesting that the Tibetans, having preserved intact the teachings of ancient Indian medicine, possess an effective medical practice of their own. This would seem to be a false assumption, for Indian medical theories, whatever their value may be, have certainly been preserved, but like so much else of the Indian scholastic inheritance, preserved as a purely literary tradition. It would be a mistake to conceive of the few monasteries where such texts are learned, notably *lCag-po-ri* on the edge of Lhasa, which is often called a 'medical college', as training centres whence medically qualified graduates go out to practice their skills amongst the layfolk. Care for the sick and suffering has never played the same part in Tibetan religion as in Christianity. Most of the inmates of *lCag-po-ri* seem to have spent their time preparing medicaments and pills or collecting herbs of which they had a real knowledge, and a few of them would make use of the experience gained, in order to make a little extra money by the way. If any medical practitioner was available at all, he was just as likely to be a layman who sold drugs and concoctions rather like a medieval apothecary. For a fee he would diagnose a patient's complaint, using the traditional methods of feeling the pulse and testing the urine (page 166). In the villages and countryside there was no medical practitioner available, either trained or untrained, and for most illnesses Tibetans put more faith in prayers, charms and amulets than in medicine. It may be that there was a lama in the vicinity, who had gained some experience in medicaments in the course of his life, and so he would give some pills or make up a concoction from his available stock of ingredients, and give a blessing as well. Struck down by a heavy cold, I (D.L.S.) accepted willingly the medicine offered me by the Dalai Lama's physician, when on a recent visit to Dharamsāla. It was a mixture of herbs and spices, among which myrobalan predominated, boiled for ten minutes, then strained and drunk hot, and it was at least as beneficial as any Western cold-cure. As for wounds, sprains and broken bones, people usually attend to these themselves, or go perhaps to someone renowned locally for his skill in helping in such matters. There is no doubt that some Tibetans possess a great deal of practical medical knowledge, derived as much as anything perhaps from the experience gained in the care of their own animals. They are probably past masters in dealing with sprains and dislocations, but all this has nothing to do with Indian medical theories. Tibetan apothecaries are glad to receive new drugs from any source, and the chief source in recent centuries has been China. From the Chinese and from those who cut up corpses (*ra-rgyab-pa*) they have gained some knowledge of the actual internal physical structure and the functioning of the human body, but no one ever seems to have shown interest in resolving the contradictions with ancient Indian psycho-physical theories, derived primarily from the practice of *yoga*. Tibetan medical practice is a study which merits serious attention, but one needs to deal with it on an empirical basis, watching the cures and testing the medicaments actually in use.

Tibetans are renowned for the absence of hygiene in their country, but the cold climate comes to their assistance. There is record of a Chinese official attempt in 1794 to improve public health arrangements. An edict of the Amban Ho Lin ordered the establishment of an isolation centre near Lhasa for the treatment of smallpox, thus superseding the former practice of simply driving smallpox victims out of the city into the hills beyond. But if ever used, the centre soon ceased to operate, for Abbé Huc records the former practice as still surviving during his visit (1846). It seems unlikely that the practice of inoculation with home-made lymph, or its use as snuff, was in vogue in Ho Lin's time, although it was certainly being used in the nineteenth century. A further enactment of his, which was quite unacceptable to the Tibetans, ordered that burial grounds should be established to replace the custom of cutting up corpses and feeding them to vultures and dogs, and of throwing infected bodies and those of criminals into rivers. In all such matters the Tibetans have gone their own way until the mid-twentieth century.

The great material changes occasioned in the first place by the British intrusion and accelerated by the effects of the Second World War scarcely touched the Tibetans' view of the world. A few who came into contact with Western visitors tended to equivocate in talking about such well-established social institutions as polyandry, which they had been led to believe were regarded unfavourably in the West. The more sophisticated might express scepticism about the usefulness of referring political matters to diviners and oracles, but they were a tiny minority, and the practice continued up to the very end. It was used in 1950 when the question whether the Dalai Lama should take refuge in India or stay in Tibet was decided by casting lots. Scrolls of paper with the alternatives written on them were rolled up in little balls of *tsam-pa* and shaken in a bowl; the decision was made in accordance with the one which came out first. A similar procedure was followed in 1956 to decide whether the Dalai Lama should stay in India, where he had gone for the celebrations of Buddhism's 2,500th year, or whether he should return to Tibet.

In some small Tibetan circles, especially among the noble families of Lhasa, there were aspirations towards change and new developments. After the death of the thirteenth Dalai Lama in 1933 it was possible for sons of these families to be sent to schools of Western type in Darjeeling, and the potential benefits of this kind of education were so obvious that the Tibetan government sanctioned the institution of an English school in Lhasa in 1944. But monastic conservatism was determined to thwart any such modernizing tendencies, and using the old arguments that such a school would endanger the religious views of the children, the abbots of 'Bras-spungs (Drepung) engineered its speedy closure. Monastic views were echoed in one of those sets of popular verses, which both express and form public opinion in Tibet:

In the holy place of Lhasa is that unholy English school.
Till our boots split we must go there, as their unwilling tool!*

But the closure of the first English school in Gyantse in 1924 had already clinched this matter. If that school had continued to develop there would have been available in the 1940s and thereafter a number of Tibetans able to understand the thoughts and ways of the non-Tibetan world, and to come to terms with them on their own ground. Now when they were needed as never before, such men did not exist or were so rare as to be totally discounted. The war years provided the Tibetan government with the last opportunity to make its case for independence known to the outside world, but through the sheer force of past circumstances it just did not possess the human means for establishing the necessary contacts. Seldom can the law of *karma*, the inevitable effects of past actions, have operated with such terrible transparency.

The continuing lack of personal contact with intelligent and thoughtful Tibetans, well educated in their traditional forms of learning, was all the more unfortunate, for Western scholars had made considerable advance in Tibetan studies since the beginning of the twentieth century. But deprived of the interested co-operation of Tibetans, they had little choice but to study Tibetan language and literature exclusively as a classical study. Owing to the great difference between the written and spoken styles of Tibetan, it was quite reasonable to study the literary language, especially in relationship with the original Sanskrit texts of Buddhist works translated into Tibetan, just as we study Latin and Greek. The chief aids in these new studies were the Tibetan-English dictionaries, which were now available thanks mainly to the devoted and self-sacrificing labours of two great Hungarian pioneers, Csoma de Körös (1784-1842) and Jäschke (1817-83).* But their efforts and those of their successors, as well as the carefully prepared editions of Tibetan texts, often with parallel Sanskrit or Chinese versions of the same Buddhist treatise, or with English, French or German translations, such as have appeared over the last few decades mainly in Europe and Japan, all these have gone unobserved by the Tibetans themselves. From 1933 onwards Professor Giuseppe Tucci of Rome made a whole succession of cultural expeditions into Western and Central Tibet. He came well equipped with a wide knowledge of Buddhist literature, of Sanskrit, classical Chinese and Tibetan, and for the first time he brilliantly brought classical Tibetan texts into some kind of living relationship with the history, architecture and iconography of the places he visited. Through historical accident, it is we Westerners who have taken the initiative in the serious study of Tibetan culture, and there is now a desperate need for trained Tibetans to continue the work, if their civilization is to survive outside our museums and libraries.

The Last Events In 1950 the great state ceremonies were still performed in Lhasa, not as mere pageantry but as religious duties, the omission or variation of which might cause national disaster. Attendance was an official duty and avoidable absence was heavily penalized. The ills of the old year were still solemnly expelled in lengthy religious dances or were transferred in all seriousness to a scapegoat who was driven from the city in strict accordance with ancient rites. Monastic pressure led to the banning of the foreign innovation of football, which tended to excite excessive passions. One particular match coincided with a sudden and ill-omened hail-storm, and this was enough to put an end to such a game, which was said to be as bad as kicking the head of the Lord Buddha. Omens were watched with anxiety, especially as relations with China went from bad to worse. The appearance of an unknown bird – in fact a painted stork driven far off course from the Indian plains – caused serious headshakings. The bird's body was kept and eventually burned ritually at a great ceremony for the averting of evil, when Communist attacks seemed imminent. I (H.E.R.) was present at the ceremony which ended most impressively with a tremendous dust-storm out of a clear blue sky. About the same time another great ceremony was held at *Sa-skya*, and there the onlookers clearly saw a white dog rush from the burning pyre; this was a sure sign of the success of the exorcism. Anxiety was roused by the persistent dripping of water in dry weather from a dragon gargoyle on one of the gold roofs of the Cathedral (*Jo-khang*), also by a bright and beautiful comet, and, perhaps more reasonably, by a fierce earthquake accompanied by reports like gunfire. Nor was there wanting a clairvoyant, a sergeant of the Dalai Lama's guard, to claim that he had seen a battle of gods and demons in the sky.

Despite such alarming portents, even the news of the Chinese attack on eastern Tibet in 1950 did not interfere with the annual holiday. All government business was suspended and the city emptied itself, while each principle officer of state entertained the others turn by turn at leisurely, costly and enjoyable picnic parties in the parks around Lhasa. Meanwhile the ordinary people of Lhasa also flocked to the riverside, smart and happy in their best clothes. The men wore robes of good broadcloth with brilliant white silk shirts showing forth, and new-fashioned high leather boots as made by Chinese craftsmen in Kalimpong. The women wore broadcloth, often Italian, and bright-coloured silk blouses. They also often wore rather unsightly Western-style shoes imported from India, although these were officially banned. Both men and women wore high felt hats, decorated with Indian brocade and gold lace. They would pitch their tents in the parks and spend a week amusing themselves, singing and playing games, eating and drinking (much *chang* was consumed), and making excursions to the river to bathe.

In a sterner vein, rivalries continued between noble cliques, sometimes involving attempted assassination. An official in disgrace would still be sent to exile dressed in homespun and riding an ox. Even an 'Incarnate Lama' could be publicly flogged for taking part in a conspiracy against the Regent. But by 1950 less was heard of charges of witchcraft and black magic, and such coups as took place were performed less spectacularly than those which followed the death of the thirteenth Dalai Lama.

Buddhism and *Bon* were mingled to the end. In the Cathedral itself, the holiest Buddhist place in Tibet, a resident *Bon-po* priest performed daily ceremonies, while on the roof a stack of juniper boughs was renewed every New Year in accordance with ancient *Bon* custom. The ancient family of *lHa-gya-ri* with its royal connections still had its *Bon-po* chaplain, who performed the naming rites of its children and the funeral ceremonies of its dead, while the Tibetan government sent an official every year to a chapel near the Yarlung Valley to burn butter-lamps and give grain to the birds, as an invitation to the cuckoo, the sacred bird of *Bon*, to return to Tibet.

When British power withdrew from India in 1947, the Tibetans lost their tenuous link with the outside world. They were assured that all the former British rights and obligations would be conveyed to the new government of India, and that the British would continue to take a friendly interest in their welfare. But in reality everything was changed. An entirely new form of government was emerging in China, and of this resuscitation of a great imperial power in Communist form, no one as yet had had any experience. On the other hand the Indian government, in the flush of its newly won independence from imperial rule, hastened to acclaim the Chinese as long lost brothers, who like them had suffered cruelly in the past from Western encroachments. The myth of two thousand years of Sino-Indian friendship was suddenly created, and the travels to India of Chinese Buddhist pilgrims during the third to eighth centuries were recalled as sure proof of it. In the fervour of political freedom, it really seemed to those who did not read their history that the makers of enmity and war were always the Westerners. They chose to overlook the warfare that had raged in India and China long before Europeans appeared on the scene, and as for the lands that lie between them, perhaps they knew nothing or very little about the events recorded in this present book. India and China had never been at war together simply because their frontiers never really touched. After the total occupation of Tibet by China in 1959, India and China were very soon at enmity and even at war. We may have suggested in the course of our story that the Tibetans were often naïve in their dealings with foreigners, and now, in all fairness to them, it must be observed that they were by no means the only ones who were victims of their own fallacies. After 1947 they were destined to be the first victims of the Indian fallacy of brotherhood with China. Until 1959 the best advice that some leading Indians could give them was to co-operate with Communist China, for the company of well-intentioned brothers can never do anyone any harm. Many leading Tibetans did their best to come to terms with the Chinese, especially the fourteenth Dalai Lama himself from the time that he assumed full authority over his government in 1950. But however sincere the attempts, co-operation was manifestly impossible, for Tibetans of all classes and Communist Chinese scarcely thought alike on a single problem. Serious conflict was therefore inevitable. Yet even under these difficult political conditions life still continued for a while in the same traditional ways.

Since the end of 1950 the Chinese government has formally claimed Tibet as an integral part of China, and their armed forces have taken physical possession of it. The Dalai Lama and his government, seeing no hope of help from others, tried to co-operate with the dominant power. There were, however, constant conflicts between ordinary Tibetans and the occupying forces, leading finally to the great commotion around the Dalai Lama's summer palace in March 1959 and his secret flight to India.*

Co-operation with the Chinese has proved quite impossible, and even the *Pan-chen* Lama, who acted for a few years in the Dalai Lama's stead, has now disappeared from the scene. Like all unwanted occupying powers, the Chinese were driven to ever sterner and more cruel repression. Their real enemies, as they have surely discovered by now, are not the nobles and rich prelates, whom they castigated as the oppressors of the Tibetan people. Nobles and rich prelates are often the first to submit so that they may keep at least part of their possessions. Their real enemies are the ordinary Tibetan people, who have little to lose but their lives, and these are so imbued and conditioned by their own special forms of culture, that for them change is impossible.

Since 1959 a heavy curtain has descended upon Tibet, which is now closed as never before. We may deduce what we can from the accounts of the very few Communist sympathizers for whom it has been raised a little. They write as though they were unaware that Tibetans ever possessed a civilization of their own, any heart-felt religion, any literature, any painting, any traditional crafts, any spontaneous song and dance. While arguing their case for the Chinese, they reveal to us unintentionally the state of cultural degradation to which this whole people has now been reduced.

Epilogue

Since 1959 the Chinese rulers have completely destroyed the main springs of Tibetan civilization. They attacked first the religious and aristocratic social order with a fury unequalled by Cromwell's henchmen in England, and their subsequent devastating onslaughts against the material and religious well-being of ordinary Tibetan farmers, herdsmen and traders may perhaps be compared in methods and results with Cromwell's invasion of Ireland. The only Tibetans who can have profited from what has now become a settled Chinese occupation are the 'have nots' and underlings who may not always have had too happy a time under the *ancien régime*. But even these will have changed masters who allowed them at least the solace of religion and the joys of traditional festivals, for new masters who force upon them, when the day's work is done, attendance at political lectures and the vindictive denunciation of fellow Tibetans whose humiliation happens to suit local group leaders. The tried methods of Chinese Communist domination have been brought to bear with destructive effect upon the whole pattern of Tibetan social life. Leaving aside the debatable question of whether this will result eventually in the higher material living standards, which the Communists promise to those who co-operate with them, we may fairly observe that the present harsh process can only result in the total destruction of the whole culture and civilization whose origin and development we have been attempting to trace. A new generation of young Tibetans, taken early from their parents, has been systematically trained to despise all traditional social and religious values, and to work with the new rulers towards the development of an entirely different material order. Every village has been visited and purged by teams of ideological workers; the village temple has ceased to exist; the Tibetan propensity for travel has been confined by the need to obtain a permit to leave one's village; the landlord and the religious state have been replaced by 'The People' and 'The Party'. One can imagine what slant has been given to the formerly uninhibited songs and to the stories of the *a-che lha-mo*. Apologists may point to claims of material and mechanical progress, but even if these promised benefits ever reach the Tibetan population, the fact remains that they were not sought by the Tibetans themselves and have been introduced in such a way as to represent the total negation of Tibetan civilization and culture.

A small minority of Tibetans, perhaps some five per cent, have sought refuge in India and neighbouring Himalayan lands. Led by the Dalai Lama and other leaders of lay and religious groups, they have sought to re-establish themselves wherever conditions have been made propitious for them. But they seem to be hampered by the very strength of their attachment to their own traditional ways, which makes adaptation to changed circumstances of life a slow and difficult process, and by the development of factional interests such as seem to bedevil the efforts of all those who try to rebuild the fortunes of uprooted refugees from any country whatsoever. By common consent the Tibetans possess an apparent equanimity and cheerfulness of demeanour in the most distressing of circumstances, but this calm exterior often conceals an inner sense of utter hopelessness and loss of all purpose in life. With few exceptions, such hopes as they dare to express, are set not on rebuilding new lives for themselves and their fellow sufferers in foreign lands, but on a speedy return to a liberated Tibet, and they forget, understandably enough, that the Tibet they knew has by now been swept away for ever, and if ever they return there, they will presumably have to come to terms with an entirely new generation of Tibetans who, however glad they may be to escape from the Chinese yoke, will nonetheless be trained in the ways of their present Communist rulers.

There are happily some exceptions such as the settlement of lay Tibetans now well established as a more or less self-supporting agricultural community at Bylakuppe in southern Mysore (India) or the much smaller groups in various places in northern India and Nepal who earn a living for themselves by weaving carpets in traditional Tibetan designs or by producing carved tables, domestic vessels, ornate swords and daggers and such things as may make a ready appeal in a tourist market. There are also small groups of lamas and monks who continue to publish copies of Tibetan religious texts which are needed for liturgical purposes or for study by their fellow exiles in India. One or two new works of Tibetan literature have also appeared, such as a description of the U.S.A. by one Tibetan visitor to that country, or in a more traditional vein the history of the *rNying-ma-pa* order by a distinguished lama of that school (see page 246). All these activities are helping to keep alive for some time longer ways of living which have now become impossible in Tibet itself.

As for the lands around Tibet which have been permeated by Tibetan Buddhist civilization in the past, few still follow the traditional ways with any creative zeal. Mongolia, the main field of Tibetan missionary activity, has emerged since 1924 as an independent Communist country, showing the way perhaps that Tibet may eventually go, if ever the Chinese relax their grip. The outward signs of traditional culture in the form of a few temples with contents intact, some small groups of elderly monks, collections of religious paintings and books, these are now preserved as part of the Mongolian national heritage, but with the lifelessness of a museum collection. As for the several small semi-independent kingdoms of the Sino-Tibetan borderlands, these were all swept away in the early 1950s when the Chinese Communists first moved to seize control of Tibet itself. They have disappeared utterly from history, practically unknown to the outside world.

Other Tibetan-speaking borders lands have been saved from the Communists thanks to their inclusion within the political frontiers of India and Nepal. These are the Indian territories of Ladakh, Spiti and Lahul, and the northern Nepalese districts from Mugu, Dolpo and Mustang in the west to Solu-Khumbu and Walung in the east. But with the remarkable exception of Solu-Khumbu all these regions seem to be in cultural decline, due mainly perhaps to lack of local aristocratic leadership and wealthy lay patronage, such as was once provided by the kings of Ladakh (now absorbed into Kashmir) or the kings of Jumla and Mustang (absorbed since the end of the eighteenth century into the new Gorkha kingdom of Nepal). To the east of Nepal lies the little state of Sikkim, which boasts a large number of small monasteries and temples, and where religious life has recently been revived by the arrival of refugee Tibetan monks and lamas of the older religious orders, notably the *rGyal-ba Karma-pa*, head of the *Karma bKa'-brgyud-pa* order, for whom a large new monastery has recently been built near Gangtok.

Next to Sikkim is the kingdom of Bhutan ('*Brug* pronounced 'Druk'), which since the seventeenth century has become and remained the stronghold of the '*Brug-pa bKa'-brgyud-pa* (Druk-pa Ka-gyü-pa) order, whence the local name of the country is derived. Since that time Bhutan was ruled by a succession of reincarnating lamas and their regents, just as was Tibet itself until 1959. But earlier this century the Bhutanese line of reincarnating lamas was replaced by an hereditary line of kings, and this lay dominance in the government may well help Bhutan to come to terms more easily with the outside twentieth-century world, which is just now beginning to make its presence felt in the country. At the same time the royal family of Bhutan patronizes generously the traditional cultural and religious life of the land. In Bhutan there are still great fort-like monasteries whose inmates can be counted in their hundreds. Both lay and religious buildings are still being constructed in traditional styles and often too with skilful adaptations of traditional designs to modern needs. These buildings, like much else of the national culture of Bhutan, represent special local developments of earlier Tibetan forms. Thus the great fort-like monasteries (*rdzong*) in the main valleys seem to take one back to that period in Tibet preceding the *dGe-lugs-pa* domination, when the older religious orders were established in rival monastic strongholds. Likewise the houses of the lay officials and farmers, who together with the monks make up almost the whole of the Bhutanese population, are manifestly local variations of the Tibetan multistoreyed house with its massive walls of stone and earth, but distinguished by the far freer use of wood, so plentiful in Bhutan. Meanwhile the great monastic forts, as well as the smaller temples and simpler domestic architecture, continue to give scope for the crafts of stone-masonry, wood-joinery and carving, painting and traditional interior decoration.

In marked contrast with Bhutan, all the other surviving regions of Tibetan culture ranged along the southern frontiers of Tibet are now simply fringe districts of either India or Nepal, remote from the main centres of government, which in any case have more immediate interests than the fostering of what is to them a totally alien culture. These distant frontier regions are usually left in peace to pursue their traditional ways of life, but through the lack of inspired local leadership and interested patronage their cultural and religious life has sunk to a very low ebb. There are scattered exceptions such as the monastery and the nunnery in Tshum (northern Nepal), both sponsored significantly by the Bhutanese and, even more remarkable, the several small Sherpa monasteries of Solu-Khumbu, all founded this century and maintained by the Sherpas themselves. But with only some ten or twenty inmates, all these places are very small, and hardly sufficient to make a strong cultural impact upon a whole region. In the far west Ladakh still possesses a number of quite large monasteries, but they have declined sadly during the last hundred years and can now hardly be considered centres of cultural and religious inspiration. What all these regions lack is the directing force of a local authority, whether lay or religious, which has an interest and stake in the survival and development of what have now become little more than odd remnants of Tibetan culture and religion.

Thus of the whole enormous area which was once the spirited domain of Tibetan culture and religion, stretching from Ladakh in the west to the borders of the Chinese provinces of Szechuan and Yunnan in the east, from the Himalayas in the south to the Mongolian steppes and the vast wastes of northern Tibet, now only Bhutan seems to survive as the one resolute and self-contained representative of a fast disappearing civilization.

Aftermath

Eleven years have passed since we completed work on the first edition of this book, and nineteen years since the present Dalai Lama, then only twenty-three years old, left Tibet for India, whither he was followed by many thousands of Tibetan refugees, representing all classes of society, thus leaving his country in the control of Chinese Communist authorities and those few leading Tibetans who were prepared to co-operate with them. There can be little doubt that the Dalai Lama himself and those who advised him to flee the country, expected an early return, and that they were primarily concerned that the one person who was seen in all times of foreign intervention as representing unequivocally the independence of Tibet, should not fall into Chinese hands. In a similar way, which was certainly not forgotten by the Tibetans, the 13th Dalai Lama had fled the country in 1904 on the occasion of the British invasion, and he had remained absent five years in Mongolia and then in China, until a better understanding of British intentions led to his return to Lhasa in 1909. Again the following year when the Chinese invaded, he fled for refuge to his newly found British friends, living for two years in India as their guest, and returning to Lhasa in 1912, when revolution in China had weakened to nothingness any Chinese hold on Tibet. On these previous occasions external political events operated entirely in the Tibetans' favour, but since 1959 political attitudes and events have shown themselves as largely unfavourable to their case, and what was intended as a brief exile has now every appearance of having become a more or less permanent arrangement. It has been a hard lesson to learn for all present-day Tibetan exiles that they should plan their lives abroad with no prospect of return.

The weakness of the Tibetan case on this occasion derives primarily from the hesitating and even overtly pro-Chinese stand adopted by her other neighbours. Whereas Mongolia won her independence from Chinese tutelage because of Russian intervention and Russian concern that Mongolia should not be part of China, the break-up in 1947 of the British Indian Empire destroyed at once all hope of a united front on Tibet's southern borders, just when the final test of strength with China was fast approaching. The British authorities in India, following a formula devised at the Simla Conference of 1914 were prepared to admit the theoretical suzerainty of China over Tibet on condition that the Chinese respected Tibetan autonomy. In practice they dealt with Tibet as an autonomous government and they would scarcely have tolerated the replacement of that peaceful buffer state by a Chinese militarily occupied zone resulting in a hostile and disputed frontier stretching the length of India's northern borders. After 1947 this northern frontier was shared by three fully independent nations, Pakistan, India and Nepal, with the little kingdom of Bhutan as a potential fourth. Pakistan and Nepal showed themselves entirely unsympathetic to the Tibetan political cause, and hastened to make frontier agreements with the newly established Chinese authorities in Tibet. India alone prevaricated, never really making a firm stand, preventing the hearing of the Dalai Lama's appeal to the United Nations in 1950 and remaining neutral when the Tibetan issue was raised in the United Nations in 1959 by Eire and Malaya. She has merely earned thereby the increasing hostility of China, resulting in the Chinese invasion of India in 1962, without serving the Tibetan political cause in any useful way. She now has to bear with threatened Himalayan frontiers at considerable cost on the far N.W. and N.E. parts of her territory. Britain, better informed than any other country apart from India about Tibet's actual political status, has simply ignored the problem, and there does not now appear to be a single Asian or African or Western Government prepared to support the Tibetan case. In fact China's only claim rests upon asserted rights of possession of Tibet as a dependent territory, rights which ceased to have any de facto validity in 1912, and which no one would be prepared to admit nowadays in the case of any western imperialist power. By the same argument Britain should still be ruling the whole of Ireland, not to mention India as well, and France still in control of all her former North African territories. Tibet's right to a genuine state of autonomy rests upon an historical cultural background, the very subject of this book, which has developed certainly over the last thousand years very differently from that of China, based as it is upon a separate language and literature, a separate form of Buddhism, a separate economy and form of government, and distinct forms of art and architecture. In order to make Tibet really part of China, such differences have to be effaced as rapidly as possible, and such has been the policy of the present Chinese Communist régime. Whereas other imperial powers chose to envisage the development of their colonies as a step towards eventual self-determination, the Chinese clearly have no such intention in the case of Tibet, which is declared as representing merely a 'national minority' and a permanent part of China. Thus all individual characteristics have to be firmly eliminated. It follows therefore that the changes that have taken place in Tibet over the last nineteen years are largely irrelevant to the subject-matter of this book. We note, however, that the present régime has sought to repair the damage to its reputation abroad which was caused by the destructive excesses of the Cultural Revolution, and that some of the more sacred buildings in and near Lhasa have now been restored as cultural museums for the carefully selected western travellers who have recently been permitted to visit Lhasa in very small numbers. But religion as a creative cultural force and as the centre of life in every village and every house in Tibet is no more; off the carefully controlled tourist tracks hundreds of monasteries and temples are desecrated as barracks and grain-stores, or used as schools and political meeting-places. Meanwhile the former agricultural and nomadic pastoral ways of life, which formed the basis of the Tibetan economy, have been supplanted by a regular pattern of communes. As for architecture, the use of concrete replaces traditional styles, and the religious art of Tibet, perhaps the main expression of Tibetian genius, has been cut off at its roots. Being non-religious in intention, traditional styles of carpet weaving have survived. It is usual nowadays to weigh the loss of traditional cultures against the advantages of modernization, and the Tibetans are by no means the only people to have lost rather heavily on such a deal, although few can have lost so much in so very short a time. Social and political changes were certainly overdue in Tibet, but it would have been possible to introduce desirable changes without subverting the whole traditional culture of the country. We have drawn attention above (pp. 228–30) to weaknesses and injustices inherent in the old Tibetan system of government (we note in fairness to the Tibetans that there are now many independent countries represented at the United Nations with far worse records of injustice to their own peoples), but we would recall one feature quite peculiar to Tibet, which continues, even amongst the many Tibetans who now live in exile, to detract from that sense of national unity, which alone can fortify a people in its struggle for independence. Since 1642 Tibet was ruled by a particular religious order, the *dGe-lugs-pa* or 'Yellow Hats', and other religious orders inevitably resented this kind of domination, although there was little overt expression of such resentment. The situation was thus far more complex than Chinese Communist propagandists have represented it, namely as a simplified antagonism between aristocrats and religious prelates, painted in the most hideous colours, on the one side, and serfs, in the most deplorable, on the other. Thus anyone who wanted to remove social injustice in Tibet would have to confront entrenched religious positions, especially those of one particular order. Operating with greater knowledge of the situation and with more sympathy for the Tibetans, the Chinese could in theory have forced a change of government in Tibet by establishing a lay administration, making use of the best talent available, and depriving the *dGe-lugs-pa* Order of its privileged political and economic position, while allowing them to continue their religious life just as the several other Tibetan Buddhist orders have had to do for the last three hundred years or more. However, such was the strength of the *dGe-lugs-pa* position on the one hand and of Chinese Communist ideology on the other, that a workable compromise would have been very difficult to achieve. Violent confrontation would seem to have been inevitable, and the overthrow of the *dGe-lugs-pa* strongholds was accompanied by the destruction of every other religious order in Tibet. With their well known antipathy to religion generally the new rulers can have had no regrets.

Bearing in mind this particular feature of Tibetan political life, one may pass briefly under review the situation of Tibetans in exile, probably some 80,000 of them, living mainly in India, but also quite large numbers in Nepal. Both these countries, especially India, have done much to alleviate the distress of many of these refugees, and India has offered the Dalai Lama a base for his operations at Dharamsala, while carefully avoiding recognizing his administration in any sense as a government in exile. Usually his advice and that of his 'ministers' have been sought by the Government of India and by foreign refugee organizations concerning the resettlement of Tibetans in exile and general aid programmes. This however has tended to have a divisive effect, for while the Dalai Lama himself is on excellent personal terms with the leaders of the other religious orders, his administration, being in its origins the direct continuation of the old Lhasa régime, inevitably has favoured their own religious order to the general exclusion of the others. In order to gain assistance these have had to forge their direct links with the Indian authorities and with those refugee organizations who did not insist on channelling aid through the Dharamsala administration, and certainly in the earlier years of exile this was not so easy. Large and now flourishing settlements have been established in Orissa and Mysore under the general control of Tibetan officers appointed by Dharamsala, and they have been the recipients of large amounts of Indian and foreign aid. Organized as far as is practicable along Tibetan traditional social and governmental ideas, they seem to preserve to a remarkable extent a purely Tibetan way of life. Of the independent establishments, we may mention the interesting case of the Bon-po settlement near Simla, which began to get going in 1964 and has proved a great success. Also noteworthy are the main Sakyapa settlement at Dehra Dun and the Karmapa centre in Sikkim. The Dalai Lama and his advisers have certainly shown an active concern for the preservation of Tibetan religion, art and literature and a great achievement has been the establishing of the Library of Tibetan Works and Archives at Dharamsala. But here too a great deal has been achieved by the representatives of the other religious orders, operating quite independently. A considerable amount of Tibetan literature has been reprinted in India mainly on the personal initiative of Tibetan monk-scholars, who have naturally shown a predilection for works of their own particular school. To a great extent their work has been co-ordinated in Delhi by Mr Gene Smith, an American scholar, who has worked with Tibetan *literati* of all schools since 1960, when a small group of Sakyapa lamas settled in Seattle at the invitation of the University of Washington. Thanks to funds provided from U.S. Indian-blocked assets it has been possible to assist in the work by granting subsidies towards the cost of printing Tibetan works in India. Mr Gene Smith has organized this indirect and most beneficial form of aid to the advantage not only of the Tibetans themselves but of all scholars throughout the world who are concerned with Tibetan studies. At the same time the presence of Tibetan monks and learned laymen at various academic centres throughout the western world and in Japan have given considerable impetus to Tibetan studies in general and to Buddhist studies in particular. From 1960 onwards specially qualified Tibetans were invited as academic assistants not only to Seattle, as mentioned above, but to London, Paris, Rome, Munich, Leiden and Tokyo, and later to other German Universities as well as to Scandinavia. The great generosity shown by Swiss organizations to Tibetan refugees has led to a large influx into Switzerland of ordinary Tibetan folk chiefly now employed in small manufacturing concerns and living in small communities mainly in the region of Zürich. With the intention of serving their religious needs, an academic centre, modelled on a traditional Tibetan monastery, has been founded at Rikon nearby. However, the United States has now become the most sought after haven for Tibetan lamas intent on establishing a following amongst westerners. Following in the wake of Indian yoga schools and the very successful Zen Buddhism movement, they have learned rapidly how to best adapt their teachings to an American audience. Thus Trungpa Rinpoche, representing the Kargyupa Sect, now has a network of religious groups spread over the country with his headquarters at Boulder (Colorado). The Nyingmapas are found in great strength at Berkeley (California), while other smaller groups strive to make headway in proximity to New York. The presence of so many Tibetans now outside Tibet, whether in India or Nepal, Europe or the United States, provides an ease of access to them such as has been available to very few travellers and scholars in the past when Tibet presented itself as a closed land to all but a privileged few. Tibet itself is still a closed land except on the Chinese and Nepalese frontiers, where entry continues to be controlled quite as strictly as in previous times. Thus the many Tibetan exiles, who suffer the loss of their country, have gained the no small advantage of freedom of converse with peoples of other countries, the lack of which in the past does much to explain the ineffectiveness of the old Tibetan government in dealing with foreign problems resulting in the present loss of independence.

Western students and scholars of Tibet will now be found wherever Tibetans are congregated and in those regions, south of the Himalayas and in Ladakh, where a Tibetan way of life and Tibetan religion survive. For their part young Tibetans have won the opportunity of following modern courses of education, whether in India, Japan, Europe or the USA. Thus gradually a new generation of educated Tibetans is emerging, strongly nationalistic and respectful of their own traditions, while learning to test them according to non-Tibetan standards of value. Some are thus acquiring a mastery of supple expressive English, equally essential for works treating of recent social and political conditions in Tibet (e.g. Dawa Norbu's *Red Star over Tibet*) or for workers concerned with traditional religious and historical themes (e.g. Samten G. Karmay's *The Treasury of Good Sayings, a Tibetan History of Bon*). Other works are appearing as exercizes in collaboration between Tibetan lamas and western disciples, and here one may note especially *The Wisdom of*

Tibet Series sponsored by the Library of Tibetan Works & Archives, or such a work as *The Practice and Theory of Tibetan Buddhism* by Geshe Lhundup Sopa and Jeffrey Hopkins. Meanwhile those few European universities, where Tibetan studies are now well established, pre-eminently perhaps London and Paris, Rome and Bonn, but also Munich, Hamburg, Prague and Budapest, continue their work of publication and teaching, often with the assistance of Tibetan members of staff. The bibliography given below serves to illustrate the wide scope of interest. In the USA students of Tibetan language and literature, history and religion, will be found not only at Seattle, but also at Berkeley (University of California), Bloomington (Indiana) and Harvard. The complexity of Tibetan social life, bound up as it has been with elaborate forms of religious practice and requiring a prior knowledge of Tibetan, both literary and colloquial, seems to have proved daunting to western anthropologists with the notable exception of Melvyn Goldstein (Cleveland, Ohio).* Tibetan art is altogether another matter, for this can have a direct appeal to the non-initiated, and such has been the growth of interest in this particular aspect of Tibetan culture over the last two decades, that it demands some rather more detailed treatment.

Until 1960 or so Tibetan art was known outside Tibet from scattered museum collections and those of the very few westerners who had visited the country on official missions or as travellers and scholars. A sure indication of the lack of general knowledge and interest in the subject is the very low price for which fine paintings in the form of temple-banners (*thangka*) could occasionally be purchased in the 1950s in India and Nepal. Twenty years later the situation is very different indeed. Dealers in London, Paris, Stuttgart, New York and elsewhere now have Tibetan paintings, images and other works of art for sale at what must seem to those who knew the earlier times really incredibly high prices, often a thousand times higher and more. Very well produced catalogues have appeared on the market, and would-be purchasers all over the western world are now able to discuss dates and styles and problems of iconography.† Such a greatly increased general interest has had the excellent effect of bringing the earlier museum collections, most of which date back to the end of the 19th and beginning of the 20th centuries, from the seclusion, to which lack of public interest had often relegated them. The collections in England began to be built up mainly as a result of the British expedition into Tibet in 1904 and the subsequent establishing of trade relations with British India. The British Museum, where still today a very small part of the total collection is on display, and the Victoria & Albert Museum, were the main recipients. The earliest American collection seems to be the one at Newark Museum in New Jersey, the result of the travels of Dr Albert Shelton and his wife throughout Tibetan-Chinese borderlands. Another large and early collection is that of the Metropolitan Museum in New York. In more recent years important collections have been made mainly by purchase at the Boston Museum of Fine Arts, the Los Angeles County Museum of Art and at the Philadelphia Museum. Similarly in England small but good collections will be found at the Ashmolean Museum in Oxford, and also in Liverpool. The very fine collection, probably the best displayed in the world, at the Musée Guimet in Paris results from the travels of Monsieur Jacques Bacot, also in the Tibetan-Chinese borderlands, early this century, and from the high scholarly interest which he himself took in Tibetan literature, religion and art. The best Russian collection, deriving mainly from the Tsarist expansion into Central Asia during the second half of the 19th century, is at the Hermitage Museum in Leningrad. This collection is especially interesting for the links that it helps to establish between Buddhist art of the ancient city-states of the Takla-makan and the newly emerging styles of Tibetan art round about 1,000 A.D. The most recent collections of all are those brought together by the present Dalai Lama in New Delhi and Dharamsala, where excellent pieces can be seen, and the collection of Heinrich Harrer now purchased by the Ethnological Museum of Zürich University, where it is now on display. In 1977 the largest exhibition of Tibetan art ever held was organized in Paris at the Grand Palais and subsequently at the Haus der Kunst in Munich.* This brought together many of the finest and most significant pieces from all the museums listed above as well as from other smaller public and private collections. There is no doubt that Tibetan art has now gained the kind of publicity which it certainly deserves.

The first serious studies of the history of Tibetan art were initiated by Professor Tucci as the result of his travels in western and central Tibet in the 1930s (see above p. 140), his collections at the Istituto del Medio ed Estremo Oriente in Rome, and his subsequent publications. It is now generally agreed that the external influences which have brought Tibetan religious art into being, thus accounting for ninety per cent or more of all Tibetan art, are those from Central Asia, from China, from India transmitted mainly through Kashmir and Nepal, and from Iran also transmitted through Kashmir but during the earlier period through Central Asia as well. However, while it is easy to write in such general terms, it becomes more difficult to be precise in one's particular examples. The influence of the Buddhist city-states of Central Asia upon the developing Tibetan Buddhist culture was likely to have been considerable during the Tibetan occupation of the whole area from the mid-7th to the mid-9th century A.D. However very little remains in Tibet from this period. Especially significant would seem to be some paintings discovered at Karakhoto (illustrated in the catalogue of the Paris and Munich exhibition, nos: 22 to 33) near Turfan on that section of the old silk route where it passes to the north of the Takla-makan. These represent a style of Indo-Tibetan art of which related examples are found in old western Tibet, and specifically at the 11th/12th century monastery of Alchi in Ladakh. This ancient western

Tibetan kingdom, since 1834 effectively taken over by the Indian state of Jammu & Kashmir, has been reopened to foreign visitors since 1974, and much early material of great interest can now be added to all that was made known by Professor Tucci forty years earlier. Alchi is particularly interesting for the examples of Tibetan murals of major Buddhist divinities set against a background of subsidiary human and animal figures, where Persian and the later Moghul influence cannot be in doubt, especially in the 16th century redecorations.* It should be emphasized that the earlier Central Asian styles themselves derive on the one side from India, the source of Buddhist religious and cultural traditions, and from western Asia, especially Iran, whence passed the old silk route, along which travelled not only merchants and traders, but also propagators of Nestorian Christianity and of Mani's eclectic religion. Christians as well as Manichees were thoroughly imbued with Persian culture. At the same time Chinese influences penetrated ever deeper along the same routes but from the eastern direction. All these various influences were certainly present when the Tibetans began to develop a religious art of their own from the 8th century onwards, and it is clear that Central Asian models provided them already with several varieties of style, from which they gradually forged their own distinctive Tibetan forms. As in most evolutionary processes many of the links in the chain are lost, and Tibetan art presents itself now as something quite distinct from that of all its neighbours except for Nepal. This comes about because of all their one time surrounding Buddhist neighbours, only Nepal has maintained an active Buddhist, as well as a Hindu, culture, and Nepalese Buddhist craftsmen were working in Lhasa right up until 1959 (see above pp. 202, 226–7). Relations between Nepalese and Tibetan Buddhism have always been particularly close because they drew upon identical late Indian Buddhist traditions as preserved in Mahāyāna and Vajrayāna literature.

We have already referred above (pp. 156–8) to Chinese artistic and cultural influence which was considerable, but although their special interpretations of Buddhist teachings were certainly propagated in Tibet in the 8th century (see above p. 79), this particular influence largely disappears during later centuries, when the Tibetans were occupied in importing Buddhism direct from India, the land of its origins. Thus the later artistic influence so far as painting is concerned, is generally incidental, affecting, however noticeably, mainly the subsidiary figures and designs in an exactly analogous way to the effects of Persian influences at Alchi, already mentioned above. But this later Chinese influence, incidental as it may be, became very wide spread, and Tibetan painting styles even in far-away Ladakh are clearly affected by it. This again serves to show how impossible it is to describe Tibetan styles according to different areas. Monks and religious painters, who were often themselves monks, were very mobile, and styles were carried rapidly from one part of the Tibetan cultural world to another, where quite different styles, e.g. the more stereotyped Indian one and the far freer Chinese (see p. 157) could continue to flourish side by side. In every case, however, the main figures in paintings and images, usually bronze, were expected to follow carefully established patterns. We observed in our preface (p. 10) that comparisons between European and Tibetan cultural history break down from the end of our Middle Ages, simply because the culture typical of our world up to the 15th century or so, continued to be typical of Tibet right up to the mid-20th century. Thus there is nothing whatsoever corresponding to our Renaissance, leading to such freedom of style and production in art as much as in literature. A skilful Tibetan painter might well introduce into his work delightful little subsidiary scenes showing parks and mountains, palace and monastic interiors, even domestic scenes when they refer to the life-story of a revered lama, but his clientèle expected his work generally to conform to conventional standards and thus his freedom was effectively limited. The only portrait painting is that devoted to important lamas, teachers and yogins, and they are shown in a conventionalized style. This is altogether so in case of representations of those from the past whose actual physiognomy is quite unknown. In the case of contemporary painting portraits of this kind are actual or at least so intended. The only buildings to be depicted as central to a work are monasteries and fine examples exist of these. The combined effect of different painting traditions existing side by side and of the conventionalized religious aspects which pervade the whole, tend to make nonsense of recent outside attempts to place Tibetan works of art in periods and even in particular western century-datings, which have little or no relevance to the Tibetan scene. Tibetan murals can sometimes be dated satisfactorily thanks to the occasional presence of inscriptions. Images and temple-banners are even more occasionally dated precisely accounting to a Chinese reign year. Most pieces are quite undated and many of them are undatable. In any case few temple-banners (*thangkas*) are older than the eighteenth century simply because of their fragile nature. Some rare examples of what have been described as an Indo-Tibetan or a Nepalese style are attributed variously to the end of the 12th century (catalogue of the Paris and Munich exhibition, no: 20) or to the 13th–14th century (catalogue of the Heeranmaneck Collection, no: 121),* and of these stylistically related murals are known in Ladakh (Alchi) and in western Tibet. All would agree that we are concerned in such cases with relatively early Tibetan styles of painting, but it would seem to be impossible to fix a firm date for any particular example, especially when there is no certain way of knowing how long paintings of such a kind continued to be executed. The same state of affairs exists in the case of free standing images, usually of copper or brass alloy, silver and even gold, unless they happen to be dated. The craft of such image-making has come to an end in Tibet itself since 1959, but it continues active amongst the Nepalese (Newar) Buddhist craftsmen of Nepal. Collectors are now often hard pressed when it comes to distinguishing a newly made image (especially when it has been skilfully treated so as to appear old) from an older one, or as they might prefer to say, the fakes from the genuine examples. Here, however, a terminology is perhaps being wrongly applied to a traditional culture which still remains very much alive. Produced according to traditional forms and methods, the modern example is in no proper sense a fake, any more than a newly woven Tibetan carpet or a newly painted temple-banner can properly be so described. The would-be purchaser should be able to judge whether such a work is well executed or not. The notion that a Tibetan work of art should be worth more just because it can be claimed to be three or more centuries old, seems to have come as a surprise to the Tibetans themselves, but curio-sellers have been quick to take advantage of this imported standard of values. However, the fact that Tibetan art continues to be a living tradition, even on the present reduced scale, offers hope for the future of the whole culture, despite the bewilderment sometimes caused to present-day collectors.

Other aspects of Tibetan culture which have evoked growing interest over the last decade are music and dancing. Like artistic representation, these can have some kind of direct appeal even to the uninitiated, and of Tibetan music, both lay and religious, some very fine recordings have been made, the most noteworthy probably being the set of records compiled by the late John Levy from his recordings made in Bhutan and produced under the sponsorship of UNESCO. However, it must be noted that Tibetan religious music and chant are highly specialized studies, requiring not only a musicological training but also knowledge of the Tibetan language and of the actual rites and liturgies involved. It is only very recently that a serious effort has been made to understand the systems of Tibetan musical notation with the combined help of the relevant theoretical literature in Tibetan and of the very few Tibetan 'choir-master' monks who are capable of explaining its peculiar methods.* It would seem that Tibetan religious music is more indebted to earlier West Asian styles of pre-Muslim Persia and even maybe far-away Byzantium than to music and chant which were once in use in the great Buddhist monasteries of northern India. Perhaps more than any other aspect of this remarkable culture music serves to emphasize the difficulties involved in finding origins and identifying influences which led to its eventual formation. This comes about because music is not only transmitted more easily than any other aspect of a culture from one people to another, but also because its forms tend to be transitory when confronted with a new kind of cultural invasion. Since the twelfth century or so, by when Tibet had completed its absorption of Buddhist civilization, taking what it chose from all its various neighbours, there was no serious cultural invasion of any kind until Chinese Communist doctrines were introduced from the 1950s onwards. Thus the Tibetans preserved very ancient styles of music, just as of art-forms, the actual origins of which were presumably quite diverse. However, these had long since been moulded into something distinctively Tibetan. But while the Tibetans were able to remain for so many centuries secure in the possession of their own cultural heritage, all the surrounding countries had experienced long periods of turmoil and change especially from the 13th century onwards (see pp. 144-7 above). The rich cultural heritages in other lands, upon which the Tibetans had been drawing, were often entirely dissipated, such as the vast accumulations of Buddhist literature, of rituals, of imagery and painting and of music and chant, which had been preserved in so many monasteries and temples of northern India prior to the Moslem invasions. Further west Sassanian culture had been to a large extent absorbed by the Moslem Arab conquerors several centuries earlier, but this now suffered devastating destruction at the hands of Mongol hordes. The old silk route linking China and Byzantium along which so many cultural influences had passed, many of them finding their way into Tibet, was disrupted for ever. Since those times change after change has ensued in all the lands whence the Tibetans had found materials to enrich their own style of civilization, and thus in so many aspects of her culture, and especially in music, Tibet appears quite unique. While the conservative nature of Tibetan religion generally has protected religious music from change, popular lay music in the first half of this century was showing the clear effects of direct Chinese and Indian influences. Here processes of change and adaptation continue with young Tibetans in exile becoming rapid enthusiasts for modern 'beat' music.

Traditional dances have been preserved by at least two Tibetan groups in India. One sponsored by Dharamsala and known as Dö-gar Tshok-pa (*Zlos-gar Tshogs-pa*) has made successful tours in Switzerland, Australia and the United States. Another group has been centred on Kalimpong where we may also note the existence of an Indo-Tibet Buddhist Cultural Institute. All the participants are otherwise employed, coming together from other work for their performances and tours, and they seem to be in need of that further encouragement and support which could enable them to perform as 'professionals'. They alone seem now to be keeping alive the traditional court music of Lhasa and the *a-che lha-mo* performances to which we have referred above (p. 258). Religious dances (*'cham*) remain the special preserve of monastic communities and these continue to be performed by Tibetan monastic groups in exile, one of which, the Gyu-tö (*rGyud-stod*) has visited London and Paris.

Another subject of considerable interest is that of Tibetan medicine. A precise study of this is probably more demanding even than that of Tibetan music. The competent researcher requires a thorough knowledge of medicine and of botany as well as proficiency in classical and spoken Tibetan and the time and patience to work together with a competent Tibetan practitioner. That the Tibetans themselves are quite capable of preserving and developing their own traditional practices is proved not only by the medical school which has been established at Dharamsala but also by the several practitioners who work independently. It is only the evaluation of their theories and practices which is difficult in that it requires considerable competence both on the Tibetan and the modern scientific side. An introduction to the whole theory is provided by a such a work as the *rGyud-bźi* on which western scholars have worked (see for example R. E. Emmerick and Elisabeth Finckh in the bibliography below) but also necessary is that practical knowledge which can identify the medicaments and herbs nowadays in use. To my knowledge only one well trained European physician has worked together with a Tibetan practitioner for a long period, two to three years, and we await with interest the results of his research.* Any Tibetan presentation of their medicine in western form lacks the western forms of knowledge necessary for an adequate interpretation, and the more popular western interpretations of Tibetan medicine all too often reveal very little detailed knowledge of the Tibetan side.

Tibet itself is now going through a period of revolution, resulting in the loss of most of its ancient heritage. The whole of China has been going through the same destructive process for the last several decades, while Mongolia suffered similar experiences during the 1920s. Just as Mongolia has since been attempting to reconstruct something of its own Buddhist heritage, so the time will almost certainly come when Tibet will attempt to reassemble fragments of its lost past and rebuild in mosaic-like form this ancient culture of which there is every reason to be proud. This task will be all the better accomplished thanks to the many Tibetans now in exile who are able to keep actively alive so many of its manifestations. Nor must we forget the very important part played in this work of preservation by the artists and craftsmen of Bhutan and especially of the old Buddhist town of Pātan in Nepal (see pp. 141, 202), where so many painters, metal-workers and even a few wood-carvers are still at work, operating according to very similar cultural traditions.

Notes

PAGE

23 *Bacot, Thomas & Toussaint, *Documents de Touen Houang relatifs à l'histoire du Tibet*, Paris 1940, p. 113, lines 25-9 and p. 151. We refer to these works generally as the Tun-huang documents and abbreviate hereafter this edition of the Tibetan 'Annals' and 'Chronicle' as THD

† R. A. Stein, *Les tribus anciennes des marches sino-tibétaines*, Paris 1959, p. 10 ff.

25 *THD pp. 81 and 85-6

26 *See the important article by John Brough, 'Comments on third-century Shan-shan and the history of Buddhism', *Bulletin of the School of Oriental and African Studies*, XXVIII (1965) pp. 582-612

28 *THD p. 110, lines 21-34 and pp. 146-7

29 *See P. Pelliot, *Histoire ancienne du Tibet*, Paris 1961, pp. 1-3 and 79-82. We have rearranged the information given here, so as to provide a single account

31 *Ibid., p. 21

32 *The *Blon-po bka'-thang-yig*, f. 8b ff. See also F. W. Thomas, *Tibetan Texts and Documents*, 1, p. 276 ff. Concerning these 'rediscovered texts' see below pp. 153-4

51 *This is illustrated in E. E. Koch, *Auf dem Dach der Welt*, Frankfurt-am-Maine 1960, p. 273

53 *From the *rGyal-po bka'-thang*, 39b-40b

54 *See D. L. Snellgrove, *Buddhist Himālaya*, pp. 271-2

55 *See D. L. Snellgrove, *Nine Ways of Bon*, O.U.P. 1967, p. 37

† Tibetan *nam-mkha'*. The term *mdos*, which is often translated as 'thread-cross', has the rather wider meaning of 'ritual device'

56 *Ibid., p. 49

57 *Ibid., pp. 61-3

58 *Ibid., p. 71

† Ibid., p. 61

59 *With regard to the origin of these kings it is interesting to note that they worshipped the gods in the 'T'ang-lo-ye-yi Mountain' some 450 li north-west of Lhasa. (See P. Pelliot, *Histoire ancienne du Tibet*, p. 142.) This seems to be the *Thang-lha*, whose god *gNyen chen Thang-lha* is often involved in *rNying-ma-pa* rituals. (See D. L. Snellgrove, *Buddhist Himālaya*, pp. 239-42)

† F. W. Thomas, *Ancient Folk-Literature*, Berlin 1957, p. 108, vv. 66-9

60 *See D. L. Snellgrove, *Nine Ways of Bon*, p. 29

† THD, pp. 116 and 155

62 *THD, pp. 120-2 and 167-9

63 *THD, pp. 118 and 162

64 *See P. Pelliot, *Histoire ancienne du Tibet*, p. 83

† Ibid., pp. 130-1

90 *See H. E. Richardson, 'A Ninth Century Inscription from *rKong-po*', *Journal of the Royal Asiatic Society*, October 1954, pp. 166-71

91 *See H. E. Richardson, *Ancient Historical Edicts at Lhasa*, Luzac & Co., 1952

97 *We have retained the spelling of the king's name as it occurs in the *Padma thang-yig*, although it differs from the earlier spelling

98 *Padma thang-yig, f. 128b⁴-129b⁴ and 131b⁵-132a¹; THD, pp. 248-50 and 255-6

100 *Zhang-zhung snyan-rgyud (Snellgrove's MS), section *ga*, *snyan-rgyud ma nub-pa'i bstan-tshigs*, ff. 2b⁵-4a⁸

102   * *Ibid.* ff. 6a¹-9a²

104   * *Zhang-zhung snyan-rgyud*, section *ka*, *bla-ma rgyud-pa'i rnam-thar*, ff. 26a⁵-27b⁵

106   * *rDzogs-chen bsGrags-pa skor-gsum* (Snellgrove's MS), section *tha 3*, *lung-drug*,
       ff. 1b¹-2a⁷

107   * *rDzogs-chen bsGrags-pa skor-gsum-pa*, section *pa dong-sprugs*, folio 22b

111   * H. E. Richardson, *Ancient Historical Edicts at Lhasa*, p. 60
       † P. Pelliot, *Histoire ancienne du Tibet*, p. 139
       ‡ R. A. Stein, *L'épopée et le barde au Tibet*, p. 231

115   * The Sanskrit and Tibetan versions of this *tantra* have been edited and trans-
       lated by D. L. Snellgrove. See his *Hevajra-Tantra*, O.U.P., 1959

129   * *bKa'-rgyud bla-ma-rnams kyi rdo-rje-mgur* 58b⁶-59b³

132   * See W. Y. Evans-Wentz, *Tibet's Great Yogi Milarepa*, O.U.P., 1928, and J.
       Bacot, *Le poète tibétain Milarépa*, Paris 1925

134   * From the *bKa'-rgyud bla-ma-rnams kyi rdo-rje mgur* 84a⁵-85b²
       † See H. V. Guenther, *The Life and Teaching of Nāropa*, Oxford 1963

136   * The name *Karma-pa*, 'Man of *Karma*', viz. one who understands the causes
       and effects of acts throughout past, present and future, was used as a kind of
       nickname of *Dus-gsum-mkhyen-pa* and his successors. The name was probably
       derived, however, from association with the monastery of *Karma gDan-sa*,
       which he founded in *Khams* in 1147. See H. E. Richardson, 'The Karma-pa
       Sect', *Journal of the Royal Asiatic Society*, Oct. 1958

138   * As an example of an Indian yogin who lived to a great age in modern times
       there is Shrī Govindānanda, born in Kerala in 1826 and who died in Nepal in
       1963. He too spent several decades in solitary meditation and was also a great
       traveller. See J. G. Bennett, *Long Pilgrimage*, London 1965

141   * D. L. Snellgrove, 'Shrines and Temples in Nepal', *Arts Asiatiques* VIII (1961)

146   * A notable exception is *Chag Lo-tsa-ba*, who passed through Nepal to Bihar
       in the first half of the thirteenth century and has left valuable first-hand
       descriptions of the sites of the great Indian Buddhist centres after they had
       been ravaged by the Muslim invaders. See G. Roerich, *Biography of Dharma-
       svāmin*, Patna (India) 1959

150   * For the complete biographies of some typical Tibetan lamas see D. L. Snell-
       grove, *Four Lamas of Dolpo*, Cassirer, Oxford 1967

153   * For a brief account of his quite extraordinary career, see W. D. Shakabpa, *Tibet
       —a Political History*, pp. 74-82

169   * See H. V. Guenther, *The Jewel Ornament of Liberation*, London 1959

171   * Concerning this set, see D. L. Snellgrove, *Buddhist Himālaya*, p. 228 ff.

174   * See D. L. Snellgrove, *Nine Ways of Bon*
       † *Blue Annals*, p. 682, corrected by reference to Tibetan text (*nya* 123a-b)

175   * *Ibid.*, p. 594, Tib. text *nya* 83b-84a

178   * The one great authority on the *Ge-sar* epic is Professor R. A. Stein. See his
       L'épopée tibétaine de Gesar, Presses Universitaires de France, Paris 1956, and
       Recherches sur l'épopée et le barde au Tibet, Paris 1959

196   * His history is available in German translation by A. Schiefner, entitled
       Tāranātha's Geschichte des Buddhismus in Indien, St Petersburg 1869. Tibetan
       text edited by Schiefner, St Petersburg 1868

197   * See D. L. Snellgrove, *Four Lamas of Dolpo*, pp. 247-56

201   * For an account of this unusual and interesting piece of deception, see W. D. Shakabpa, *Tibet—a Political History*, pp. 125-8

202   * *ba-re* is the Newar form of Sanskrit *vandya*, 'worthy', used as a respectful term for Buddhist priests and monks. In Nepal they became from the thirteenth century onwards the Buddhist equivalents of Brahmans, for they were no longer celibate (see p. 147) but were recognized as the highest Buddhist caste. They were silversmiths and goldsmiths for a large part, although some of them continued to function as priests

207   * The most convenient edition of these songs is that published as *Love Songs of the Sixth Dalai Lama*, translated into Chinese and English by Yu Dawchyuan, Peiping 1930. For the verses we have selected and retranslated from the original Tibetan, see his edition pp. 46-55 and 76-79

217   * *Ibid* pp. 156-7

222   * *Documenti dei missionari italiani nel Tibet e nel Nepal* (i-vii) in 'Nuovo Ramuso', Rome 1952-6
        † Published by Routledge, London 1931, revised edition 1937

225   * For a detailed account of the historical events covered so far in our Chapter 8 see Luciano Petech, *China and Tibet in the early 18th Century*, Brill, Leiden 1950. This is the finest detailed monograph published so far on a specific period of Tibetan history

226   * For further details see H. E. Richardson, *Tibet and its History*, pp. 64-68

227   * *Ibid*, p. 72
        † The spelling *Thibet* was adopted by the authors and is used in all French editions of their work. Two new editions have recently appeared in France, that of *Club des Libraires de France* 1962, and of *Le Livre de Poche Chrétien*, *Librairie Générale Française* 1962. The English translated edition, *Travels in Tartary and Tibet*, London 1928, is out of print

235   * *Three Years in Tibet*, Madras 1909
        † *Tibet Past and Present*, Oxford 1924, *The People of Tibet*, Oxford 1928, *The Religion of Tibet*, Oxford 1931 and *Portrait of the Dalai Lama*, London 1942

247   * For details, see the interesting article by R. A. Stein, 'Le *Linga* des dances masquées lamaïques et la théorie des âmes' in *Liebenthal Festschrift*, *Sino-Indian Studies*, vol. v, nos. 3-4, pp. 1-36

248   * The first wheeled vehicles to enter Central Tibet were the horse-drawn traps and soon afterwards the cars, all introduced by the British at the beginning of the twentieth century. Subsequently bicycles were brought in by Nepalese residents. In the extreme eastern parts of Tibet which were under some kind of direct Chinese administration, carts were already in use.

257   * For such a ceremony, see D. L. Snellgrove, *Buddhist Himālaya*, pp. 262-74

263   * *dag pa'i zhing gi lha sar/ma dag dbyin ji slob sgra/*
        lham gog rdol du 'gro dgos/khong tshos byed pa'i las red
        The last phrase, translated freely so as to achieve a jingle, means literally: 'this is the work that they are doing'

264   * See the article by Walter Simon, 'Tibetan Lexicography and Etymological Research' in *Transactions of the Philological Society*, 1964

267   * For a detailed description of these and subsequent events see H. E. Richardson, *Tibet and its History*, pp. 183 ff.

PAGE

277 *We draw attention also to the work of Barbara Aziz just published (see the Bibliography below) on the structure of Tibetan rural society, and of Eva Dargyay (Munich) on structure and change within a group of Tibetan villages (not yet published).

277
278 †The most important catalogue is that published in Paris (1977) under the *auspices of the Musée Guimet, entitled *Dieux et démons de l'Himalaya*, and subsequently in an improved German edition with a more apt title *Tibet, Kunst des Buddhismus*, Munich 1977. Another very informative catalogue is that of the Newark Museum, New Jersey, produced by Eleanor Olson in five volumes, published and reprinted at varying dates: I–1950, 1971; II–1950, 1972; III–1971; IV–1961; V–1971. One may also note some other catalogues produced for local exhibitions of Tibetan art: Zürich 1969, New York 1974, Berlin 1976, Cologne 1977, Brussels 1975 and 1978.

279 *See D. L. Snellgrove & T. Skorupski, *The Cultural Heritage of Ladakh*, vol. I, Boulder 1977, pp. 31, 56.

280 **The Arts of India & Nepal, The Nasli & Alice Heeramaneck Collection*, Museum of Fine Arts, Boston 1966.

281 *We have in mind especially the work being done in London by Mr Ricardo Canzio on the Sakya Paṇḍita's 'Treatise on Music' (*Rol-mo'i bstan-bcos*) and its relevance to present-day Tibetan liturgy and chant. We also note a small work produced by Mr Jampel Kaldhen on the Indo-Tibet Buddhist Cultural Institute in Kalimpong, entitled *Rang-re'i dbyangs kyi lde-mig* ('The Key of our Music'), as evidence of Tibetan interest in this work of elucidation. The works on Mme Mireille Helffer are listed in the Bibliography to the Revised Edition.

283 *This is Monsieur Fernand Meyer who is completing a thesis on the subject for the University of Strasbourg. See his article 'Médecine tibétaine' as listed in the Bibliography to the Revised Edition. He draws attention to the many divergences between theory and practice, especially the manner in which Tibetan medicinal/botanical names may be transferred to very different plants simply because certain characteristics appear similar. Such lack of scientific exactitude makes the task of a scientifically minded researcher all the more difficult.

Chronological Table

Manchu Overlordship

1720 Ch'ing Emperor, K'ang Hsi, drives out Dzungars and establishes his authority at Lhasa.

1723 Civil war follows withdrawal of Chinese from Lhasa.

1728 *Pho-lha bSod-nams s Tobs-rgyas* (b. 1689) defeats rivals; governs Tibet with Chinese approval and support. Imperial representatives (Ambans) re-established at Lhasa.

1737 IIIrd Pan-chen Lama, *Blo-bzang dPal-ldan Ye-shes*, born.

1740 *Pho-lha* given title of 'King'.

1745 End of Christian mission at Lhasa.

1747 *Pho-lha* dies; his son *Gyur-med rNam-rgyal* succeeds.

1750 Assassination of *Gyur-med rNam-rgyal*: murder of Ambans: further Chinese military expedition.

1757 Death of VIIth Dalai Lama: appointment of first of almost continuous series of monk regents.

1758 VIIIth Dalai Lama, *'Jam-dpal rGya-mtsho*, born.

1775 Warren Hastings sends George Bogle to Tibet.

1781 IV Pan-chen Lama, *Blo-bzang bs Tan-pa'i Nyi-ma*, born.

1792 Gorkha invasion evicted by army of Emperor Ch'ien Lung. Policy of excluding foreigners adopted.

1806 IXth Dalai Lama, *Lung-rtogs rGya-mtsho*, born.

1816 Xth Dalai Lama, *Tshul-khrims rGya-mtsho*, born.

1838 XIth Dalai Lama, *mKhas-grub rGya-mtsho*, born.

1842 The Dogra War.

1854 Vth Pan-chen Lama, *bs Tan-pa'i dBang-phyug*, born.

1856 XIIth Dalai Lama, *'Phrin-las rGya-mtsho*, born. War with Nepal.

1876 XIIIth Dalai Lama, *Thub-bstan rGya-mtsho*, born.

1883 VIth Pan-chen Lama, *Chos-kyi Grags-pa*, born, died 1937.

British Interests

1888 First clash between Britain and Tibet, in Sikkim.

1904 The Younghusband Expedition. Treaty between Britain and Tibet.

1906 Sino-British treaty about Tibet. Revival of Chinese activity.

1910 Chao Erh-feng's troops occupy Lhasa. Dalai Lama flees to India. Former relationship with Emperor denounced by Tibetans.

Renewal of Independence

1911 End of Ch'ing dynasty.

1913 Eviction of Chinese from Tibet.

1914 Tripartite Conference at Simla: Agreement between Tibet and Britain only: hostilities with Chinese continue.

1934 Death of XIIIth Dalai Lama.

1935 XIVth Dalai Lama, *bsTan-'dzin rGya-mtsho*, born. Chinese and British missions at Lhasa.

1947 Tibetans accept Indian assumption of former British relationship.

Communist Domination

1950 Chinese Communists attack Tibet.

1951 Sino-Tibetan Agreement allows Chinese occupation of Tibet.

1954 Sino-Indian Agreement about Tibet.

1959 Abortive rising against Chinese at Lhasa. Dalai Lama flees to India. Many refugees follow. Tibetan Government replaced by Chinese dictatorship. Decay of culture and religion.

1967 Red Guards complete destruction of holy places.

Succession of Religious Schools

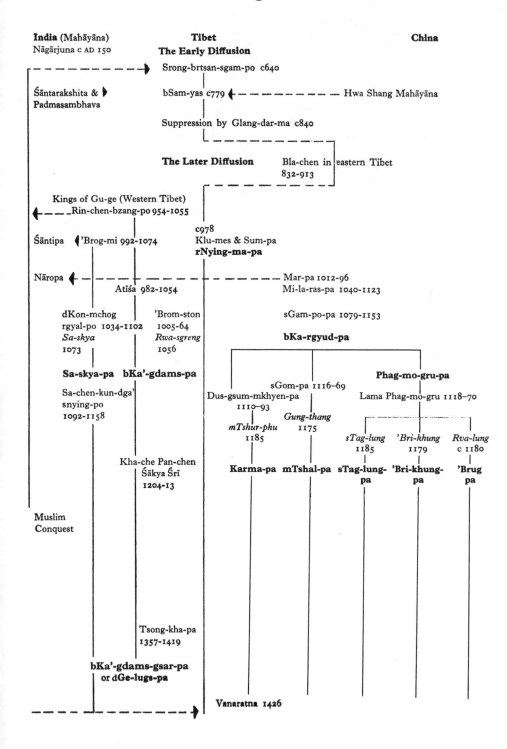

India (Mahāyāna)
Nāgārjuna c AD 150

Tibet
The Early Diffusion

China

Srong-brtsan-sgam-po c640

Śāntarakshita &
Padmasambhava

bSam-yas c779 ←——————— Hwa Shang Mahāyāna

Suppression by Glang-dar-ma c840

The Later Diffusion   Bla-chen in eastern Tibet
832-913

Kings of Gu-ge (Western Tibet)
Rin-chen-bzang-po 954-1055

c978
Klu-mes & Sum-pa
rNying-ma-pa

Śāntipa   'Brog-mi 992-1074

Nāropa ←——————————— Mar-pa 1012-96
Mi-la-ras-pa 1040-1123

Atīśa 982-1054

dKon-mchog   'Brom-ston   sGam-po-pa 1079-1153
rgyal-po 1034-1102   1005-64
Sa-skya   *Rwa-sgreng*   **bKa-rgyud-pa**
1073   1056

Sa-skya-pa bKa'-gdams-pa
Phag-mo-gru-pa

Sa-chen-kun-dga'
snying-po
1092-1158

sGom-pa 1116-69
Dus-gsum-mkhyen-pa   Lama Phag-mo-gru 1118-70
1110-93
Gung-thang
mTshur-phu   1175
1185   *sTag-lung* *'Bri-khung* *Rva-lung*
1185   1179   c 1180

Kha-che Pan-chen
Śākya Śrī
1204-13

**Karma-pa mTshal-pa sTag-lung- 'Bri-khung- 'Brug
pa   pa   pa**

Muslim
Conquest

Tsong-kha-pa
1357-1419

**bKa'-gdams-gsar-pa
or dGe-lugs-pa**

Vanaratna 1426

Pronunciation Rules

Like all simplified forms of phonetic spelling, the results are only approximate, for it is not practicable to attempt to cover all the subtle changes of vowel and consonant harmony which occur in Tibetan words of more than one syllable.

1. There are eight prefixed letters, *g, d, b, m, r, s, l* and the apostrophe ' which represents a distinct letter in the Tibetan alphabet. All these eight 'prefixes' may be ignored for the purpose of an approximate pronunciation.
E.g. *dKar-gdung-pa* is pronounced 'Kar-dung-pa'.
    bsTan-'gyur is pronounced 'Tan-gyur' or better 'Ten-jur'
                         (see notes 3 and 7 below)
Thus in our index, as in all Tibetan dictionaries, Tibetan words are given under their 'radical' letters, and not under prefixed letters. E.g. *dKar-gdung-pa* appears under K.

2. Ignoring these prefixes, one may pronounce the radical letters much as in English, but note that:
    c is pronounced as a lightly pronounced 'j'.
E.g. *lCag-po-ri* is pronounced 'Jag-po-ri' with 'j' pronounced as in English 'June'.
    th represents an aspirated 't', *viz* 't-h' (and not English 'th') just as *kh, ph* (which does not = 'f') and *tsh* represent aspirated 'k', 'p' and 'ts'.
E.g. *Thub-bstan rnam-rgyal* is pronounced 'T-hub-ten nam-gyel'

    z is pronounced as 's'.
    zh is pronounced as 'sh' (words beginning with *z* and *zh* are in fact pronounced on a lower tone, but we have kept tone out of these rules).
    ng is often an initial in Tibetan, whereas it occurs only in a medial or final position in English.

3. Some combinations of consonants are simplified into single sounds:
    gy is sometimes pronounced as an English 'j',
    py by the same process of palatalization is pronounced like Tibetan *c* (*viz.* a lightly pronounced English 'j'),
  phya similarly is pronounced as *ch*,
   bya is pronounced as *j* (a deep English 'ch'),
  mya is pronounced as *nya*,
    tr and *dr* are usually pronounced so that the 'r' is scarcely heard.
    mr is simply pronounced as *m*,
    sr is usually pronounced as *s*,

v as the last element of compound consonants is not pronounced:
Zhva-nag pronounced 'Sha-nag'.

4. Other combinations of consonants are pronounced in ways seemingly little connected with the written style, for while spellings have remained fixed since the seventh century, sound values have changed in varying degrees in the different parts of Tibet. The language of Central Tibet tends always to be the standard, and this has undergone the most marked phonetic changes.

db is pronounced as 'w' and *dby* as 'y',

kr is pronounced like *tr* (see note 3 above),

khr and *phra* are pronounced as 'trh' *viz.* aspirated *tr*,

gr and *br* are pronounced like *dr*.

E.g. *Khri-srong-de-brtsan* is pronounced as 'Tri-song-de-tsan', simplified still further by some authors to 'Tri-song-de-tsen' or even 'Ti-song-de-tsen'. (When different authors embark upon simplified 'phonetic' spellings for the use of Western readers, it becomes impossible to keep to a generally accepted form in names such as this.)

'Brog-mi is pronounced as 'Drog-mi',

'Bras-spungs is pronounced as 'Drä-pung', often written in Western works simply as Drepung. (For the vowel change see note 7.)

Whereas the combinations *kla, gla, bla, rla* and *sla* are all pronounced simply as 'la', *zla* is pronounced as 'da'.

E.g. *Zla-ba* is pronounced 'Da-wa',

Gling is pronounced 'Ling'.

(This example is written with capital G, because the Tibetans themselves treat it as the radical letter in their dictionaries. See note 1 above.)

5. There are ten possible final letters, namely: *g, ng, d, n, b, m, r, s, l* and the letter '. Of these *d* and *s* are not pronounced, while *g, r,* and *l* are sometimes so lightly pronounced that they may be omitted in phonetic spellings. The letter ' which is treated as the sign of the pure vowel 'a' by Tibetans, often produces an intruding nasal sound in compound words. E.g. *bKa'-'gyur* pronounced 'Kanjur'.

6. One may note that letters which come in the middle of compound words, whether finals of the first syllable or initials (even the normally silent prefixes) of the second syllable, tend to be preserved in pronunciation. E.g. *Blo-bzang* may be pronounced 'Lo-sang' or 'Lobsang'. Here again the Tibetans regard *B* as the radical letter in the combination *Bl.* Compare *Gling* above.

7. As in English (compare the quality of the vowel *a* in *pa* and *pan*), certain consonants modify the preceding vowel. Thus *a* comes to be pronounced like open *e* or German *ä*, *o* may be modified to *ö*, and *u* to *ü*

Bibliography

BACOT, J. *Le poète tibétain Milarépa*, Paris 1925
Le Tibet révolté, Paris 1912
Trois mystères tibétains, Paris 1921
La vie de Marpa le 'traducteur', Paris 1937
BACOT, J., THOMAS, F. W. & TOUSSAINT, *Documents de Touen-houang relatifs à l'histoire du Tibet*, Paris 1940
BAILEY, F. M. *No passport for Tibet*, London 1957
BELL, SIR C. *The people of Tibet*, Oxford 1928
Portrait of the Dalai Lama, London 1946
The religion of Tibet, Oxford 1931
Tibet: Past and Present, Oxford 1924
BROUGH, J. 'Comments on third-century Shan-shan and the history of Buddhism', *Bulletin of the School of Oriental and African Studies*, xxviii(1965), pp. 582–612
CHANG, G. C. C. *The Hundred Thousand Songs of Milarepa*, New York 1962
CHAPMAN, F. S. *Lhasa, the Holy city*, London 1938
CONZE, E. *Buddhism*, Oxford 1951
Buddhist Wisdom Books, London 1958
The Prajñāpāramitā Literature, The Hague 1960
DALAI LAMA, XIVth *My Land and my People*, London 1962
DAS, S. C. *Indian Pandits in the Land of Snow*, Calcutta 1893: reprint 1965
Journey to Lhasa and Central Tibet, London 1904
DASGUPTA, S. B. *An introduction to Tāntric Buddhism*, Calcutta 1950
DAVID-NEIL, A. *Initiations and Initiates in Tibet*, London 1931: 2nd. ed. 1958
The superhuman life of Gesar of Ling, London 1933: 2nd ed. 1959
With mystics and magicians in Tibet, London 1931
DEMIÉVILLE, P. *Le Concile de Lhasa*, Paris 1952
DESIDERI, I. *An account of Tibet*, London 1937
EKVALL, R. B. *Religious observances in Tibet*, Chicago 1964
EVANS-WENTZ, W. Y. *Tibetan yoga and secret doctrines*, Oxford 1935
The Tibetan Book of the Dead, 3rd ed. London 1957
The Tibetan Book of the Great Liberation, London 1954
Tibet's great Yogi Milarepa, 2nd ed. London 1951
FERRARI, A. *mK'yen-brtse's Guide to the Holy Places of Central Tibet*: completed and edited by L. Petech and H. E. Richardson, Rome 1958
FLEMING, P. *Bayonets to Lhasa*, London 1961
FRANCKE, A. H. *Antiquities of Indian Tibet* (2 vols), Calcutta 1914 & 1926
A history of Western Tibet, London 1907
FÜRER-HAIMENDORF, C. *Himalayan Barbary*, London 1955
GETTY, A. *The Gods of Northern Buddhism*, Oxford 1928: reprint 1963
GOLDSTEIN, M.C. 'Study of the *ldab-ldob*', *Central Asian Journal*, ix (1964), pp. 123–41

GROUSSET, R. *In the footsteps of the Buddha*, London 1932
GUENTHER, H. V. *The Jewel Ornament of Liberation, by sGam-po-pa*, London 1959
The Life and teaching of Nāropa, London 1963
HAARH, E. 'The identity of Tsu-chi-chien, the Tibetan "king" who died in 804 AD', *Acta Orientalia*, xxv (1–2), pp 121–70
HARRER, H. *Seven years in Tibet*, London 1952
HEDIN, S. *Trans-Himalaya*, London 1909–1913
HOFFMANN, H. *Quellen zur Geschichte der tibetischen Bon-Religion*, Wiesbaden 1950
The religions of Tibet, London 1961
HUC, R.-E. *Souvenirs d'un voyage dans la Tartarie et le Thibet*, 1844–48. 2nd ed. Paris 1962. English translation *Travels in Tartary, Thibet and China*, 1844–48. London 1879 & 1928
KAWAGUCHI, E. *Three years in Tibet*, Madras 1909
LANDON, P. *Lhasa* (2 vols), London 1905
LI AN-CHE. 'The Sakya sect of Lamaism', *Journal of the West China Research Society*, xvi A (1945), pp. 72–86 'Dege: a study of Tibetan population', *Southwestern Journal of Anthropology*, iii (1947), pp. 279–94
'Bon: the magico-religious belief of Tibetan-speaking peoples', *ibid.* iv (1948), pp. 31–42
'rNying-ma-pa, the early form of Lamaism', *Journal of the Royal Asiatic Society*, 1948 pp. 142–63
'The bKa'-brgyud sect of Lamaism', *Journal of the American Oriental Society*, 69 ii (1949), pp. 51–59
MACDONALD, D. *The land of the Lama*, London 1928
MARAINI, F. *Secret Tibet*, London 1952
MARKHAM, SIR C. *Narrative of the mission of G. Bogle to Tibet, and the journey of J. Manning to Lhasa, with notes and lives*, London 1879
MIGOT, A. *Tibetan Marches*, London 1955
NEBESKY-WOJKOWITZ, R. *Oracles and demons of Tibet*, The Hague 1956
Where the Gods are mountains, London 1956
NORBU, T. J. *Tibet is my Country*, London 1960
OBERMILLER, E. *History of Buddhism by Bu-ston*, Heidelberg 1931
PALLIS, M. *Peaks and Lamas*, London 1939: 4th ed. 1946
PELLIOT, P. *Histoire ancienne du Tibet*, Paris 1961
PETECH, L. 'Dalai Lamas and Regents of Tibet', *T'oung Pao*, xlvii, pp. 368–394
China and Tibet in the early eighteenth century, Leiden 1950
A study on the Chronicles of Ladakh, Calcutta 1939
Documenti dei missionari italiani nel Tibet e nel Nepal (vols. i-vii), Rome 1952–6
RICHARDSON, H. E. *Ancient historical Edicts at Lhasa*, London 1953
Tibet and its history, London 1962. American ed., *A short history of Tibet*, New York 1962
'Three ancient inscriptions from Tibet', *Journal of the Asiatic Society of Bengal*, 1949, pp. 45–65
'Tibetan inscriptions at the *Zhva'i lha-khang*', *ibid.*, 1952, pp. 133–54 & 1953, pp. 1–12
'A ninth-century inscription from *rKong-po*', *ibid.*, 1954, pp. 57–73

'The *Karma-pa* Sect', *ibid.*, 1958, pp. 139–64, & 1959, pp. 1–17

ROCKHILL, W. W. *Land of the Lamas*, New York 1891

ROERICH, G. N. *The Blue Annals of gZhon-nu-dpal* (2 vols), Calcutta 1949 & 1953
Biography of Dharmasvāmin, Delhi 1959

RONA TAS, A. 'Social terms in the List of grants of the Tibetan Tun-Huang Chronicle', *Acta Orientalia Hung.*, v (1955), pp. 249–70
'Tally-stick and divination-dice in the iconography of Lha-mo', *ibid.* vi (1956), pp. 163–79

RUEGG, D. S. *The Life of Bu-ston Rin-po-che*, Rome 1966

SCHULEMANN, G. *Geschichte der Dalai-Lamas*, Leipzig 1958

SHAKABPA, W. D. *Tibet—a political history*, New Haven & London

SHEN, T.-L. & LIU, S. CH. *Tibet and the Tibetans*, Stanford, Cal. & London 1952

SNELLGROVE, D. L. *Buddhist Himālaya*, Oxford 1957
Four Lamas of Dolpo (2 vols), Oxford 1967 & 1968
The Hevajra-Tantra (2 vols), London 1959
Himalayan Pilgrimage, Oxford 1961
Nine Ways of Bon, London 1967

STEIN, SIR A. *On ancient Central Asian tracks*, London 1933

STEIN, R. A. *La civilisation tibétaine*, Paris 1962
L'épopée tibétaine de Gésar dans sa version lamaïque de Ling, Paris 1956
Recherches sur l'épopée et le barde au Tibet, Paris 1959
Les tribus anciennes des marches sino-tibétaines, Paris 1959
'Le liṅgau des dances masquées lamaïques et la théories des âmes', *Liebenthal Festschrift*, *Sino-Indian Studies*, v, nos. 3–4, pp. 1–36

TEICHMAN, SIR E. *Travels of a Consular Officer in Eastern Tibet*, Cambridge 1921

THOMAS, F. W. *Ancient folk-literature from North-Eastern Tibet*, Berlin 1957
Tibetan literary texts and documents concerning Chinese Turkestan (4 vols), London 1935, 1951, 1953 & 1963

TOUSSAINT, G. C. *Le Dict de Padma* (*Padma thang-yig*), Paris 1933

TUCCI, G. *Indo-Tibetica* (4 vols), Rome 1932–1941
Minor Buddhist texts (2 vols), Rome 1956 & 1958
Preliminary report on two scientific expeditions in Nepal, Rome 1956
Teoria e pratica del Mandala, Rome 1949: English translation, *Theory and practice of the Mandala*, London 1961
Tibet, London 1967
Tibetan painted scrolls (3 vols), Rome 1949
A Lhasa e oltre, Rome 1950: English translation, *To Lhasa and beyond*, Rome 1956
Tombs of the Tibetan Kings, Rome 1950
Travels of Tibetan pilgrims in the Swat Valley, Calcutta 1940

TUCCI, G. & GHERSI, E. *Secrets of Tibet*, London 1935

TURNER, S. *An account of an Embassy to the Court of the Teshoo Lama in Tibet*, London 1800

URAY, G. 'On the Tibetan letters *Ba* and *Wa*', *Acta Orientalia Hung.*, v (1955), pp. 101–21
'The four horns of Tibet according to the Royal Annals', *ibid.*, x (1960), pp. 33–57

WADDELL, L. A. *The Buddhism of Tibet or Lamaism*, London 1895: 2nd ed. Cambridge 1934
Lhasa and its mysteries, London 1906

WYLIE, T. V. *The geography of Tibet according to the 'Dzam-ling rgyas-bshad*, Rome 1963

YOUNGHUSBAND, SIR F. *India and Tibet*, London 1910

YU DAWCHYUAN. *Love songs of the Sixth Dalai Lama*, Peiping 1930

Bibliography to the 1978 Edition

With few exceptions this bibliography lists books and articles published since the first edition (1968) of *The Cultural History of Tibet*. It cannot claim to be complete but it attempts to be fairly representative of the large amount of original research work which has been undertaken on the subject over the last decade. We draw special attention to the following journals:

Kailash, A Journal of Himalayan Studies, published under the editorship of Mr Hallvard K. Kuloy, in Kathmandu, Nepal, since 1972;

The Tibet Journal, published by the Library of Tibetan Works and Archives in Dharamsala, India, since 1975;

Zentralasiatische Studien, produced by the Institute for Central Asian Studies (Seminar für Sprach- und Kulturwissenschaft Zentralasien) of Bonn University, and published by Otto Harrassowitz, Wiesbaden, since 1967.

It seems unnecessary to list the many articles concerned with various aspects of Tibetan culture in such journals which are largely devoted to the subject. One may note also: *Acta Asiatica, Bulletin of the Institute of Eastern Culture*, vol. 29, Tokyo, 1975, which was devoted almost exclusively to articles on Tibet. Thus these have not all been listed separately.

Also one must note *The Bulletin of Tibetology*, published by the Sikkim (formerly Namgyal) Institute of Tibetology, under the editorship of Mr N. C. Sinha since 1964.

Short articles, some of considerable interest, have appeared in *The Tibetan Review*, a monthly paper published in Delhi.

AHMAD, ZAHIRUDDIN *Sino-Tibetan relations in the seventeenth century*, Rome 1970

ARDUSSI, J. A. 'Brewing and drinking the beer of enlightenment in Tibetan Buddhism', *Journal of the American Oriental Society* 97 (1977), pp. 115–24

ARIS, MICHAEL 'The admonition of the thunderbolt cannon ball and its place in the Bhutanese New Year festival', *Bulletin of the School of Oriental and African Studies*, XXXIX (1976), pp. 601–35

'Report on the University of California Expedition to Kutang and Nubri in Northern Nepal in Autumn 1973', *Contributions to Nepalese Studies*, Kirtipur (Nepal), 2 (1975), pp. 45–87

Bhutan, the Early History of a Himalayan Kingdom, Warminster 1978

AZIZ, BARBARA *Tibetan Frontier Families*, New Delhi 1978

BECKWITH, C. L. 'Tibet and the early medival *florissance* in Eurasia: a preliminary note on the economic history of the Tibetan empire', *Central Asiatic Journal*, XXI (1977), pp. 89–104

BEYER, S. *The Buddhist Experience*, Belmont, California 1974

The Cult of Tārā, Berkeley, Los Angeles, London 1973

BLONDEAU, ANNE MARIE *Matériaux pour l'étude de l'hippologie et de l'hippiatrie tibétaines*, Geneva 1972

'Les religions du Tibet' in *Histoire des Religions 3*, Encyclopédie de la Pléiade, Paris 1976, pp. 233–330

La Vie de Pema-öbar, drame tibétain, Paris 1973

BOGOSLOSKIJ, V. A. *Essai sur l'histoire du peuple tibétain ou la naissance d'une société de classes*, Paris 1972

BOSSON, J. E. *A Treasury of Aphoristic Jewels, the Subhaṣitaratnanidhi of Sa-skya Paṇḍita in Tibetan and Mongolian*, Indian University, Uralic and Altaic Studies, vol. 92, 1969

BRAUEN, M. *Impressionen aus Tibet*, Innsbruck 1974

BRAUEN, M. & KVÆRNE, P. *Tibetan Studies*, Zürich 1978

CARRARELLI, P. M. V. 'Il linguaggio architettonico del Tibet e la sua diffusione nell'Asia Orientale', *Rivista degli Studi Orientali*, Rome 1976, pp. 197–240

CASSINELLI, C. W. & EKVALL, R. B. *A Tibetan Principality, The Political System of Sa sKya*, Ithaca and New York 1969

DAGYAB, LODEN SHERPA *Tibetan Religious Art*, 2 vols, Wiesbaden 1977

DEMIÉVILLE, P. 'Récents travaux sur Touen-houang', *T'oung Pao*, LVI (1970), pp. 1–95

DE JONG, J. W. 'Notes à propos des colophons du Kanjur', *Zentralasiatische Studien*, 6 (1972), pp. 505–559

DENWOOD, P. T. *The Tibetan Carpet*, Warminster 1974

'Bhutanese Architecture', *Asian Affairs*, LVIII (1971), pp. 24–33

'Tibetan temple-art in its architectural setting' in *Mahāyānist Art after A.D.900*, School of Oriental & African Studies, London 1972, pp. 47–55

'A Greek Bowl from Tibet', *Iran*, XI (1973), pp. 121–7

DE ROSSI FILIBECK, ELENA 'Testi tibetani riguardanti i Gorkha', *Atti della Accademia Nazionale dei Lincei*, 1977, Memorie, series VIII, vol. XXI, pp. 1–57

DOUGLAS, N. & WHITE, M. *Karmapa: the Black Hat Lama of Tibet*, London 1976

EKVALL, R. B. *Fields on the Hoof. Nexus of Tibetan Nomadic Pastoralism*, New York 1968

EIMER, H. *Berichte über das Leben des Atīśa (Dīpaṃkaraśrījñāna)*, Wiesbaden 1977

'Die Gar log Episode bei Padma dkar po und ihre Quellen', *Orientalia Suecana*, Uppsala, XXIII–XXIV (1974–5), pp. 182–199

Skizzen des Erlösungsweges in buddhistischen Begriffsreihen, Bonn 1976

EMMERICK, R. E. 'A chapter from the rgyud-bźi', *Asia Major*, XIX (1973), pp. 141–62

'Sources of the rgyud-bźi', *Zeitschrift der Deut-*

schen *Morgenländischen Gesellschaft*, Supplement III, 2, 1977, pp. 1135–42
Tibetan Texts concerning Khotan, London 1967
FREMANTLE, FRANCESCA & TRUNGPA, CHÖGYAM, *The Tibetan Book of the Dead*, Boulder & London 1975
GABORIEAU, M. *Récit d'un voyageur musulman au Tibet*, Paris 1973
GOLDSTEIN, M. C. 'The balance between centralization and decentralization in the traditional Tibetan political system', *Central Asiatic Journal*, xv (1971), pp. 170–182
'Taxation and the structure of a Tibetan village', *Central Asiatic Society*, xv (1971), pp. 1–27
'Serfdom and mobility: an examination of the institution of "human lease" in traditional Tibetan society', *Journal of Asian Studies*, xxx (1971), pp. 521–34
'Stratification, polyandry, and family structure in Central Tibet', *Southwestern Journal of Anthropology*, 27 (1971), pp. 64–74
Modern colloquial Tibetan—Lhasa dialect, Seattle, University of Washington 1970
Modern literary Tibetan, Urbana, University of Illinois 1973
Dictionary of modern literary Tibetan, Kathmandu 1975
GUENTHER, H. V. *Buddhist Philosophy, Theory and Practice*, Boulder 1976
HAHN, M. *Lehrbuch der klassischen tibetischen schriftsprache*, Bonn 1974
HAARH, E. *The Yar-luṅ dynasty. A study with particular regard to the contribution of myths and legends to the history of ancient Tibet and the origin and nature of its kings*, Copenhagen 1969
HELFFER, MIREILLE, *Les chants dans l'épopée tibétaine de Ge-sar d'après le livre de la course de cheval*, Geneva, Paris 1977
'Traditions musicales des Sa-skya-pa relatives au culte des Mgon-po', *Journal Asiatique* 264 (1976), pp. 357–404
HOFFMANN, H. (editor) *Tibet, a handbook*, Bloomington 1975
HOPKINS, J. *Tantra in Tibet, the Great Exposition of Secret Mantra* by Tsong-ka-pa, introduced by H.H. the 14th Dalai Lama, trans. & ed. by Jeffrey Hopkins, London 1977
IMAEDA, Y. 'Documents tibétains de Touen-houang concernant la concile du Tibet', *Journal Asiatique* 263 (1975), pp. 125–46
JEST, C. 'A technical note on the Tibetan method of block-carving', *Man* 61 (1961), pp. 83–5
Dolpo, communautés de langue tibétaine du Népal, Paris 1975
KARMAY, HEATHER *Early Sino-Tibetan Art*, Warminster 1975
KARMAY, SAMTEN G. *The Treasury of Good Sayings: a Tibetan history of Bon*, London 1972
'A discussion on the doctrinal position of the rDzogs-chen from the 10th to the 13th centuries', *Journal Asiatique* 263 (1975), pp. 147–56
'A general introduction to the history and doctrines of Bon', *Memoirs of the Research Department of the Toyo Bunko* 33 (1975), pp. 171–217
KASCHEWSKY. R. *Das Leben des lamaistischen Heiligen Tsongkhapa Blo-bzang-grags-pa (1357–1419)*, Wiesbaden 1971

KASCHEWSKY, R. & TSERING, P. *Das Leben der Himmelsfee, 'Gro-ba bzaṅ-mo*, Vienna 1975
KVÆRNE, P. *An Anthology of Buddhist Tantric Songs, a study of the Caryāgīti*, Oslo 1977
'Aspects of the origin of the Buddhist tradition in Tibet', *Numen*, XIX, Leiden 1972, pp. 22–40
'Bonpo Studies, the *A Khrid* System of Meditation', part I, *Kailash*, Kathmandu, I (1973), pp. 19–50; part II, *id*, pp. 247–32
'The Canon of the Tibetan Bonpos', part I, *Indo-Iranian Journal*, The Hague, XVI (1974), pp. 18–56; part II, *id*, pp. 96–144
'A Chronological table of the Bonpo: the *bstan-rcis* of *Ñi-ma bstan-' jin*', *Acta Orientalia*, Copenhagen, XXXIII (1971), pp. 205–82
'On the Concept of Sahaja in Indian Buddhist Tantric Literature', *Temenos*, Turku (Finland), 11 (1975), pp. 88–135
'Remarques sur l'administration d'un monastère bon-po', *Journal Asiatique*, 258 (1980), pp. 187–208
A Norwegian Traveller in Tibet, New Delhi 1973
LALOU, MARCELLE *Etudes tibétaines dédiées à la mémoire de Marcelle Lalou*, Paris 1977
LODRÖ, GESHE G. *Geschichte der Kloster-Universität Drepung*, vol. I, Wiesbaden 1974
LOWRY, J. *Tibetan Art*, Victoria & Albert Museum, London 1973
'Three seventeenth century Tibetan thankas', *Victoria & Albert Museum Bulletin* IV (1968), pp. 106–112
MACDONALD, ARIANE *Etudes tibétaines* (Actes du XXIX Congrès International des orientalistes), Paris 1973
MACDONALD, ARIANE & IMAEDA, Y. *L'Art du Tibet*, Paris 1977
MACDONALD, A. W. *Matériaux pour l'étude de la littérature populaire tibétaine*, Paris, vol. I, 1967; vol. II, 1972
MACGREGOR, J. *Tibet, a chronicle of exploration*, London 1970
MARAZZI, A. *Tibetani in Svizzera, Analisi di una distanza culturale*, Milan 1975
MEYER, F. 'Médecine tibétaine—l'homme et son milieu', *Colloques internationaux du Centre National de la Recherche Scientifique*, no. 268, *Himalaya, Écologie-ethnologie*, Paris 1976 (December), pp. 195–205
MILLER, R. A. *Studies in the Grammatical Tradition in Tibet*, Amsterdam
Studies in the History of Linguistics, vol. 6, Amsterdam 1976
NADOU, J. *Les bouddhistes kāśmīriens au moyen âge*, Paris 1968
NAGAO, G. 'Reflections on Tibetan Studies in Japan', *Acta Asiatica* 29 (1975), pp. 107–28
NEBESKY-WOJKOWITZ, R. DE, *Tibetan Religious Dances*, The Hague 1976
NEUMAIER, EVA 'bKa'-brgyad raṅ byuṅ raṅ śar, ein rJogs-ćʼen-Tantra', *Zeitschrift der Deutschen Morgenländischen Gesellschaft*, 120 (1970), pp. 131–163
NORBU, DAWA *Red Star over Tibet*, London 1974
NORBU, THUBTEN JIGME & TURNBULL, C. *Tibet*, New York 1968
OLSHAK, BLANCHE C. & WANGYAL, GESHE THUPTEN *Mystic Art in Ancient Tibet*, London 1973

OTT-MARTI, A. E. *Tibeter in der Schweiz. Kulturelle Verhaltensweisen im Wandel*, Zürich 1971

PETECH, L. *Aristocracy and Government in Tibet*, Rome 1973

A History of Ladakh, Rome 1977

'China and the European travellers to Tibet, 1860–1880', *T'oung Pao*, LXII (1976), pp. 219–52

RAHUL, RAM *The Government and Politics of Tibet*, Delhi 1969

The Himalayan Borderlands, Delhi 1970

RAUBER, HANNA *Der Schmied und sein Handwerk im traditionellen Tibet*, Zürich 1976

RECHUNG RINPOCHE *Tibetan Medicine*, London 1973

RICHARDSON, H. E. *Ch'ing Dynasty Inscriptions at Lhasa*, Rome 1975

' "The Dharma that Came Down from Heaven": a Tun-huang Fragment', *Buddhist Thought & Asian Civilization*, California 1977, pp. 219–229

'Early Burial Grounds in Tibet and Tibetan decorative art of the VIIIth and IXth centuries', *Central Asiatic Journal*, VIII (1963), pp. 73–92

'The rKong-po inscription', *Journal of the Royal Asiatic Society*, 1972, pp. 30–39

'The Growth of a Legend', *Asia Major*, XVI (1971), 169–77

'The Inscription at the Tomb of Khri Lde Srong Brtsan', *Journal of the Royal Asiatic Society*, 1969, pp. 29–38

'A new inscription of Khri Srong Lde Brtsan', *Journal of the Royal Asiatic Society*, 1964, pp. 1–13

'The Skar Cung Inscription', *Journal of the Royal Asiatic Society*, 1973, pp. 12–20

ROSE, L. E. *The Politics of Bhutan*, Ithaca and London 1977

RUEGG, D. S. *Le traité de Tathāgatagarbha de Bu-ston Rin chen grub*, Paris 1973

SCHUH, D. *Erlasse und Sendschreiben mongolisher Herrscher für tibetische Geistliche*, St. Augustin, Bonn 1977

Urkunden und Sendschreiben aus Zentraltibet, Ladakh und Zangskar, vol. I, St. Augustin, Bonn 1976

Untersuchungen zur Geschichte der Tibetischen Kalenderrechnung, Wiesbaden 1973.

SERRUYS, H. 'Early Lamaism in Mongolia', *Oriens Extremus*, Oct. 1963, pp. 181–216

SINHA, N. C. *An Introduction to the History and Religion of Tibet*, Calcutta 1975

SNELLGROVE, D. L. & SKORUPSKI, T. *The Cultural Heritage of Ladakh*, vol. I, Boulder 1977

SOPA, GESHE L. & HOPKINS, J. *Practice and Theory of Tibetan Buddhism*, London 1976

STEIN, R. A. *Tibetan Civilization*, London 1972

Vie et Chants de 'Brug-pa Kun-legs le Yogin, Paris 1972

'Le texte tibétain de 'Brug-pa kun-legs', *Zentralasiatische Studien*, 7 (1973), pp. 9–219

'Un document ancien relatif aux rites funéraires des bon-po tibétains', *Journal Asiatique*, 258 (1970), pp. 155–86

TARING, RINCHEN DROLMA *Daughter of Tibet*, London 1970

TUCCI, G. *The Ancient Civilization of Transhimalaya*, London 1973

Deb-t'er dmar-po gsar-ma, Tibetan chronicle by bSod-nams grags-pa, vol. I, Rome 1971

TUCCI, G. & HEISSIG, W. *Les religions du Tibet et de la Mongolie*, Paris 1973

URAY, G. 'L'annalistique et la pratique bureaucratique au Tibet ancien', *Journal Asiatique*, 263 (1975), pp. 157–70

'The narrative of legislation and organisation of the *mKhas-pa'i dga'-ston*. The origins of the traditions concerning Sroń-brcan sgam-po as first legislator and organiser of Tibet', *Acta Orientalia Academiae Scientarum Hungaricae* 26 (1972), pp. 11–68

VOSTRIKOV, A. I. *Tibetan Historical Literature. Soviet Indology Series 4*, Calcutta 1970

WANGYAL, GESHE *The Door of Libration, essential teachings of the Tibetan Buddhist tradition*, New York 1973

WAYMAN, A. *The Buddhist Tantras*, London 1974

WAYMAN, A. & LESSING, F. D. *Fundamentals of the Buddhist Tantras* (Indo-Iranian Monographs, Vol. VIII), The Hague, Paris 1968

WILHELM, *Prüfung und Initiation im Buche Pauṣya und in der Biographie des Nāropa*, Wiesbaden 1965

WOODCOCK, G. *Into Tibet, the early British explorers*, London 1971

WYLIE, T. V. 'The first Mongol conquest of Tibet reinterpreted', *The Harvard Journal of Asiatic Studies*, 37 (1977), pp. 103–133

Reprints of earlier works

In the series *Bibliotheca Himalayica*, as edited by H. K. Kuløy and published by the Mañjuśrī Publishing House, New Delhi:

DAS, SARAT CHANDRA *Contributions of the Religion and History of Tibet*, 1970

Journey to Lhasa and Central Tibet, 1970

DUKA, T. *Life and Works of Alexander Csoma de Körös*, 1972

EDGAR, J. W. *Report on a visit to Sikhim and the Tibetan Frontier*, 1969

Gazetteer of Sikhim, 1972

HODGSON, B. H. *Essays on the Languages Literature and Religion of Nepal and Tibet*, 1972

MARKHAM, C. *The Mission of George Bogle to Tibet and the Journey of Thomas Manning to Lhasa*, 1971

TURNER, S. *An Account of an Embassy to the Court of the Teshoo Lama in Tibet*, 1971

Other reprints:

BELL, SIR CHARLES *The Religion of Tibet*, London 1970

CARRASCO, P. *Land and Polity in Tibet*, Seattle 1972

DASGUPTA, S. B. *An Introduction to Tantric Buddhism*, Boulder 1974

FRANCKE, A. H. *Antiquities of Indian Tibet*, 2 vols, New Delhi 1972

NEBESKY-WOJKOWITZ, R. DE *Oracles and Demons of Tibet*, Graz 1975

OBERMILLER, E. *History of Buddhism*, Tokyo, no date (Suzuki Research Foundation Reprint series 5)

PALLIS, M. *Peaks and Lamas*, 3rd revised edition, London 1974

PETECH, L. *China and Tibet in the early eighteenth century*, revised edition, Leiden 1972

ROERICH, G. N. *The Blue Annals* in one volume, Delhi 1976

SHEN, T.-L. & LIU, S. CH. *Tibet and the Tibetans*, New York 1973

WADDELL, L. A. *The Buddhism of Tibet or Lamaism*, London 1971

Bibliography to the 1995 Edition

ARIS, M. *Hidden Treasures and Secret Lives. A Study of Pemalingpa (1450–1521) and the Sixth Dalai Lama (1683–1706)*, London 1989

ARIS, M., & BOOZ, P. *Lamas, Princes, and Brigands. Joseph Rock's Photographs of the Tibetan Borderlands of China*, New York 1992

BASS, C. *Inside the Treasure House. A Time in Tibet*. London 1990

BECKWITH, C. I. *The Tibetan Empire in Central Asia*, Princeton 1987

BÉGUIN, G. *Art ésoterique de l'Himâlaya. La donation Lionel Fournier*, Paris 1990

BÉGUIN, G. (ed.) *Dieux et démons de l'Himâlaya*, Paris 1977

BLONDEAU, A.-M. "Le 'découvreur' du *Mani bka'-bum* était-il bon-po?", in L. Ligeti (ed.), *Tibetan and Buddhist Studies Commemorating the 200th Anniversary of the Birth of Alexander Csoma de Körös*, vol. I, Budapest 1984, pp. 77–123

BOORD, M. *The Cult of the Deity Vajrakīla, According to the Texts of the Northern Treasures Tradition of Tibet (Byang-gter phur ba)*, Tring 1993

BUFFETRILLE, K. "La restauration du monastère de bSam yas: un exemple de continuité dans la relation chapelain-donateur au Tibet?" *Journal Asiatique*, CCLXXVII/3–4(1989), pp. 363–411

BUFFETRILLE, K. "Questions soulevées par la restauration de bSam yas," in S. Ihara & Z. Yamaguchi (eds.), *Tibetan Studies: Proceedings of the 5th Seminar of the International Association for Tibetan Studies*, vol. 2, Narita 1992, pp. 378–386

CHAN, V. *Tibet Handbook: A Pilgrimage Guide*, Chico, Calif. 1994

CHANDRA, LOKESH. *Buddhist Iconography*, New Delhi 1991

CHAYET, A. *Art et Archéologie du Tibet*, Paris, 1994
"Le monastère de bSam-yas: Sources architecturales," *Arts Asiatiques*, XLIII (1988), pp. 19–29

DALAI LAMA, 14th. *Freedom in Exile*, London 1990

DOWMAN, K. *The Power-places of Central Tibet: The Pilgrim's Guide*, London & New York 1988

DUDJOM RINPOCHE JIKDREL YESHE DORJE. *The Nyingma School of Tibetan Buddhism: Its Fundamentals and History* (G. Dorje & M. Kapstein, eds.), 2 vols., Boston 1991

ESSEN, G.-W., & THINGO, T. T. *Die Götter des Himalaya*, 2 vols., Munich 1989

GOLDSTEIN, M. C. *A History of Modern Tibet, 1913–1951: The Demise of the Lamaist State*, London 1989

GOLDSTEIN, M. C. & BEALL, M. *Nomads of Western Tibet*, London 1989

GRÖNBOLD, G. *Tibetische Buchdeckel*, Munich 1991

GYATSO, J. "The Development of the *Gcod* Tradition," in B. Aziz & M. Kapstein (eds.), *Soundings in Tibetan Civilization*, New Delhi 1985, pp. 320–341

HARRER, H. *Zeitdokumente aus den Jahren 1944–1951*, Zurich 1981

HARRISON, P. *Druma-kinnara-rāja-paripṛcchā-sūtra. A Critical Edition of the Tibetan Text (Recension A) based on Eight Editions of the Kanjur and the Dunhuang Manuscript Fragment*, Tokyo 1992
"In search of the source of the Tibetan Bka' 'gyur: A reconnaissance report," in P. Kvaerne (ed.), *Tibetan Studies: Proceedings of the 6th Seminar of the International Association for Tibetan Studies*, vol. I, Oslo 1994, pp. 295–317

HELLER, A. "Ninth-century Buddhist images carved at lDan-ma-brag to commemorate Tibeto-Chinese negotiations," in P. Kvaerne (ed.), *Tibetan Studies: Proceedings of the 6th Seminar of the International Association for Tibetan Studies*, vol. I & Appendix, Oslo 1994, pp. 335–349 & 12–19

HERUKA, TSANG NYÖN. *The Life of Marpa the Translator*, Boulder 1982

IMAEDA, Y. *Histoire du cycle de la naissance et de la mort: Étude d'un texte tibétain de Touen-houang*, Geneva 1981

IMAEDA, Y. & TAKEUCHI, T. *Choix de documents tibétains conservés à la Bibliothèque Nationale*, vol. III, *Corpus Syllabique*, Paris 1990

JACKSON, D. P. "The Identification of Individual Teachers in Paintings of Sa-skya-pa Lineages," in T. Skorupski (ed.), *Indo-Tibetan Studies*, Tring 1990, pp. 129–144
The Early Abbots of 'Phan-po Na-lendra: The Vicissitudes of a Great Tibetan Monastery in the 15th Century, Vienna 1989
The Entrance Gate for the Wise (Section III): Sakya Paṇḍita on Indian and Tibetan Traditions of Pramāṇa and Philosophical Debate, 2 vols., Vienna 1987
The Mollas of Mustang: Historical, Religious and Oratorial Traditions of the Nepalese–Tibetan Borderland, Dharamsala 1984

JACKSON, D. P. & JACKSON, J. A. *Tibetan Thangka Painting: Methods and Materials*, London 1984

KARMAY, S. G. "A Pilgrimage to Kongpo Bon-ri," in S. Ihara & Z. Yamaguchi (eds.), *Tibetan Studies: Proceedings of the 5th Seminar of the International Association for Tibetan Studies*, vol. 2, Narita 1992, pp. 527–539
"L'homme et le boeuf: le rituel de *glud* ('rançon')," *Journal Asiatique*, CCLXXIX/3–4 (1991), pp. 327–381
Secret Visions of the Fifth Dalai Lama, London 1988

KEWLEY, V. *Tibet: Behind the Ice Curtain*. London 1990

KHOSLA, R. *Buddhist Monasteries in the Western Himalaya*, Kathmandu 1979

KLIMBURG-SALTER, D. "The Tucci Archives Preliminary Study, 1: Notes on the Chronology of Ta pho *'Du Khaṅ*," *East and West*, 35/1–3 (1985), pp. 11–41

"Tucci Himalayan Archives Report, 2: The 1991 Expedition to Himachal Pradesh," *East and West*, 44/1 (1994), pp. 13–82

KVAERNE, P. "Tibet. Bon Religion. A Death Ritual of the Tibetan Bonpos," in Th. P. van Baaren, L. P. van den Bosch, *et al.* (eds.), *Iconography of Religions*, section XII, fasc. 13, Leiden 1985

Tibetan Studies: Proceedings of the 6th Seminar of the International Association for Tibetan Studies, 2 vols. & appendix, Oslo 1994

LAMOTHE, M.-J. *Milarepa: Les cent mille chants*, Paris, vol. I, 1985; vol. II, 1989; vol. III, 1993

LO BUE, E. *Tesori del Tibet: oggetti d'arte dai monasteri di Lhasa*, Milan 1994

"The Princes of Gyantse and their Role as Builders and Patrons of Arts," in S. Ihara & Z. Yamaguchi (eds.), *Tibetan Studies: Proceedings of the 5th Seminar of the International Association for Tibetan Studies*, vol. 2. Narita 1992, pp. 559–573

LO BUE, E. & RICCA, F. *Gyantse Revisited*, Florence 1990

MEYER, F. "The Potala Palace of the Dalai Lamas in Lhasa," *Orientations*, XVII/7 (1987), pp. 14–32

MEYER, F. (ed.) *Tibet: Civilisation et Société*, Paris 1990

MORTARI VERGARA, P. & BÉGUIN, G. (eds.), *Dimore umane, santuari divini. Origini, sviluppo e diffusione dell'architettura tibetana/ Demeures des hommes, sanctuaires des dieux. Sources, développement et rayonnement de l'architecture tibétaine*, Rome & Paris 1987

MÜLLER, C. C., & RAUNIG, W. *Der Weg zum Dach der Welt*, Innsbruck 1982

NATIONAL HISTORY MUSEUM, TAIPEI & STATE MUSEUM OF ETHNOLOGY MUNICH, *Catalogue of Tibetan Artifacts Exhibition*, Taipei 1994

NORBU, J. *Zlos-gar. Performing Traditions of Tibet*, Dharamsala 1986

PAL, P. *Art of Tibet*, Berkeley & Los Angeles 1983
Tibetan Paintings, Basel 1984

PANGLUNG, J. L. "Die metrischen Berichte über die Grabmäler der tibetischen Könige," in H. Uebach & J. L. Panglung (eds.), *Tibetan Studies: Proceedings of the 4th Seminar of the International Association for Tibetan Studies*, Munich 1988, pp. 321–367

PARFIONOVITCH, Y., DORJE, G., & F. MEYER, *Tibetan Medical Paintings*, 2 vols., London 1992

PETECH, L. *Central Tibet and the Mongols. The Yüan–Sa-skya Period of Tibetan History*, Rome 1990
Selected Papers on Asian History, Rome 1988

POMMARET, F. *Les Revenants de L'Au-Delà dans le Monde Tibétain*, Paris 1989

RHIE, M. M., & THURMAN, R. A. F. *Wisdom and Compassion. The Sacred Art of Tibet*, New York 1991

RICCA, F., & LO BUE, E. *The Great Stupa of Gyantse. A Complete Tibetan Pantheon of the Fifteenth Century*, London 1993

RICHARDSON, H. E. *A Corpus of Early Tibetan Inscriptions*, Hertford 1985
Ceremonies of the Lhasa Year, London, 1993

RONGE, V. *Das Tibetische Handwerkertum Vor 1959*, Wiesbaden 1978

SEYFORT RUEGG, D. "*mchod yon, yon mchod and mchod gnas/yon gnas*. On the Historiography and Semantics of a Tibetan Religio-social and Religio-political

Concept," in E. Steinkellner (ed.), *Tibetan History and Language. Studies dedicated to Uray Géza on his Seventieth Birthday*, Vienna 1991, pp. 441–453

SKORUPSKI, T. *A Catalogue of the Stog Palace Kanjur*, Tokyo 1985

SNELLGROVE, D. L. *Indo-Tibetan Buddhism*, Boston & London 1987

SNELLGROVE, D. L., & SKORUPSKI, T. *The Cultural Heritage of Ladakh*, vol. 2, Warminster 1980

SØRENSEN, P. K. *Divinity Secularized. An Inquiry into the Nature and Form of the Songs Ascribed to the 6th Dalai Lama*, Vienna 1990
The Mirror Illuminating the Royal Genealogies, Wiesbaden 1994

SPANIEN MACDONALD, A., & Y. IMAEDA. *Choix de documents tibétains conservés à la Bibilothèque Nationale*, Paris, vol. I, 1978; vol. II, 1979

SPERLING, E. "Lama to the King of Hsia," *The Journal of the Tibet Society*, 7 (1987), pp. 31–50

STEIN, R. "Tibetica Antiqua" (I–V), *Bulletin de l'École Française d'Extrême-Orient*, LXXII (1983), pp. 150–236, LXXIII (1984), pp. 257–272, LXXIV (1985), pp. 83–133, LXXV (1986), pp. 169–196, LVII (1988), pp. 27–56

STEINKELLNER, E. *Tibetan History and Language. Studies dedicated to Uray Géza on his Seventieth Birthday*, Vienna 1991

STODDARD, H. *Le mediant de l'Amdo*, Paris 1985
"The Long Life of rDo-sbis dGe-bśes Śes-rab rGya-mcho (1884–1968)," in H. Uebach & J. L. Panglung (eds.), *Tibetan Studies: Proceedings of the 4th Seminar of the International Association for Tibetan Studies*, Munich 1988, pp. 465–471

SZERB, J. *Bu ston's History of Buddhism in Tibet*, Vienna 1990

TEMPLEMAN, D. *Tāranātha's Life of Kṛṣṇācārya/ Kāṇha*, Dharamsala 1989

TSYBIKOV, G. T. *Un pélérin bouddhiste au Tibet*, Paris 1992

UEBACH, H. *Nel-pa Paṇḍitas Chronik Me-tog Phreṅba*, Munich 1987
"On Dharma-Colleges and their Teachers in the Ninth Century Tibetan Empire," in P. Daffinà (ed.), *Indo-Sino-Tibetica. Studi in onore di Luciano Petech*, Rome 1990

URAY, G. "The Earliest Evidence of the Use of the Chinese Sexagenary Cycle in Tibetan," in L. Ligeti (ed.), *Tibetan and Buddhist Studies Commemorating the 200th Anniversary of the Birth of Alexander Csoma de Körös*, Budapest 1984, vol. 2, pp. 341–360
"Tibet's connections with Nestorianism and Manicheism in the 8th–10th centuries," in E. Steinkellner & H. Tauscher (eds.), *Contributions on Tibetan Language, History and Culture*, vol. I, Vienna 1983, pp. 399–429

VITALI, R. *Early Temples of Central Tibet*, London 1990

VAN WALT-VAN PRAAG, M. C. *The Status of Tibet*, London 1987

WAYMAN, A. *Calming the Mind and Discerning the Real. Buddhist Meditation and the Middle View. From the Lam rim chen mo of Tsoṅ-kha-pa*. New York 1978

WHITFIELD, R., & FARRER, A. *Caves of the Thousand Buddhas*, London 1990

YUTHOK, D. Y. *House of the Turquoise Roof*, Ithaca 1990

ZWALF, W. *Heritage of Tibet*, London 1981

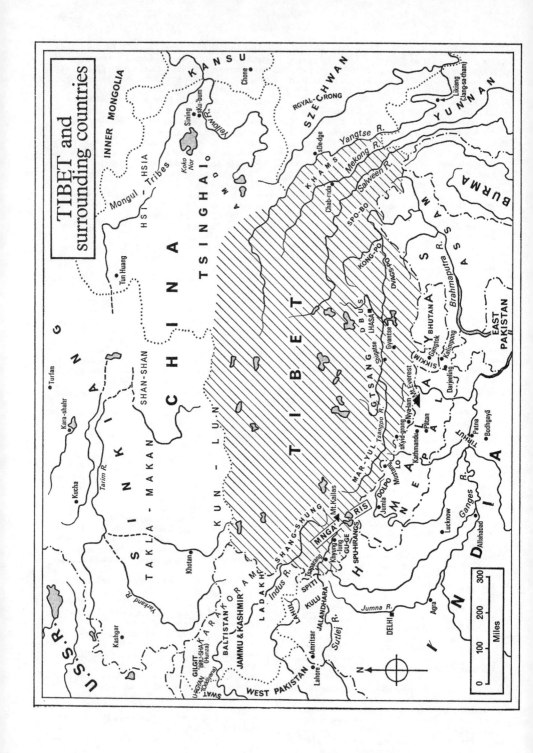

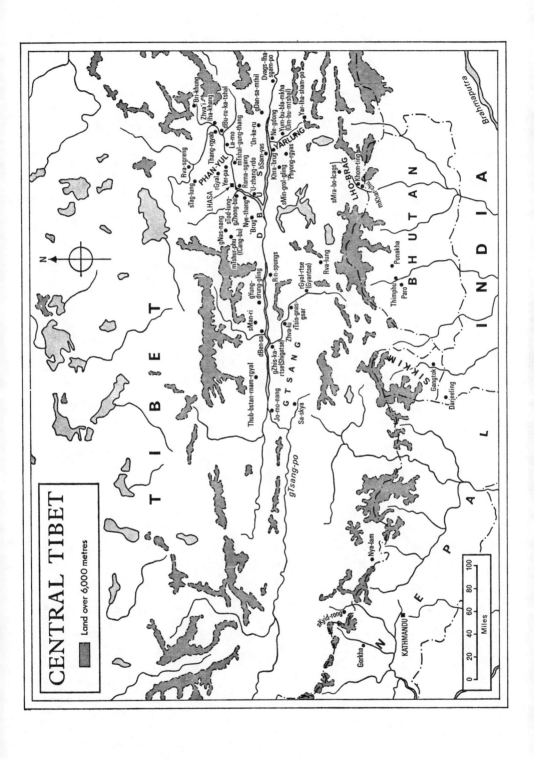

CENTRAL TIBET

Land over 6,000 metres

Miles
0 20 40 60 80 100

Brahmaputra

INDIA

BHUTAN

Thimphu
Paro
Punakha

SIKKIM

Gangtok
Darjeeling

N E P A L

KATHMANDU

Gorkha

sKyid-rong

Nya-lam

Jo-mo-nang

Sa-skya

Thub-bstan-rnam-rgyal

gTsang-po

G T S A N G

gZhis-ka-rtse(Shigatse)

Zhva-lu

rTsis-gnas-gsar

dBen-sa

sMan-ri

g.Yung-drung-gling

Ri-ri-spungs

rGyal-rtse
(Gyantse)

Rva-lung

mKhar-chu

Khom-ting

LHO-BRAG

sMra-bo-lcags

sMin-grol-gling

Phyong-rgyas

Yar-lha-sham-po

Yum-bu-bla-mkha
(Om-bu-mtshal)

YARLUNG

Ne-gdong

Dvags-lha-
sgam-po

gDan-sa-mthil

Yar-pa

Ra-mo

mTshaI-gung-thang

'On-ke-ru

Rama-sgang

bSam-yas

Kbra-brug

U-zhang-rdo

Nye-thang

'Brug

D B U S

mTshur-phu
('Cang-bu)

gZhong-ba

sTod-lung

gNas-nang

LHASA

rGyal

Thang-rgyal

PHAN-YUL

sTag-lung

Rva-sgreng

Zhva'i-
lha-khang

Bri-khung

dBu-ru-ka-tshal

N

T I B E T

Index